The
Principal's Guide
to
MANAGING
SCHOOL
PERSONNEL

The
Principal's Guide
to
MANAGING
SCHOOL
PERSONNEL

Richard D.
SORENSON

Lloyd M.
GOLDSMITH

**CORWIN
PRESS**
A SAGE Company

For information:

Corwin Press
A SAGE Company
2455 Teller Road
Thousand Oaks, California 91320
www.corwinpress.com

SAGE Ltd.
1 Oliver's Yard
55 City Road
London, EC1Y 1SP
United Kingdom

SAGE India Pvt. Ltd.
B 1/I 1 Mohan Cooperative
   Industrial Area
Mathura Road, New Delhi
India 110 044

SAGE Asia-Pacific Pte. Ltd.
33 Pekin Street #02-01
Far East Square
Singapore 048763

Printed in the United States of America

Library of Congress Cataloging-in-Publication Data

Sorenson, Richard D.
The principal's guide to managing school personnel/Richard D. Sorenson,
Lloyd M. Goldsmith.
     p. cm.
Includes bibliographical references and index.
ISBN 978-1-4129-6122-6 (cloth)
ISBN 978-1-4129-6123-3 (pbk.)
   1. School personnel management—United States. I. Goldsmith, Lloyd Milton. II. Title.

LB2831.58.S67 2009
371.2'012—dc22   2008027697

This book is printed on acid-free paper.

08   09   10   11   12   10   9   8   7   6   5   4   3   2   1

Acquisitions Editor:	Arnis Burvikovs
Associate Editor:	Desirée A. Bartlett
Production Editor:	Jane Haenel
Copy Editor:	Claire Larson
Typesetter:	C&M Digitals (P) Ltd.
Proofreader:	Annette Pagliaro Sweeney
Indexer:	Kirsten Kite
Cover Designer:	Michael Dubowe
Graphic Designer:	Karine Hovsepian

Contents

List of Tables

List of Figures

Preface

A school's principal and personnel determine its success. High expectations, accountability standards, legislative dictates for highly qualified personnel, as well as a changing and demanding workforce have increased pressure on principals. Rapidly evolving technology is influencing how schools recruit, select, and retain personnel. Principals must shape their schools' culture to inspire and motivate personnel to provide the best service possible for the students served.

Building on the concepts introduced in *The Principal's Guide to School Budgeting* (2006), *The Principal's Guide to Managing School Personnel* further assists public and private school administrators who desire to enhance their personnel management expertise. Policies, procedures, and techniques needed to manage personnel as they create effective learning environments are examined throughout the book.

Educational leaders who desire to strengthen their personnel management skills will value this book. The book's usefulness extends beyond that of a desk resource. Not only have effective human resource/personnel management techniques been described, application and management strategies have also been included. The book contains numerous practical scenarios, examples, and case studies to better assist principals in understanding the leader's role from a personnel perspective. Principals have a variety of experiences when managing personnel. *The Principal's Guide to Managing School Personnel* provides real examples to illustrate issues associated with the supervision of personnel.

To enhance the book's usefulness, it has been purposely organized into brief, single-topic-focused chapters. Each chapter begins with an appropriate quote and general overview and includes numerous visuals, tables, figures, and relevant activities.

Chapter 1, *Personnel and the National Standards*, contains an examination of the Interstate School Leaders Licensure Consortium Standards, the national standards for school leaders. The personnel dimension of the standards is explored.

Chapter 2, *Personnel and School Culture*, investigates the relationship between culture and personnel. The authors created the Personnel Success Model to demonstrate how culture and personnel factors can be aligned to create success for campus personnel. Strategies to shape school culture are also explored.

Chapter 3, *Personnel and the Principal*, examines the concept of quality principal leadership as related to effective interaction with school personnel. The Principled Personnel Model is introduced in this chapter, examining six personnel principles: respect, trust, honesty, responsibility, rights, and expectations.

Chapter 4, *Personnel and Communication*, considers the importance of communication relative to managing school personnel. Factors of communication such as richness and media are reviewed. The Personnel Success Model, introduced in Chapter 2, is expanded to include communication.

Chapter 5, *Personnel and Conflict Resolution*, presents an examination of effective school leadership in the midst of personnel conflict. This chapter introduces The Principal's Peace Primer, which identifies eight platforms essential to managing and resolving personnel conflict: preserve purpose, protect process, practice patience, promote people, prize perceptions, praise progress, produce a plan, and perfect peace.

Chapter 6, *Personnel and Recruitment and Selection*, acknowledges that effective principals seek the right personnel for the right positions by incorporating recruitment and selection procedures such as conducting a position analysis, utilizing résumés, interviewing potential candidates, conducting reference checks, and by developing strong faculty-administrator relationships through collaborative leadership.

Chapter 7, *Personnel and Induction and Mentoring Programs*, recognizes that the appropriate implementation of induction and mentoring programs serves as an important step in the maximization of school personnel. Beginning teachers need assistance, and this chapter examines important induction and mentoring issues that help a principal create a school environment that ensures everyone matters.

Chapter 8, *Personnel and Adverse Situations*, permits the reader to understand that no other aspect of public school administration is subject to the plethora of policies, regulations, and legal mandates as is the management of school personnel. Nevertheless, this chapter reveals how court rulings, district policies, and school regulations have appropriately eased the administrative burden and associated principal worries relative to the handling of personnel and personnel issues.

Special features of the book include the following:

- Discussion questions
- Case study applications and problems
- Experiential activities and exercises
- References and resources

Working with school personnel can be a difficult prospect for principals who neither anticipate nor prepare for the numerous challenges, persistent individual needs, and unremitting situations that evolve when confronted with the leadership role of maintaining and improving the capabilities of a campus workforce. Therefore, *The Principal's Guide to Managing School Personnel* was written to provide the school leader with the necessary information and basic skills essential to the successful principal-personnel relationship. As a result, readers will note that while the book is not an exhaustive study of the human resource subject, it does incorporate practical and relevant information, strategies and techniques for principals and prospective school leaders to assiduously incorporate into their own school settings. Principals who successfully partner with campus personnel serve as the front line of defense between student achievement and failure, between programmatic quality and mediocrity, and between educational reform and stagnation.

We commend you to the rich and descriptive methods of effectively leading school personnel that come from the reading and analysis of the contents within this book. We also welcome your ideas and suggestions for making the next edition of the book more relevant and informative. To share your comments, please write or e-mail us through the Corwin Press offices, 2455 Teller Road, Thousand Oaks, California 91320–2218 (CorwinPress.com).

Acknowledgments

We express our deep appreciation to the many wonderful individuals who over the years were the "personnel" serving the professional learning communities at T. M. Clark Elementary School and W. C. Andrews Elementary School. Without these dedicated individuals, our professional success would be limited, and our personal lives would have been far from enriched. We extend our utmost respect and gratitude to those with whom we have worked, as they have contributed both directly and indirectly to our book, *The Principal's Guide to Managing School Personnel*.

We are most indebted to a dear and dedicated friend and colleague, Dr. Karen Maxwell of Abilene Christian University, who gave so generously of her time to read and edit our manuscript in its numerous incarnations. Karen, your editorial talents have made this book a better read!

—RDS & LMG

Always, I am thankful for my wife of more than three decades: Donna, my best friend, partner, the love of my life, and the wonderful mother of my two grown "kiddos" —Lisa (Do you remember me?!) and Ryan (Para guiar otros fuera de las tenieblas de pecado; que vean ellos la luz de Cristo en tí). A special acknowledgment is extended to the graduate students in the Educational Leadership and Foundations Department at The University of Texas at El Paso, who serve as "gluttons for punishment" by allowing me to indoctrinate them, through personal musings and scholarly activities, about school personnel.

—RDS

A special thanks to my wife, Mary, for her patience with me as I get absorbed in writing and forget what is going on around me. She is always a source of inspiration to me. I thank God for bringing us together. Abbi, Ellie, and Nelson: you inspire me to be my best. I hope I inspire you to be your best.

Finally, I thank the development team of ACU Online for accommodating my schedule to combine university responsibilities with my writing obligations.

—LMG

PUBLISHER'S ACKNOWLEDGMENTS

Corwin Press gratefully acknowledges the contributions of the following individuals:

Carolyn Banks
Regional Director of Teacher
   Education
University of La Verne
La Verne, CA

Claire Coleman
Assistant Professor of Education
University of La Verne
La Verne, CA

Gerald Dery
Principal
Nessacus Regional Middle
   School
Dalton, MA

Boyd Dressler
Professor
Montana State University
Bozeman, MT

Patricia M. Richardson
Professor of Practice
University of Maryland
College Park, MD

Leslie Standerfer
Principal
Estrella Foothills High School
Goodyear, AZ

Rosemarie Young
Principal
Watson Lane Elementary
Louisville, KY

About the Authors and Contributing Author

Dr. Richard D. Sorenson is an associate professor in the Educational Leadership and Foundations Department at The University of Texas at El Paso (UTEP). He received his EdD from Texas A&M University–Corpus Christi in the area of educational leadership. Dr. Sorenson served public schools for 25 years as a social studies teacher, principal, and associate superintendent for personnel. Currently, Dr. Sorenson works with graduate students at UTEP in the areas of school personnel, school-based budgeting, educational law, and leadership development. He was named The University of Texas at El Paso College of Education Professor of the Year in 2005, is involved in several educational initiatives on the U.S./Mexico border, and is an active writer with numerous professional journal publications. Dr. Sorenson has also authored textbooks, teacher resource guides, and workbooks in the area of the elementary and secondary school social studies curricula. He conducts workshops at the state and national levels on topics such as principal preparation, instructional leadership, and effective teaching practices. He has been actively involved with the Texas Elementary Principals and Supervisors Association, the Texas Association of Secondary School Principals, for which he conducts annual New Principal Academy seminars, and the Texas Council for the Social Studies. Dr. Sorenson has based his professional life and career on the Biblical principle found in Proverbs 16:3, "Commit your works to the Lord and your plans will be established" (New American Standard Bible). His research interest is in the area of the school principalship, specifically the examination of conditions and factors that inhibit and discourage lead teachers from seeking the school principalship as a career option. Dr. Sorenson has been married to his wife, Donna, a medical coder, for the past 33 years and has two children, Lisa, an elementary school teacher, and Ryan, a college student—all of whom are the pride and joy of his life.

Lloyd M. Goldsmith is associate professor and chair of the Department of Graduate Studies in Education at Abilene Christian University. He earned his EdD in educational leadership from Baylor University. Dr. Goldsmith is currently involved in developing online graduate education degrees that incorporate faith principles. He teaches courses in school culture, professional development, and continuous school improvement. He served public schools for 29 years as an elementary science teacher, middle school assistant principal, and elementary school principal. He and a fellow chemistry professor, Dr. Kim Pamplin, codirect a program to facilitate high school chemistry teachers in effective instructional strategies. Dr. Goldsmith has served on several state committees for the Texas Education Agency. He currently serves as a consultant on a project to migrate mandated state principal training to an online format. He is president of the Texas Council of Professors of Educational Administration. Dr. Goldsmith has presented at numerous state, national, and international conferences. He is active in Kiwanis International and Boy Scouts of America. He is active in his local church, where he teaches Sunday school to lively fourth graders, works with the Boy Scouts, and leads a life group. Dr. Goldsmith has been married to his wife, Mary, a high school science teacher, for 22 years. They have three children: Abigail, who is majoring in elementary education; Ellie, a serious violinist studying to be a music teacher; and Nelson, a high school student interested in sports and hunting.

CONTRIBUTING AUTHOR

Joe L. Cope is an associate professor and chair of the Department of Conflict Resolution at Abilene Christian University (ACU). A practicing Texas attorney and mediator, he earned his juris doctorate from Texas Tech University School of Law and a graduate certificate in dispute resolution from the Pepperdine University School of Law. Dr. Cope has developed a unique online master's degree program in conflict resolution and reconciliation that was designed for wide application in a variety of careers, including education. He teaches courses in negotiation and mediation, legal systems, and advanced dispute resolution. Dr. Cope is a member of the Texas Mediation Trainers Roundtable and is currently serving on the council of the Alternative Dispute Resolution Section of the State Bar of Texas. Dr. Cope also serves as the executive director of the Center for Conflict Resolution at ACU. He specializes in interventions in multiple party and organizational conflict. He has conducted training seminars and interventions throughout the United States and Canada, as well as serving as visiting professor at the University of Arkansas at Little Rock. Dr. Cope has been married to his wife, Nancy (his high school sweetheart), for the past 33 years and has two sons, two wonderful daughters-in-law, a precocious granddaughter, a fantastic dog, and four granddogs.

1

Personnel and the National Standards

So, as fast as you can,
Think of something to do!
You will have to get rid of
Thing One and Thing Two!

—The fish in *The Cat in the Hat*

It was one of those days. You know, *those days.* A thought runs across your mind: "If school didn't have children and employees with all their problems and issues, then it wouldn't be such a bad place to work!" It was a thought birthed in a moment of absolute frustration. After all, it was one of those days.

You became an educator to make life better for the world. It's a calling, not just a job. But somewhere along the way you discovered that people are, well, just messy—whether they are 6 or 66 years old.

Let's bring to light another thought: "Sometimes the adults at my school are worse than the students! They argue and bicker, they do the minimum and expect the maximum, and they are more interested in themselves than helping the students. I'm a people person," you think to yourself. "How can I have these kinds of thoughts about people, especially people I care about?"

Figure 1.1   A Chain Letter

Dear Colleague,

This chain letter is meant to bring happiness to you. Unlike other chain letters, it does not cost any money. Just send a copy of this letter to six other schools that are tired of their principals. Then bundle up your principal and send him/her to the school at the bottom of the list. In one week you will receive 16,436 principals, and one of them should be a dandy. Have faith in this letter!

P.S. One man broke the chain and got his old principal back.

If similar thoughts have crossed your mind, welcome to the club. It is part of our human condition.

Theodor Geisel, better known as Dr. Seuss, introduced us to several unique characters in his classic book, *The Cat in the Hat.* Thing 1 and Thing 2 are two characters who wreak havoc in Sally's home on that cold, cold, wet day. The truth of the matter is Thing 1 and Thing 2 were accomplices of another instigator of chaos—the Cat in the Hat. All three of these characters had an undiagnosed case of listening deficit disorder (LDD) compounded by a compulsive behavior driven by their own selfish agendas. This troublesome trio had taken up residence in Sally's home, much to her chagrin.

The antics of Thing 1 and Thing 2 evoked pleas from the fish to evict this destructive duo. But being a victim of LDD, the Cat in the Hat repeatedly ignored the fish's pleas. Only when Sally and her brother took strong overt action, involving the use of a net, were Thing 1 and Thing 2 brought under control. (Throughout history, the net has proven to be an excellent intervention strategy when dealing with out-of-control things.)

School personnel have all types of needs, characteristics, and personalities. How do we effectively lead employees resembling the Cat in the Hat and his sidekicks, Thing 1 and Thing 2? Unlike the Cat in the Hat, we don't have the option of placing our Thing 1 and Thing 2 in a locked box no matter how much we wish to do so.

A few years ago, a chain letter made the e-mail rounds (Figure 1.1). The consequence of breaking the chain reminds us that personnel matters need to be resolved using proven strategies. Unlike the Cat in the Hat's solution, we can't ship our personnel problems far, far away.

A typical school budget allocates over three-fourths of its revenue for human resources (Sorenson & Goldsmith, 2006). This means the majority of a school's resources are expended on this one item. Principals must be good financial stewards. Whether or not the school's vision will be achieved depends on the wise use of human resources. Effective school leaders exude a passion for empowering and promoting growth in the adults in their buildings—the *school personnel.*

Who are the personnel on a campus? *The Random House Unabridged Dictionary* (Stein, 1967) defines personnel as "the body of persons employed in any work, undertaking, or service." Using this definition, personnel on a school campus include teachers, diagnosticians, counselors, cafeteria staff, custodians, bus drivers, librarians, coaches, security staff, and principals. Has anyone been left out? If so, we must include them as well. Simply stated, the term school personnel means all the adults who have some compensated role on the campus.

Personnel is not a stand-alone concept. Other concepts closely associated with personnel include the following:

Professional development—informal and formal activities designed to improve the skills, abilities, and attitudes of the personnel

Professional development needs—needs that arise in the assorted employee groups for an assortment of reasons

Personnel administration—the activities involved in attaining individual, group, or school goals through acceptable use of the school's human resources

Personnel policy—the written rules and regulations stating the general aims and intentions of the school district governing the working relationships and rules

INTERSTATE SCHOOL LEADERS LICENSURE CONSORTIUM STANDARDS AND PERSONNEL

The Interstate School Leaders Licensure Consortium (ISLLC) standards are a logical place to begin a discussion on the relationship between leaders and personnel. Yet these standards can appear distant to leaders engaged in the heat of battle in leading schools.

A brief examination of the ISLLC standards provides an overview of the authors' assertion that the ISLLC standards address personnel issues and do indeed speak loudly to leaders engaged in the heat of battle. The lofty goals of the standards *are* connected to the reality of leading schools. The 2008 ISLLC standards and their accompanying functions can be downloaded at www.ccsso.org/content/pdfs/elps_isllc2008.pdf. The 1996 ISLLC standards are available at www.educ.ksu.edu/EDADL928/ISLLCStandards.pdf.

ISLLC STANDARDS

1. An education leader promotes the success of every student by *facilitating the development, articulation, implementation, and stewardship of a vision of learning that is shared and supported by all stakeholders.*

(Continued)

(Continued)

2. An education leader promotes the success of every student by *advocating, nurturing, and sustaining a school culture and instructional program conducive to student learning and staff professional growth.*

3. An education leader promotes the success of every student by *ensuring management of the organization, operation, and resources for a safe, efficient, and effective learning environment.*

4. An education leader promotes the success of every student by *collaborating with faculty and community members, responding to diverse community interests and needs, and mobilizing community resources.*

5. An education leader promotes the success of every student by *acting with integrity, fairness, and in an ethical manner.*

6. An education leader promotes the success of every student by *understanding, responding to, and influencing the political, social, economic, legal, and cultural context.*

Source: Council of Chief State School Officers, 2008. (Italics added.)

The Council of Chief State School Officers (CCSSO), a national organization of state-level education leaders, created the ISLLC (Murphy & Shipman, 1998; Shipman, Topps, & Murphy, 1998). The Consortium spent years developing a set of standards that codify the skills that effective principals possess. These standards, revised in 2007, remind leaders that improving teaching and learning is a central responsibility of those in leadership positions. The standards demand active, not passive, leadership. The standards assume that leaders are collaborative and inclusive in leading their schools. Finally, the standards do not subscribe to any particular theory of leadership. No one leadership theory has proven to be adequate to be franchised as *the* leadership theory for school administrators. The necessary skills and characteristics of leadership must still be developed and fostered in school leaders (National Policy Board for Educational Administration, 2002).

To facilitate our examination of the ISLLC standards, we have assigned a moniker to each standard that condenses the underlying principle of the ISLLC standard into one word (see Table 1.1). This moniker provides a "mental shoulder tapping" to remind us of the underlying concept behind the standard, which is typically referenced numerically.

The ISLLC standards are examined through a personnel lens in an effort to explore how the national leadership standards address personnel matters. This examination will provide us with some guiding principles for personnel matters.

Table 1.1	Monikers for the ISLLC Standards for School Leaders
Standard 1	Vision
Standard 2	Learning
Standard 3	Environment
Standard 4	Community
Standard 5	Ethics
Standard 6	Global

ISLLC Standard 1: The Vision Standard

An education leader promotes the success of every student by *facilitating the development, articulation, implementation, and stewardship of a vision of learning that is shared and supported by all stakeholders.*

Each of the six standards begins with the words, "An education leader promotes the success of every student by." These standards exist to promote student success.

A particularly intriguing word in this standard is *stewardship.* Peter Block defines stewardship as "the willingness to be accountable for the well-being of the larger organization by operating in service rather than in control, of those around us" (quoted in Smith & Piele, 2006, p. 138). This sobering thought places a mantle of responsibility on leaders to *serve* the personnel in an effort to mold the school's vision, which drives all aspects of the school. Table 1.2 provides examples of principal behaviors from ISLLC Standard 1 that demonstrate how principals assist personnel with vision.

The first ISLLC standard is purposefully about vision because clearly defined visions are hallmarks of effective organizations. The connection between the ISLLC vision standard and personnel management is obvious even to the casual observer. School personnel must have ownership of the school's vision. This happens when each person in the school has a personal vision that is aligned with the school's vision *and* also has the requisite skills and talents to turn the vision into reality.

Introduction to the Personnel Success Model

The Personnel Success Model in Figure 1.2 provides a graphic representation of the relationship between school vision, personal vision, and

Table 1.2   Select Ways Leaders Assist Personnel With Vision

Leaders work with personnel to

- Use existing resources to support the vision and goals
- Develop the vision with and among the stakeholders
- Identify, clarify, and address barriers to achieving the vision
- Use the vision to shape educational programs, plans, and activities
- Monitor and evaluate progress and revise plans with personnel
- Promote continuous and sustainable improvement
- Recognize and celebrate the contributions of personnel toward the realization of the vision

Source: Council of Chief State School Officers (1996, 2008).

Figure 1.2   Personnel Success Model

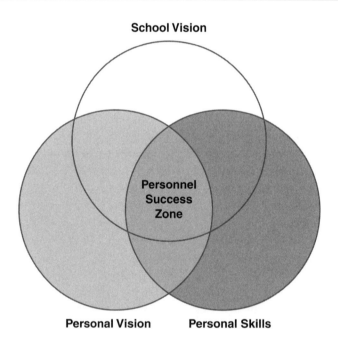

personal skills. The alignment of these three factors produces the Personnel Success Zone. As the alignment of these three factors increases, the size of the Personnel Success Zone increases. If 100% alignment of the three factors could be achieved, the three circles that represent them in the model would be positioned on top of each other, making the Personnel Success Zone appear as a single circle.

When considering this model, it is important to remember once again that dealing with people is messy. Although the model is "frozen" on the printed page, in practice it is anything but static. The three factors are in constant motion, affecting the size of the Personnel Success Zone, which in turn impacts personnel success, which impacts fulfilling the school's vision, which . . . you get the idea.

Leaders facilitate the vision process when they involve stakeholders in creating a school vision that everyone owns. Beautifully framed vision statements hanging on school walls or printed in personnel handbooks are useless unless the personnel carry similar personal visions and recognize a purpose in what they do.

People need a purpose in life. Rick Warren (2002) emphasizes this in his best-selling book, *The Purpose Driven Life.* Warren proposes that many people's lives are driven by guilt, resentment, anger, materialism, and the need for approval. He asserts, "Without a purpose, life is trivial, petty, and pointless" (p. 30). According to Warren, living a purpose-driven life provides meaning, adds focus, provides motivation, and simplifies life. Warren's *purpose in life* is analogous to the Personnel Success Model's personal vision component. People need to know how their personal skills assist them in fulfilling their personal vision and the school's vision. School leaders assist personnel in this process in a variety of ways including school visioning activities, formative and summative evaluations, general conversations, faculty and grade/department meetings, and private conversations. As people discover strengths and weaknesses in their personal skills, some will seek intervention because their personal skills and their personal vision are not aligned. Personal skills need continuous improvement.

Effective leaders help personnel discover their purpose in life, develop their personal skills, and own the school's vision. They also show how these three factors intersect to create personnel success.

Principaling a school is a lot like pastoring a church. Both principals and pastors help people discover their purpose in life, support them, and offer advice. Often people seek advice about issues not directly associated with their jobs but with private issues that affect their job performance. Principals, like pastors, celebrate successes of their personnel, share in the joy of births, mourn deaths, and comfort in times of frustration and illness. They also serve as sounding boards and benevolent taskmasters when needed.

Two Case Studies

The following case studies use the Personnel Success Model in Figure 1.2 to illustrate personnel problems that develop when misalignment occurs in the areas of personal vision, school vision, and personal skills.

THE CHEMISTRY IS GONE CASE STUDY

Mr. Coffee, a high school chemistry teacher in his early 30s, became embittered and sarcastic about his job. He knew chemistry and possessed decent instructional skills that he improved by attending professional development activities beyond what was expected.

But Mr. Coffee's personal vision was not congruent with his school's vision. He was not happy in his job. The conflict between his personal vision and the school's vision manifested itself in a "love-hate" relationship with teaching. One minute he would express his anger and frustration with the students over a litany of issues— many of which had become greatly magnified in his mind. The next moment he would be verbally debating with himself on how he could better teach stoichiometric calculations or Avogadro's principle.

One year at midterm Mr. Coffee resigned. He immediately joined a family member's construction business and is now happily building homes.

Analysis of the Chemistry Is Gone Case Study

Figure 1.3 illustrates Mr. Coffee's situation using the Personnel Success Model. His personal vision was not aligned with his school's vision. This lack of alignment caused the tension in this case study.

The personal skills circle and the school vision circle remain intersected because Mr. Coffee possessed the necessary teaching skills to help achieve the school's vision. The personal skills and the personal vision circles remain intersected because he had the necessary carpentry skills to be successful at his new construction job.

The Personnel Success Zone, the area where all three circles intersect, disappeared in Mr. Coffee's situation. (The Personnel Success Zone is depicted in Figure 1.2.) Personnel success is more than academic success because teaching also includes social and emotional components. Mr. Coffee was able to teach the course content, but he was not a contented individual. Mr. Coffee's abrupt and sarcastic manner adversely affected the learning environment.

The school was able to hire another chemistry teacher whose personal vision was aligned with that of the school's. Everyone benefited from Mr. Coffee's self-realization that teaching was not his passion.

Congratulate Mr. Coffee on having the courage to leave the teaching profession. Everyone needs to live a purpose-driven life that comes about when one's personal vision and the organization's vision are aligned.

Figure 1.3   Analysis of Mr. Coffee's Situation Using the Personnel Success Model

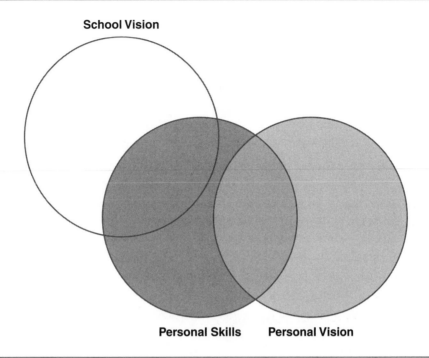

School Vision

Personal Skills   Personal Vision

THE COOKIES CRUMBLE CASE STUDY

Mrs. Field was a kind and gentle primary teacher whose students knew she loved and cared for them. Mrs. Field was also well liked by the faculty and her principal, Mrs. Pierre. Mrs. Field reminded faculty and students of a favorite aunt. Everyone loved her tasty homemade cookies.

Mrs. Field's teaching and classroom management skills, however, were not so well developed, and her classroom was frequently chaotic. Children constantly talked and moved about the room while she attempted to teach. While the activities in her lessons were appropriate, they were eclectically bundled into what she thought was a lesson.

Mrs. Field's fellow teachers expressed their concerns to the principal. They knew learning was not occurring in her classroom. Even the janitor told Mrs. Pierre, "Mrs. Field, she is not a good teacher. I can tell when I clean her room."

Other data reinforced the principal's assessment. Observations made by other school personnel, the principal's classroom walk-throughs, parent requests to have students reassigned, and academic testing data all mirrored the same concerns.

(Continued)

(Continued)

Mrs. Pierre had provided Mrs. Field with opportunities to observe effective teachers in practice on other campuses, sent her to workshops, provided her with a mentor, provided her individual feedback from formal and informal observations, and utilized other professionals to observe and provide her with feedback. None of these interventions resulted in any significant change in Mrs. Field's classroom performance. So after extensive coaching and mentoring over a significant period of time, Mrs. Pierre finally recommended the nonrenewal of Mrs. Field.

Analysis of the Cookies Crumble Case Study

When time came to dismiss Mrs. Field, Mrs. Pierre reported, "It was like firing my grandmother." Mrs. Pierre and Mrs. Field negotiated Mrs. Field's face-saving exit, and they have remained friends. Mrs. Field has moved on to other endeavors where she can use her skills successfully.

Figure 1.4 provides a graphic representation of Mrs. Field's situation using the Personnel Success Model. The school vision circle and the personal vision circle remain intersected because both the teacher and the school were interested in the children and their success. The personal skills circle is isolated because the teacher did not have the skills necessary to help the school achieve its vision, nor did she have the necessary skills to fulfill her personal mission to teach and help children. The Personnel Success Zone (see Figure 1.2) disappears because the teacher's personal skills were deficient and students were not academically successful in her classroom.

The principal's action personified the opening of each ISLLC standard, *"An education leader promotes the success of every student by."* The instructional leader's first obligation is to children and their education, not to the school's personnel. Personnel are entitled to due process and the opportunity to improve and grow professionally, but principals must not lose sight that children are the innocents in the system. No amount of rationalization by adults can change this fact. Adults must advocate for children.

School leaders are obligated to help personnel discover and develop their professional skills. One way principals accomplish this is through professional development designed to meet the instructional needs of the students and personnel. These needs are identified using multiple sources of data including the following:

- Conversations
- Personnel surveys
- Teacher observations and walk-throughs
- Analysis of student achievement data

Figure 1.4   Analysis of Mrs. Field's Situation Using the Personnel Success Model

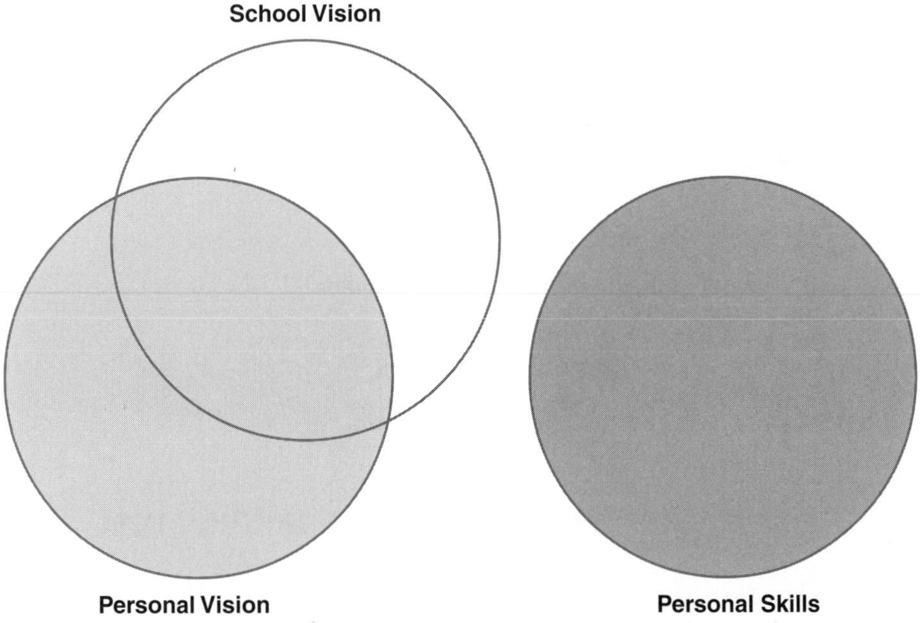

School Vision

Personal Vision   Personal Skills

Using data and giving the staff opportunities to have input into the professional development planning increases the likelihood of personnel ownership in the professional development process.

ISLLC Standard 2: The Learning Standard

An education leader promotes the success of every student by *advocating, nurturing, and sustaining a school culture and instructional program conducive to student learning and staff professional growth.*

The one-word moniker for ISLLC Standard 2 is *learning* (see Table 1.1). This ISLLC standard demands inclusivity of all the school's stakeholders. No one gets a bye in the tournament of learning. ISLLC Standard 2 calls everyone to be a learner with its "instructional program conducive to *student learning* and *staff professional growth* [italics added]" clause. Staff professional growth: Is that not a $20 term for lifelong learning? By reading this book, you are modeling lifelong learning to those in your arena of influence.

Staff professional development nails down the personnel dimension of ISLLC Standard 2 while simultaneously connecting it to the culture, to the instructional program, and to student learning at the school. Personnel matters touch every dimension of this standard. Table 1.3 lists seven principal performances associated with ISLLC Standard 2 that establish the relationship of personnel matters to this ISLLC standard.

Table 1.3   Select Ways Leaders Assist Personnel With Learning

Leaders work with personnel to

- Treat everyone with fairness, dignity, and respect
- Focus staff development on student learning consistent with the vision and goals of the school
- Ensure the staff feels valued
- Encourage lifelong learning
- Encourage high expectations for themselves and the staff
- Supervise instruction
- Monitor and evaluate the impact of the instructional program

Source: Council of Chief State School Officers (1996, 2008).

THE PROFESSIONAL DEVELOPMENT DAY FROM HELL

It's the first day of professional development at the beginning of the school year at Frostbite Falls Elementary School. The usual fare consisting of coffee, juice, and donuts is available.

The training is in the cafeteria. It could have been in the library. It doesn't really make a difference. Either place has furniture that is too small for teachers. The cafeteria contains folding tables with little stools attached to them. The slightest shift causes them to squeak. With the faculty seated, younger faculty swear they hear part of a Beyoncé song in the squeaking of the stools. The older teachers think they hear part of a Rod Stewart song. It is a generational thing. Minds run wild with thoughts like these because it is another day of forced professional development. The state legislature mandates it, but as usual doesn't adequately fund it.

While the speaker talks, teachers make mental lists of things they need to do to get ready for the first day of school. Some actually write their lists in the margins of the presenter's handout.

The squeaking and squirming continues. Do these people need pharmaceutical intervention for their hyperactive disorder caught from their students? What's up with all of this squeaking? You want to yell, "Quiet!" but it isn't your classroom. You're not the teacher. Today, you're the student. You are sitting on an uncomfortable stool. You wonder if this might be a reason students squirm a lot in your class: uncomfortable seating and a lesson that they see no reason to be studying. The thought bothers you a little bit.

The presenter is talking without a microphone and the acoustics are so bad in the cafeteria that you can't hear half of what she is saying even if you wanted to do so. You really don't want to listen, so you say nothing. You continue revising your "to do" list.

It's been 45 minutes now. The old "discretely-look-at-your-watch-to-see-what-time-it-is" behavior begins to spring up around the room. The presenter drones on. Who found this person? What in the world does this have to do with my job and me? Someone passes a note to you. It reads, "Where do you want to go for lunch?" You look at the author of the note and shrug your shoulders. Finally you write, "How about Chinese?" and send the note back. The originator of the note looks at you and nods. You pass the note to another teacher who looks at it and mouths, "Can I come too?" You nod. The communication continues to ripple through the cafeteria. In no time a group of 12 teachers are thinking about Peking Palace and their "to die for" egg rolls with sweet-and-sour sauce.

The presenter continues. You think, "If I were a cat in a hat, I could put this thing in a box with a hook and send it where no one would ever look."

A break is announced and everyone comes to life again. Free. You're free for 15 minutes. If you're good at this, you can stretch the break to 25 minutes and then beg for an extra 30 minutes for lunch. You are successful in both endeavors. The morning wasn't a total loss after all.

After a nice meal at the all-you-can-eat buffet at the Peking Palace, you return to your assigned stool again. "Will it ever end?" you think. The drone of the speaker, the warmth of the room, and your belly full of Chinese food makes it hard to stay awake.

Two younger teachers are text messaging each other. Another teacher is discretely listening to a podcast on her iPod. You are mentally organizing your "Welcome Back" bulletin board because you are older and are not high tech. You have an idea you know the kids are going to love.

But not all is lost yet on this day of professional development. The principal, who had slipped out of the room shortly after the presentation began so she could catch up on her office work, slipped back into the cafeteria just in time to dismiss you an hour early so you could work in your classroom. You immediately think, "Finally! I get to do something worthwhile today."

Before you leave the cafeteria, the principal asks everyone to complete an evaluation of the professional development using the official Frostbite Falls Professional Development Evaluation Instrument. This five-point Likert-type scale evaluation system is used to evaluate all professional development. It is convenient to use. It's on a Scantron® form, which makes compiling the results quick and easy. You wonder what ever happens to these data.

You start to mark the form to indicate how you really feel about the professional development, but you hesitate for a moment. You quickly mark 5, the high-end score, on all the standard indicators. After all, you received longer breaks, an extended lunch, and they let you go an hour early. If the evaluations aren't good, you might be assigned to a committee to plan the professional development for next year. That would be the kiss of death.

You stop by the soda machine, get a diet soda, and walk to your classroom. Now you can finally start working. Except for the Chinese food, it has been a wasted day.

Professional Development

For the sake of brevity, the examination of the personnel dimension of ISLLC Standard 2 is limited to the concept of professional development. The Professional Development Day From Hell no doubt brought to mind some of your own excruciating experiences with professional development.

- Did that professional development day remind you of professional development that you have had to endure or assign personnel to attend?
- Does it meet with the intention for professional development that is embedded in ISLLC Standard 2?
- Do you ever cringe at the thought of professional development? Why?
- Have you ever had to present professional development?
- What was that experience like?

As professional development leaders, principals possess a mental model of professional development. This model is based on prior experiences with professional development. In many cases our mental model for professional development is something we *do* to personnel instead of *with* personnel. When personnel are *do-ed* instead of *with-ed* in professional development, attitudes become extremely negative. Without ownership, resentment develops as evidenced in the Professional Development Day From Hell scenario.

Professional development has never been more important for educators than it is in today's exponential growth of knowledge and information. The roles of educators are changing; new roles must be learned. Research strongly supports the notion that changes in education "almost never take place *in the absence* of professional development" (Guskey, 2000, p. 4; italics added).

Marilyn Tallerico (2005), in her book *Supporting and Sustaining Teachers' Professional Development,* suggests that staff professional development priorities must be driven by student learning priorities. Tallerico further writes that "micro- and macro-level student needs' analysis can help define [professional development] priorities" (p. 4). To accomplish this, existing student data must be gathered; longitudinal data is even better. Professional development designed around student learning data is much more likely to be viewed as relevant to the vision and mission of the school. In their analysis of 25 national and state studies, Shannon and Bylsma (2007) noted that focused staff professional development was one of nine prevalent themes. Holcomb (2004) encourages school leaders to get excited about data as they meet learner needs. The importance of student learning outcomes and professional development is echoed in the Guskey and Spark's model of the relationship between professional development and improvements in student learning (Guskey, 2000).

Data must be considered in designing professional development within the context of the school's mission and vision. This connects ISLLC Standard 1 (vision) and ISLLC Standard 2 (learning). Personnel issues are one of the areas that web together the six ISLLC standards.

Lindstrom and Speck (2004) caution principals not to view professional development as an "add on." (That's what happened in the Professional Development Day From Hell scenario.) Lindstrom and Speck make an important point that "it is clear from recent educational research that site-based, job-embedded professional development that becomes an integrated part of the daily work with the school can better serve the learning process of the adults and thus improve student learning" (p. xiii).

Teacher Quality Program. The Teacher Quality Program is an example of professional development that meets the demands for staff professional development called for in ISLLC Standard 2 (learning) and espoused by Lindstrom and Speck. This federal program provides financial resources to higher education institutions and nonprofit organizations to promote improved instruction in mathematics and science. It was most recently reauthorized in 2002 as Title II of the No Child Left Behind Act.

Professional development in this program is tethered to state student performance data and state content standards. It must also reflect recent scientifically based research on teaching and learning while incorporating activities and strategies targeting underserved and underrepresented populations (Charles A. Dana Center, 2006).

Dr. Kim Pamplin, a chemistry professor, and Dr. Lloyd Goldsmith, a former principal and current education leadership professor, provide professional development for high school chemistry teachers through the Teacher Quality Grant Program administered by Abilene Christian University and funded through the Charles A. Dana Research Center for Mathematics and Science Education located at the University of Texas at Austin. The professional development activities in Pamplin and Goldsmith's grants are based on analysis of student achievement data in the targeted service area and data gathered on the grant participants' needs. Teachers come to the university for 12 days of content and pedagogy training in the summer. They receive stipends as well as equipment such as computers, AV projectors, and Vernier instruments associated with the training for their schools.

Teachers return to the university campus several times during the academic year for additional training, follow-up, and professional networking. The professors likewise visit each of the high school campuses to provide additional assistance and to gather data. Teachers model how they are incorporating the professional development content in their teaching strategies and lesson designs.

Evaluations from teachers, school district administrators, and external grant reviewers have been very positive. Most of the teachers reapply to attend the training for multiple years. This longitudinal relationship with

Table 1.4   Partial List of the Code of Ethics for Staff Development Leaders

Staff development leaders

- Are committed to achieving school and district goals, particularly those addressing high levels of learning and performance for all students and staff members
- Select staff development content and processes that are research-based and proven in practice after examining various types of information about student and educator learning needs
- Continuously improve their work through the ongoing evaluation of staff development's effectiveness in achieving school system and school goals for student learning
- Continuously improve their knowledge and skills

Source: National Staff Development Council (2006).

the teachers has allowed Goldsmith and Pamplin to see the skills learned in the grant become embedded in the participants' teaching repertoire.

Staff Development Leaders Code of Ethics. The National Staff Development Council (NSDC) has developed a code of ethics for professional development leaders. This code can be downloaded from http://www.nsdc .org/connect/about/ethics.cfm. An abridged version of this code of ethics is located in Table 1.4. The principles in this code of ethics support the ISLLC standards as viewed through the personnel lens employed in this book. This code of ethics is another illustration of the connectedness of the ISLLC standards for educational leaders to the broader community of the stakeholders in public education.

ISLLC Standard 3: The Environment Standard

An education leader promotes the success of every student by *ensuring management of the organization, operation, and resources for a safe, efficient, and effective learning environment.*

The one-word moniker assigned to ISLLC Standard 3 is *environment* (see Table 1.1). Assigning just one word to this standard was particularly difficult because *effective* and *learning* are so attached to environment. One wants to invent the word *effectivelearningenvironment* for the one-word moniker for this ISLLC standard.

Senge et al. (2000) wrote in *Schools That Learn*, "Improving the numbers and providing safe learning spaces are legitimate goals, but they can't replace the power of a larger vision, personal and shared as the driving force behind improving schools" (p. 22). Senge et al.'s observation immediately

Table 1.5   Select Ways Leaders Assist Personnel With the
Learning Environment

Leaders work with personnel to

- Monitor and evaluate the management and operation systems
- Identify potential problems and opportunities
- Align financial, human, and material resources to the goals of the school
- Confront and resolve problems in a timely manner
- Involve personnel in decisions affecting the school
- Share responsibility to maximize ownership and accountability
- Use effective conflict resolution skills
- Use effective communication skills
- Ensure human resource functions
- Support the attainment of school goals
- Develop the capacity for distributed leadership

Source: Council of Chief State School Officers (1996, 2008).

melds this standard with the previous two ISLLC standards (vision and learning). What's the purpose in having a "safe, efficient, and effective learning environment" if we do not achieve our school's vision and students do not learn?

Table 1.5 contains an abbreviated list of principal behaviors associated with the learning environment. Proactive behavior is required on behalf of the school leader to assist in fulfilling ISLLC Standard 3. Principals must be involved in the day-to-day operation of the school. While this may not be the most exciting part of leadership, it is a necessary one. Data management systems must be in place, expenditures must be monitored, schedules must be developed, people and programs must be evaluated, and personnel must be hired. These, along with a myriad of other daily obligations, are necessary to create the safe, efficient, and effective learning environment called for in this ISLLC standard. Principals do this fueled by the compelling force behind shared vision.

AN AQUARIUM STORY

An aquarium is a safe, efficient, and effective environment for marine life. Maintaining an aquarium environment takes constant tending by its owner. It helps if the owner has a passion for aquatic life. Every two to four weeks, the aquarium's filter cartridge must be replaced and 25% of the water must be exchanged. When adding water to the aquarium, a water conditioner must be added to neutralize chlorine, chloramines, and heavy metals harmful to fish.

(Continued)

(Continued)

The gravel must also be vacuumed to remove dirt and uneaten food. The owner must constantly guard the aquarium from being overcrowded and must avoid overfeeding the fish, because food that isn't eaten pollutes the aquarium. The water temperature must be monitored so it remains in a specified range for the fish to survive.

Consideration must be given to the location of the aquarium. It should be located on a structure that can adequately support its weight, in a place where it won't be accidentally damaged, and where it can be constantly observed. Fish must be selected that are compatible with each other. Failure to adequately monitor and immediately take corrective action could lead to a major catastrophe for the aquarium's inhabitants.

Finally, care should be given to the aquarium's décor. Aquatic plants (live or artificial) and decorative rocks or ornaments add to the aquarium's visual appeal.

Like the individual who tends to an aquarium's environment, the person who tends to a school's environment exhibits many of the same behaviors. Principals, like aquarium owners, identify potential problems. If the aquarium's water starts turning green, the owner takes immediate steps to intervene for the safety of the marine life. When the situation stabilizes, the aquarium owner must review the standard operating procedures to determine what went wrong and what, if any, procedures must be modified. In a school, the principal exhibits similar behaviors. If smoke appears in the building, the fire alarm sounds and the students exit according to the emergency plan. After everyone's safety is secured and the system is brought back to normalcy, the principal reviews the standard operating procedures to see if the situation could have been prevented or if procedures should be modified.

ISLLC Standard 4: The Community Standard

An education leader promotes the success of every student by collaborating with faculty and community members, responding to diverse community interest and needs, and mobilizing community resources.

The one-word moniker assigned to ISLLC Standard 4 is *community* (see Table 1.1). Once again, the crafting of the words in the ISLLC standards is of paramount importance.

How different this ISLLC standard would have been had it focused on *organization* instead of *community*. The exchange of one word would have resulted in a totally different standard demanding a different set of skills.

An organization is an organized body of people with a particular purpose. Businesses, associations, and schools are examples of organizations. (Are visions of a graduate course in organizational theory dancing in your head—Contingency theory, Western Electric studies, Myers-Briggs Type Indicator, transforming leadership, decision making?) Yes, schools do meet the criteria of formal organizations that bring people together from an external force—state law. And yes, principals need to understand organizational theory. But ISLLC Standard 4 is calling us to consider our school from a community perspective and not an organizational perspective.

A community is "a group of people living together in one place, especially one practicing common ownership: *a community of nuns*" and "all the people living in a particular area or place: *local communities*" (Stein, 1967). A school is a community. All of the people (students and personnel) live and practice ownership. Like nuns in the community of a convent, who live committed to a vision and mission, the students and personnel live in a school building committed to a vision and mission (ISLLC Standard 1—vision).

People with a myopic view of community would stop at this point and miss the full understanding of ISLLC Standard 4. A school's community is much broader than the personnel and students who are brought together by organizational forces. A school's community is more inclusive than a convent's community. A school's community is about "all the people living in a particular area." Adopting this broader definition of community requires a school to collaborate with its students, personnel, families, and members of the school's broader community. This broader definition requires schools to be an integral part of the larger community, inform the public, collaborate and partner with families, and involve the community in the school decision-making process (Council of Chief State School Officers, 2008).

The personnel connection to ISLLC Standard 4 has been established. If Standard 4 is to become a reality, school personnel must become key agents in the process. Principals work with personnel to help them understand their role in the ISLLC community standard. Table 1.6 provides behaviors principals exhibit to help personnel fulfill their obligation to ISLLC Standard 4.

Table 1.6   Select Ways Leaders Assist Personnel With Community Resources

Leaders work with personnel to:

- Provide personnel with the opportunity to develop collaborative skills
- Provide opportunities for personnel to model community collaboration
- Encourage high visibility, active involvement, and communication with the larger community
- Build and sustain positive relationships with families and caregivers
- Build and sustain productive relationships with community partners

Source: Council of Chief State School Officers (1996, 2008).

AQUARIUM STORY 2: A FISHY STORY OF A FOWL WHOSE LIFE HAD GONE AFOUL

An elementary school in a coastal community became involved with its state aquarium because of Diablo, a red wing falcon. Diablo received his name when he was found injured on State Highway 666 in a ranching area of the state. The animal lover who discovered the injured falcon brought the bird to the state aquarium. After all, an aquarium is a place that cares for animals. The aquarium welcomed Diablo into its aquatic culture, but the aquarium did not have the financial resources to care for its unexpected feathered guest.

A teacher brought this need to the attention of her school's principal. Together, the faculty and students decided that the school should adopt the injured falcon. After all, the school's mascot was a dolphin, and there were dolphins at the aquarium, and the falcon was at the aquarium. With such irrefutable and grand logic in place, a bond was formed between the school, the aquarium, and the injured raptor.

The students organized a bake sale to raise money for Diablo. The bake sale was held on the Tuesday before Thanksgiving in conjunction with the school's annual grandparent and senior citizen day. This annual event brought a sizable gathering of grandparents and senior citizens from throughout the community, state, and nation to this suburban school. With grandparents and senior citizens in tow, students wound their way to the bake sale. You guessed it. Grandparents and senior citizens winked at each other and their youthful charges and opened their wallets in response to a youngster's pitch about Diablo's need. The bake sale sold out. Some items sold for more than the asking price. Enough money was raised from the sale to take care of Diablo's needs for one year.

The following spring the aquarium staff brought Diablo to the school for a visit. The staff explained Diablo's injury and talked to the students about raptors in general, falcons in particular. A local photographer took a picture of Diablo and had a near life-size print made. A local frame shop framed the picture, which was hung in the school's library. Children were visually reminded of Diablo on a daily basis.

When grandparent and senior citizen day came around that year, Diablo's bake sale was open. At that point, it was inculcated into the school's culture. The aquarium deepened the tradition by annually inviting the entire fourth-grade class to a free aquarium VIP visit. This provided the students in this kindergarten-through-fourth-grade campus something to look forward to during their final year at the school. The highlight of this trip for the students was to visit Diablo's home at the aquarium.

Sometimes an opportunity to respond to diverse interests and needs and mobilize community resources manifests itself in unique ways. Who would have ever thought meeting the needs of an injured red wing falcon would bring a state aquarium, an elementary school, and the school's broader community together? Raising funds to support Diablo, while important, could be argued from an ISLLC Standard 4's vantage point as only one important outcome in this story.

ISLLC Standard 5: The Ethics Standard

An education leader promotes the success of every student by *acting with integrity, fairness, and in an ethical manner.*

The one-word moniker assigned to ISLLC Standard 5 is *ethics* (see Table 1.1). This standard, of all the ISLLC standards, is most likely to elicit passionate opinions from leaders, since ethical issues often appear to be ambiguous. For example, a very popular and successful coach is an extremely poor teacher. Parents complain about the coach's classroom performance. The principal knows the coach has tremendous political and parental support because of his strong winning record. What needs to happen? Our personal perspectives are interjected into what is right or wrong in situations such as this one.

Our country is in a culture war. Traditional values and the meaning of "acting with integrity, fairness, and in an ethical manner" are under challenge. Educational leaders are caught in the center of this ideological war. In the midst of the national debate, there is a renewed interest in spiritual leadership. Paul Houston (executive director of the American Association of School Administrators since 1994) and Stephen Sokolow, authors of *The Spiritual Dimension of Leadership: 8 Key Principles to Leading More Effectively* (2006), challenge leaders to examine core beliefs and principles that guide, sustain, and inspire them during challenging times. The authors contend that the more leaders are aware of their spiritually rooted values and principles, the more effective leaders they will become.

ISLLC Standard 5 is about character, and it stresses that character matters. Larry Lashway, educational research analyst and writer, asserts that "acting with integrity, fairness, and in an ethical manner" requires leaders to influence the political, social, economic, and legal environment on behalf of students (Smith & Piele, 2006). If educators are to heed Lashway's challenge—and the authors believe they should—then an examination of ourselves, our motives, and how we treat personnel and other stakeholders in the school community is in order. Each individual's understanding of this standard defines that person's behavior; it imposes limits on what he or she is willing to do or not do to achieve an alignment of personal vision, school vision, and personal skills to create the Personnel Success Zone described in the Personnel Success Model.

A school leader has positional authority. With this authority comes power. The authority associated with the position is static. It is clearly defined by laws, codes, and policy. Power, on the other hand, is not static, it is fluid. The personnel and other school stakeholders give the leader

Table 1.7   Select Ways Leaders Assist Personnel With Ethics

Leaders work with personnel to

- Examine personal and professional values
- Demonstrate a personal and professional code of ethics
- Serve as a role model
- Accept responsibility for school operations
- Treat people fairly, equitably, and with dignity and respect
- Recognize and respect the legitimate authority of others
- Apply laws and procedures fairly, wisely, and considerately
- Promote social justice and ensure that individual student needs inform all aspects of schooling

Source: Council of Chief State School Officers (1996, 2008).

power. The amount of power educational leaders possess is dependent on how personnel and other school community stakeholders are treated, as well as how they use the authority provided by law. Heifetz and Linsky (2002) remind us, "We all have our hungers, which are expressions of our normal human needs. But sometimes those hungers disrupt our capacity to act wisely or purposefully" (p. 23).

Table 1.7 contains a sampling of behaviors that fulfill the calling of this ISLLC standard.

The Cookie Crumbles Case Study Revisited

Earlier in the chapter Mrs. Field was introduced in The Cookie Crumbles Case Study. Let's reexamine this case from the perspective of ISLLC Standard 5 (ethics), focusing on the ethical behavior of the principal.

The principal did not talk about Mrs. Field behind her back, nor did the principal speak to her in ambiguities concerning her job performance. Mrs. Field was made aware of her instructional and management deficits in a clear and documented manner. She was then afforded multiple opportunities over an extended period of time to increase her knowledge and competency in these areas through formal instruction, observation of behaviors being modeled appropriately, and participation in summative conferences on her teaching behaviors based on observations by her principal.

The intent of the entire process was to help the teacher improve her teaching skills; it was not to fire the teacher. The fact that Mrs. Field and the principal remained good friends at the end of this process is testimony that both of them were upholding the spirit of ISLLC Standard 5 (ethics).

The principal was bound to uphold this standard from both the personnel perspective and the student and parent perspectives. The teacher needed to be informed of her instructional deficiencies and provided with resources and opportunities to improve her performance to a satisfactory level. However, the principal's ethical obligation to the students and their parents was to ensure that the students were receiving a proper education. The competing interests between these stakeholders illustrate the challenge in fulfilling this standard's call for leaders to act "with integrity, fairness, and in an ethical manner."

ISLLC Standard 6: The Global Standard

An education leader promotes the success of every student by *understanding, responding to, and influencing the larger political, social, economic, legal, and cultural context.*

The one-word moniker assigned to ISLLC Standard 6 is *global* (see Table 1.1). Global was selected as the moniker because it encompasses not only the local, state, and national factors, but also includes international factors. Technology and communications have changed significantly since the ISLLC standards were written in 1996. In the ensuing 10+ years, the impact of these two forces has influenced education in more ways than could have been imagined.

Thomas Friedman (2005), in his book *The World Is Flat: A Brief History of the Twenty-First Century*, makes sense of the advances in technology and communications that are impacting education, foreign policy, and economic issues. Friedman asserts that the advances in technology and communications are the reasons the world is "flattening," in the sense of making opportunities equally available, and this change will at some point be viewed like the fundamental shifts that occurred with the invention of the printing press, the rise of the nation-state, and the Industrial Revolution.

The flattening of the world demands a shift in the way stakeholders in education address the *what* and *how* of education as delivered to America's young people so they will remain competitive in the flat world. Wee Theng Tan, president of Intel China, described how China's national affiliate science fair has students in almost all China's provinces competing in the fair:

We have as many as six million kids competing, although not all are competing for the top jobs. . . . [But] you know how seriously they take it. Those selected to go to the international [Intel] fair are immediately exempted from college entrance exams. (quoted in Friedman, 2005, p. 266)

Table 1.8   Select Ways Leaders Assist Personnel With the Global Context

Leaders work with personnel to

- Ensure that the school community works within the framework of policies, laws, and regulations enacted by local, state, and federal authorities
- Communicate among the school community concerning trends, issues, and potential changes in the environment in which the school operates
- Advocate for children, families, and caregivers
- Act to influence local, district, state, and national decisions affecting student learning

Source: Council of Chief State School Officers (1996, 2008).

These students can select which top university in China they want to attend.

Bill Brody, president of Johns Hopkins University, reported to Friedman that over 60% of his graduate students in the sciences were foreign-born, mostly from Asia. Tracy Koon, Intel's director of corporate affairs reminds us, "[Science and math] drive technology and our standards of living. Unless kids grow up knowing that universal language, they will not be able to compete" (p. 272). Friedman laments the fact that if Intel and other American technology firms must go overseas to meet their engineering needs, then America is in quite a crisis. Friedman opines:

> One cannot stress enough the fact that in the flat world the frontiers of knowledge get pushed out farther and farther, faster and faster. Therefore companies need the brainpower that can not only reach the new frontiers but push them still farther. (p. 274)

ISLLC Standard 6 (global) calls the principal to develop "knowledge and understanding of global issues and forces affecting teaching and learning." The references to Friedman's work illustrate the rapid change in globalization and its impact on American education. A strong case exists for the principal and personnel to work together to keep American students competitive in a global community.

Using only the global dimension of this ISLLC standard narrowed its examination, and the examination was also narrowed by this book's focus on personnel perspective. With that said, Table 1.8 provides four principal behaviors from ISLLC Standard 6 that not only directly relate to personnel but also to the global dimension of this standard.

FINAL THOUGHT

The personnel perspective review of the ISLLC standards provides a connection between theory and practice, between the ideal and life's reality. Real stories and associated information were used to provide clear and concrete examples of how these standards manifest themselves in schools. The standards provide a framework from which leaders can address school personnel matters. In the subsequent chapters, policy, law, and personnel practices will be further explored. The journey through the text will not be that of a technical personnel manual. Instead the journey will be much more like a field manual providing insights on how leaders can address personnel issues in the daily operations of a school, how to get more out of personnel, and how to make you a better leader.

DISCUSSION QUESTIONS

1. Tables 1.2, 1.3, 1.5, 1.6, 1.7, and 1.8 describe behaviors associated with the ISLLC standards. Select two of those behaviors and discuss how you have seen them manifested. Think of other ways they can be displayed.

2. The Chemistry Is Gone and The Cookies Crumble case studies were used to examine the situation of two educators. Their situations were illustrated using the Personnel Success Model depicted in Figure 1.2. Think of an educator you know. Use the Personnel Success Model to graphically represent that educator's situation. Defend your use of the Personnel Success Model.

3. Discuss how the ISLLC standards are supported by the partial list of the NSDC's Code of Ethics for Staff Development Leaders located in Table 1.4.

4. Use the Aquarium Story and the ISLLC Standard 3 principal behaviors in Table 1.5 to draw parallels between events in the aquarium story and similar events you have experienced in a school.

5. Use the Aquarium Story 2 and ISLLC Standard 4 to expand the connection between this story and ISLLC Standard 4.

6. Use the Internet to visit your state education agency's Web site. Locate your state's code of ethics for educators. Compare and contrast your state code of ethics with ISLLC Standard 5.

7. Using ISLLC Standard 6, describe how technology has impacted your school from a local, national, and international perspective.

CASE STUDY APPLICATION

THE ISLLC STANDARDS AND ME

This chapter's case study is an anomaly compared to the other case studies. Instead of providing a case study, *you* are the case study. It is hoped this will assist you in understanding the interconnectedness of the ISLLC standards as well as how the standards manifest themselves in a school environment.

Reflect on your experiences as an educator. How do your experiences connect with the ISLLC standards in general and to personnel issues specifically? Your challenge is to find a personnel-based illustration for each of the ISLLC standards pairings.

Use the *ISLLC Standards & Me Case Study Graphic Organizer* that follows to assist you in organizing your responses. Half of the organizer's boxes are shaded. This shading eliminates the duplication of the pairing of the ISLLC standards.

An example response has been completed in the vision-collaboration cell to illustrate a response. This cell is created by the intersection of the *vision* row with the *community* column. The response "Site-based planning committee develops or updates the school's vision and mission statements" was from this individual's experience serving on the school's campus planning committee. The campus planning committee (community) had reviewed the school's vision statement (vision). This example illustrates how ISLLC Standard 1 (vision) and ISLLC Standard 4 (community) are manifested in a single personnel-related activity. The site-based team (ISLLC Standard 4—community) was working on the vision and mission statements (ISLLC Standard 1—vision).

Fill the remaining graphic organizer cells with an appropriate personal personnel experience. If you have not had an experience to meet the requirement of a particular cell, consider an experience you think would be appropriate. Note in the cell that your response was not a personal experience.

When you complete the 15 cells of the *ISLLC Standards & Me Case Study Graphic Organizer,* write a self-reflection on your 15 responses examining how you view the relationship between personnel and the ISLLC standards.

The ISLLC Standards & Me Case Study Graphic Organizer

ISLLC Standard	1 Vision	2 Learning	3 Environment	4 Community	5 Ethics	6 Global
1 Vision				Site-based planning committee develops or updates the school's vision and mission statements.		
2 Learning						
3 Environment						
4 Community						
5 Ethics						
6 Global						

2

Personnel and School Culture

Principals who seek their own interests over those of their staff will breed a culture of cynicism and selfishness. . . . In contrast, principals who find their own fulfillment in the empowerment of others and in the accomplishment of group goals will inspire others to do the same.

—Stuart C. Smith (quoted in Smith & Piele, 2006, p. 181)

The aquarium is still aglow in a dimly lit room. The fish are swimming about the pirate's chest, the wrecked Spanish galleon, and the artificial plants. Could a lesson on school culture exist inside the aquarium, a lesson void of a cheesy "school of fish" analogy?

An aquarium develops its own culture. The aquatic creatures share behaviors. They swim about each other with mutual respect. They are conditioned to the abundance of food that descends when the aquarium's lid opens. This opening triggers the "get as much as you can as fast as you can" fish behavior.

Observing the aquarium makes one wonder if culture would have been a better topic for the first chapter. After all, if a school's culture is unhealthy, then personnel matters are doomed to failure. The day algae invaded the aquarium, the importance of culture quickly became apparent. The owner's extensive, dramatic, and rapid response restored the aquarium to its natural state. Being an aquarium's keeper is much like being a principal. Both jobs involve shaping and nurturing culture.

CULTURE AND CLIMATE

Culture and climate are often mistakenly used interchangeably. No uniform definition for school culture exists. Webb and Norton (2003) define school culture as "the set of important assumptions, beliefs, values, and attitudes that members of the school share" (p. 106). They define school climate as "the collective personality of a school" (p. 106; see Figure 2.1).

Figure 2.1   Culture Versus Climate

Culture – who we are

Climate – how we treat each other

Robbins (2004) defined five functions of culture. First, culture has a boundary-defining function; that is, the school's culture is unique and is what delineates one school from all other schools. Second, culture provides a sense of identity for the school's personnel. Third, culture assists in obtaining commitment of a school's personnel to something beyond their own personal interests. Fourth, culture assists in stabilizing the school's social system. Culture is the *social glue* that holds the school together. It identifies the standards for speech and action. Finally, it provides personnel a framework to guide and shape their behaviors and attitudes. Often personnel are not fully accepted into a school's culture until they learn the school's cultural rules (Robbins, 2004). This can be particularly true for a new leader such as a principal.

Borrowing again from Webb and Norton (2003), culture and climate are linked together by people, interpersonal relations, collective phenomena, environmental factors, socialization, shared goals, and influenced behaviors. These seven links between culture and climate demonstrate the influence personnel matters have on school culture and climate. They also help explain the confusion that exists between the two terms.

Culture and Personnel Factors in the Personnel Success Model

The personnel factor's presence in the ISLLC standards was established earlier. A further examination of the standards reveals a culture factor tagging along with the personnel factor in each ISLLC standard.

Standard 2 straightforwardly acknowledges its personnel and culture factor: "An education leader promotes the success of every student by advocating, nurturing, and sustaining a school culture and instructional program conducive to student learning and staff professional growth" (Council of Chief State School Officers, 2008).

ISLLC Standard 1, the vision standard, provides yet another example of culture and personnel factors residing in these national standards. The Personnel Success Model (Figure 2.2) illustrates the alignment of school vision, personal vision, and personal skills to increase the success of personnel in school. This same model demonstrates the influence of culture on personnel.

Figure 2.2   Personnel Success Model

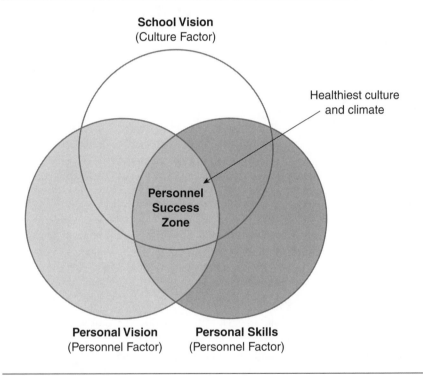

School vision functions as a culture factor in the Personnel Success Model. The school vision combined with the stakeholders' shared beliefs and values define its culture. Personal vision and personal skills serve as personnel factors. Each person's individual purpose is driven by a personal vision. Each member of the school's personnel team brings a set of individual personal skills.

The intersection of the school vision circle with either the personal vision circle or the personal skills circle represents the intersection of personnel factors with the culture factor. Healthy school culture is manifested in these two intersections. The triple-intersected Personnel Success Zone is where the healthiest culture resides. In this zone, personnel take complete ownership of the school's vision, align their personal vision with the school's vision, and possess the necessary talents and skills to turn both personal and school visions into reality.

HOME TOWN HIGH SCHOOL CASE STUDY

Home Town High School's vision statement proclaims academic success for all students. The site-based campus planning committee—in reviewing multiple years of school attendance, dropout, achievement, discipline, and grading data—discovered that the school's vision was not reality for many students, particularly the school's freshmen.

After wasting time blaming the elementary and middle school teachers, the committee decided to identify what the high school stakeholders could do to address their findings. The stakeholders began a self-reflection process. The process began with a period of self-reflection that reaffirmed the relevancy of the school's vision statement. Next the stakeholders individually reviewed their own personal vision statements. With few exceptions, the stakeholders' personal visions were congruent with the school's vision statement.

The planning committee continued to gather data beyond their campus to determine *why* their high school needed to change. Their examination of the digital society with its photo-image capability, cell phones, Web, and digital streaming led the committee to declare a need for breakthrough thinking. Business as usual would not solve Home Town High School's problems.

The planning committee then determined *what* needed to change. They came to consensus that the four roles of education as identified by the International Center for Leadership in Education could help them decide what needed to change (Daggett, 2005). The roles are:

- Fostering intellectual development
- Preparing students to be informed, caring, and productive citizens
- Preparing students for higher education
- Preparing students for the world of work

The site-based committee believed these roles reflected the students' needs at Home Town High School. Now the committee faced the challenge of gaining buy-in from the school's other stakeholders. This was a formidable task, but a supermajority of the stakeholders embraced the committee's recommendations even though some expressed uneasiness as to where this process might lead them.

The committee's final step was to determine *how* to change. The *how* led to the creation of a ninth-grade academy. As the committee explained the *how* to the school's stakeholders, it became evident a need existed to hone personal skills and acquire additional personal skills such as change management, curriculum design, and integrated accountability.

The Personnel Success Model in Figure 2.3 (p. 34) illustrates this change process. First, the committee reviewed and affirmed the school vision, the culture factor. Second, the stakeholders reviewed their own personal visions, a personnel factor. For the most part, the stakeholders' visions were congruent with the school's vision. The school vision circle and the personal vision circle substantially overlapped. Third, the stakeholders realized that even though they possessed many important personal skills, additional skills were needed for all students to succeed. The personal skills circle did not overlap as much with the personal vision and school vision circles. As the stakeholders acquire and utilize new personal skills, the personal skills circle will gravitate toward the center of the model, increasing the size of the Personnel Success Zone.

SHAPING CULTURE FOR THE COMMON GOOD

Individuals and organizations bring past experiences and beliefs, as well as their cultural histories and world views, into the process of learning; all of these influence how we interact with and interpret our encounters with new ideas and events.

—Linda Lambert (1995, p. 57)

The Home Town High School Case Study underscores the influence of culture on school operations. Schools must recognize the importance of culture to be successful in improving teaching and learning (Deal & Peterson, 1999; Fullan, 1998). A school's underlying theory of culture must be revamped to include new ways of thinking about schooling (Lashway, 2006; Sergiovanni, 1996). Culture must be considered when contemplating any change within a system (Lashway, 2006; Schlechty, 1997). Senge et al. (2000) remind us that a school's culture is not static. They assert that a school's culture "is a continual process in which attitudes, values, and skills continually reinforce each other" (p. 326). Because the school's culture is not static, the principal knows that he or she can influence it.

The Personnel Success Model illustrates Senge et al.'s assertion that culture is not static. Although the model is static on the printed page, in practice the culture factor and the two personnel factors are in constant motion as personnel interact in the school environment.

Principals know schools need to change, so they shape school culture to increase personnel effectiveness and student achievement. Change usually occurs incrementally; it *never* happens without the commitment of the personnel involved. A positive change in a school's culture has a phenomenal impact on student learning. Goals and outcomes are necessary for success, and fostering a culture where students and personnel are inspired to reach these goals and outcomes is a moral obligation.

Figure 2.3   Personnel Success Model in the Home Town High
                  School Case Study

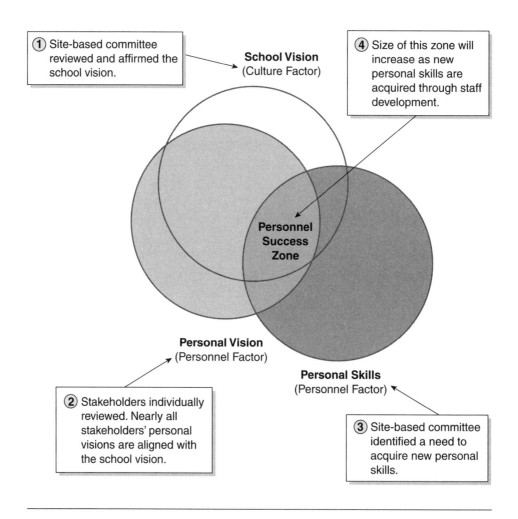

A mountain of advice exists for shaping a school's culture to support student learning. Googling "school culture" harvests about 255 million hits. Narrow the search to "school culture and the principal" and a mind-boggling 16 million hits is netted. The evidence is clear: Principals can shape school culture to increase learning and personnel self-efficacy. Principals must understand how school procedures, policies, and processes shape culture to support learning. A healthy culture must exist for learning to occur.

Filtering through all the information on culture is a daunting task for anyone, much less an educator with a demanding workload. We have created a strategy list to assist principals as they work with personnel to shape school culture. David Letterman has his Top Ten List. The FBI has its Ten Most Wanted List. Google has its aforementioned 255 million culture hits. Sorenson and Goldsmith have their 11 Ten Most Wanted Strategies for Shaping School Culture. It's not quite as catchy as the other lists, but it gets the job done! The strategies were chosen based on the authors' experience and research. Unlike other top-ten lists, this list is *not* in any particular order. Principals and their personnel know their unique situations. Astute personnel understand their schools' needs. Select strategies that best fit your school. Strategy descriptions are purposely brief, but some are expanded in subsequent chapters. Additional culture resources are listed at the end of this chapter.

11 TEN MOST WANTED STRATEGIES FOR SHAPING SCHOOL CULTURE

- *Encourage people to collaborate.* People feel valued when they have meaningful input in shaping the school's culture. A site-based planning committee is a superior method for securing participation in the planning process (Sorenson & Goldsmith, 2006). Students are served better the closer the decision is made to the student (Anderson, 2006). A properly run site-based planning committee provides a mechanism for aligning the school vision and resources. It is here that ideas are shared and teaching and learning capacity are enhanced. A campus improvement plan that is collaboratively developed, regularly referenced, and freely amended dramatically increases ownership of the plan by the personnel. Teams sharing knowledge and skills accomplish much more than individuals working alone (Hoyle, English, & Steffy, 1998). A brief discussion of this strategy does not do it justice. *The Principal's Guide to School Budgeting* (Sorenson & Goldsmith, 2006) provides detailed guidance on implementing this essential culture-shaping strategy. Two cautions: First, if this strategy is utilized, it must be done properly. Failure to do so increases distrust and cynicism among personnel. Second, if implemented properly, be prepared for a dramatic and positive change in culture.

- *Model trust and respect.* Trust and respect enable personnel to adopt innovation and risk-taking as part of the school's culture. Personnel must feel safe in examining and trying new ideas to improve student learning. Principals foster trust and respect by trying new ideas themselves.

Publicly admitting when an idea flops and seeking input from personnel and other stakeholders on why the idea flopped models risk-taking as nothing else can. When principals exhibit this professional behavior, they give personnel the courage to attempt new ideas and the knowledge that less-than-perfect results are okay. The principal sends a powerful message: Calculated risk taking is not only respected but also encouraged and will be rewarded with positive feedback and support.

• *Know yourself.* In the sixth century BCE, "Know thyself" was inscribed on the forecourt of the temple of Apollo at Delphi, Greece (Morden, 2001). Almost 3,000 years later we humans are still trying to "know ourselves." Leaders and personnel must know themselves and each other if they are to positively shape school culture. By knowing themselves, principals become more likely to have successful discussions with personnel about their strengths and weaknesses (Hoyle et al., 1998). One way leaders discover more about themselves is discovering their leadership style (see Chapter 6). A host of instruments exist to assist the principal in this endeavor. Glanz (2002) offers one such instrument in *Finding Your Leadership Style: A Guide for Educators.* Glanz utilizes a personal needs assessment to assist leaders in finding their leadership style, followed by the development of growth and improvement objectives. Glanz's process centers around seven leadership qualities and seven virtues that he identifies as necessary for school leaders. Another excellent source for self-reflection is *Leadership: Theory and Practice,* by Peter G. Northouse (2004). Northouse provides an overview of several leadership theories, their strengths and weaknesses, as well as a leadership instrument for the reader to construct a self-profile based on that leadership theory. This allows the leader to conduct a self-evaluation utilizing a variety of theories.

• *Listen.* Listen first. People have two ears and one mouth. Listen at least twice as much as you speak. Astute and sustained listening allows a principal to achieve an insight into the school's challenges. Insights assist in making course corrections and strengthen the leader's position with personnel. When principals listen, they are less likely to *react* and more likely to *reflect.* Reacting is more of an immediate response, while reflection requires deeper and more careful thought. Don't confuse hearing with listening. Hearing is merely using the ear to perceive sound. Listening, on the other hand, is intentional and takes notice of what someone is saying. One way principals know if they are listening is if they possess an attitude of understanding as they interact with others. Good listeners strengthen their relationships with their personnel as they strengthen themselves personally.

• *Use humor* (see Chapter 3). Daniel Pink (2006) asserts in his book *A Whole New Mind: Why Right-Brainers Will Rule the Future,* "humor can be a clarifying organizational elixir" (p. 199). He also believes humor is a cohesive force citing, "anyone who's ever traded jokes at the water cooler or laughed over lunch with colleagues understands" (p. 199). The brain's right hemisphere, with its big-picture capacity, ability to combine differing perspectives, and ability to place situations in context, is used for humor. Pink quotes Fabio Sala in the *Harvard Business Review*, "[Humor] reduces hostility, deflects criticism, relieves tension, improves morale, and helps communicate difficult messages" (p. 198). Sala's quote hits the bull's eye concerning issues school leaders face. Principals must be able to laugh at themselves and encourage personnel to appropriately use humor. Humor benefits personnel by balancing stress levels, motivating staff, energizing meetings, stimulating team spirit, improving communication, reducing conflict situations, increasing productivity, building self-esteem, and fostering new ideas from creativity (Gibson, 2003).

• *Improve your data collection and analysis skills.* Data analysis is powerful, but only if the school's personnel understand it and accept it. Successful school principals employ ongoing data-driven decision-making skills in a team planning process (Lambert, 1998; Picciano, 2006). It is likely personnel will need additional training in collecting and analyzing data. Be patient and realize this is a continuous project. Data-driven decision-making principles include technical adequacy of measurement, meaningful and appropriate reference, a graphic means of communication, and visual displays so interpretation can be explicit to the reader (Tindal, Duesbery, & Ketterlin-Geller, 2006). The site-based committee is an excellent place to introduce serious data analysis. This committee can change the personnel's attitudes about data. Good data gathering and analysis lead to robust discussions. A thought without data is only an opinion; it's not a fact. Effective data use erodes prejudices as it shapes school culture. An excellent data use resource is *Using Data to Close the Achievement Gap*, by Ruth S. Johnson (2002).

• *Stay current in your field.* Time is already a precious commodity. How could time be taken from a full calendar to do this self-perceived selfish strategy? Remember what your mother said: "Take care of yourself so you can take care of others." Airlines provide the same message in the flight attendants' preflight instruction, "Put the oxygen mask on yourself first. Then secure a mask on your child." Yes, Mom and the airlines are right. Subscribe to a professional magazine and read at least one article each month. Read a book of interest in your current situation. Consider forming a book study group with other principals or personnel. An accountability group such as this increases the likelihood of making the time to read. Professional reading provides inspiration for new ideas to lead personnel. Another way to stay current in the field is to download podcasts to your iPod and listen to them while exercising or traveling. Audio books are another source of professional information. Both podcasts and audio books allow multitasking as knowledge is acquired. If principals do not feed themselves, they cannot feed their personnel.

• *Attend professional development with your personnel.* Professional development promoting creation of a learning community is essential for healthy personnel and a healthy school culture. Principals need to validate professional development activities with their personnel (DuFour, 1997). Principals validate professional development by attending professional development activities with the school's personnel. This accomplishes two objectives: (1) it provides the principal with a better understanding on how professional development supports the campus instructional plan, and (2) the principal's presence sends a strong message to personnel that the training is important to the principal and the school's culture. Time spent in purposefully selected professional development with personnel is time well invested. Try this strategy at least once. It works and it will likely be repeated. When attending training, do not be in a corner on a cell phone! This too sends a message: the training is not all that important. One final consideration: Principals must attend professional development that promotes their own professional growth in leadership skills development and provides personal renewal (Brown & Irby, 1997).

• *Be a moral person.* Principals cannot exhibit moral leadership unless they are moral. It simply is not possible. This fact of life forces principals to ask themselves, "Am I moral?" Reflect deeply on your life. Recall lessons you have learned, influences you have experienced, and the people who have influenced you. Who models moral behavior to you? What is it about that person that models moral conduct? Compare yourself to this individual. Honest self-reflection is a must if you are to learn from this strategy.

• *Be an encourager.* Encouragers give support, comfort, and hope to people, and they stimulate development. Encouragement manifests itself in an infinite number of ways. Encouragement might be meeting and greeting personnel and students, sending a handwritten note, surprising them with a treat, or eating lunch with a group of students. Encouragement might be verbal praise or simply a smile or a cheerful "hello." Or it might be attending a funeral or visiting someone who is ill. Encouragement might be doing a good deed anonymously and watching what happens. Encouragement is individualized. Find methods that fit your style.

• *Have a personal wellness program.* If the school district does not have a wellness program, develop your own personal wellness program. When you feel better, you work better. People who care for their bodies have reduced absenteeism. They also have increased productivity. This leads to improved work performance (Corporate Wellness Programs and Employee Wellness, 2007). Taking care of the physical body also reduces stress. There are all kinds of creative ways to promote personal wellness. Some examples include an exercise club where school stakeholders meet to exercise, a weight control group or other 12-step groups, or a quiet place on the campus. Fit employees miss fewer days, and morale is higher among employees who participate in wellness programs (Sharkey & Gaskill, 2006).

That's the list. Is it what was expected? Disappointed? Truthfully, no program or kit exists to create a quick fix for either cultural or personnel issues. There are effective strategies for providing a framework for creating a positive change in personnel and school culture. One such strategy is professional learning communities.

Richard DuFour, Rebecca DuFour, Robert Eaker, and Gayle Karhanek (2004), in *Whatever It Takes: How Professional Learning Communities Respond When Kids Don't Learn*, promote professional learning communities as the "most powerful conceptual model for transforming schools to meet their new challenges" (p. 2). Professional learning communities' attributes, such as shared missions, collaborative teams, collective inquiry, and continuous improvement, are personnel intensive and culturally dependent. The professional learning community, with its emphasis on a culture that demands personnel stretch to be more effective, is congruent with the personnel and school culture issues raised in this chapter.

Shaping culture is hard work requiring involvement and leadership. Including step-by-step instructions would be foolish on the authors' part. Principals, not authors, are the instructional leaders, and each principal must lead and work collaboratively with the school's personnel, employing strategies appropriate for that school's culture. When a selected strategy does not work as expected, the principal's responsibility is to model the trust-and-respect strategy and openly discuss with the personnel why the selected strategy didn't work. This behavior will positively affect the school's culture.

You, Me, Hobbamock, and Massasoit

> *He was no liar, he was not bloody and cruel. . . . In anger and passion he was soon reclaimed; easy to be reconciled towards such as had offended him; [he] ruled by reason in such measure as he would not scorn the advice of mean men; and . . . he governed his men better with fewer strokes, than others did with many; truly loving where he loved.*

> —Hobbamock's eulogy of Massasoit,
> sachem of the Wampanoag, 1623

Nearly 400 years ago Europeans sailed to America and settled in the present state of Massachusetts. This was the beginning of a relationship between two very different cultures—Native American and European. The Pilgrims depended on Hobbamock, a Pokanoket, for their safety. Hobbamock was a warrior with unfailing loyalty to the Wampanoags' sachem (chief) Massasoit and to the Pilgrim leader Miles Standish. When Massasoit died in 1623, Hobbamock eulogized him (Philbrick, 2006). What he said nearly 400 years ago speaks to us as 21st century school leaders today. Consider the evidence that many if not all of the Sorenson and Goldsmith 11 Ten Most Wanted Strategies for Shaping School Culture are embedded in the Hobbamock quote from Massasoit's eulogy (see Table 2.1).

Table 2.1   11 Ten Most Wanted Strategies for Shaping School Culture in Hobbamock's Eulogy of Massasoit

Hobbamock's Quote	Connection to 11 Ten Most Wanted Strategies for Shaping School Culture
He was no liar	He could be trusted (trust and respect strategy).
He was not bloody and cruel	He took care of his people (moral person strategy).
In anger and passion he was soon reclaimed	He knew his strengths and weaknesses and worked on improving them ("know thyself" strategy).
Easy to be reconciled towards such as had offended him	He understood forgiveness (moral person strategy).
Ruled by reason in such measure as he would not scorn the advice of mean men	He listened to others, even those who offended him (data collection and analysis strategy, listening strategy).
He governed his men better with fewer strokes than others with many	This implies he listened and was an encourager. It also implies he might have encouraged collaboration as he broke from traditional beating of workers (encourager strategy, listening strategy, moral person strategy).
Truly loving where he loved	Truly loving requires listening, encouragement, trust, respect, self-awareness, humor, data collection and analysis and morality (nearly all of the 11 Ten Most Wanted Strategies for Shaping School Culture).

A 1623 burial in a New England Wampanoag village in the present day state of Massachusetts is a stark contrast to 21st century postmodern America. Yet the words of Hobbamock are haunting. They travel across time with a relevance to today, from Boston's Big Dig to Hawaii's tropical shores. Hobbamock, a non-college-educated warrior, connected with an equally uneducated leader Massasoit in much the same way we connect with good leaders today. Massasoit shaped culture by connecting personnel with vision. Principals must do the same "with fewer strokes than others."

QUARTER TILL ELEVEN

Understanding the relationship between culture and personnel is an adventure. English writer G. K. Chesterton believed "An inconvenience is only an adventure wrongly considered; an adventure is an inconvenience rightly considered" (*Quotations of G. K. Chesterton*, retrieved December 7, 2007). In J. R. R. Tolkien's *The Hobbit*, Bilbo Baggins ran from the door at a quarter till eleven, without even so much as a pocket handkerchief, and launched an adventure that would change his life forever.

It is a quarter till eleven. Unlike Bilbo Baggins, principals carry much more than a pocket handkerchief. Their adventure involves "letting go." The adventure involves "a turning"—a turning away from and a turning toward an adventure of the heart as well as the mind. This adventure can begin any day from any place.

Shaping school culture and working effectively with personnel cannot be purchased in a slick software package or by bringing in a motivational speaker or taking personnel on a retreat. It is not a program with three steps to this, and seven steps to that, and a principle for everything. It is a journey, an adventure, and a challenging task that at times is lonely and discouraging.

Principals cannot nuke school culture in a microwave; they must use a slow cooker and let it simmer, allowing the flavors to blend. No instant gratification exists in culture shaping. Once the aroma of a school's culture wafts through a school's hallways, drifts into the classrooms, and filters through the nostrils of its stakeholders and stirs their souls, the principal knows positive culture shaping has occurred and personnel have been changed. The adventure has started.

It is a quarter till eleven. Start the adventure to shape your school's culture and develop personnel for learning. Take the first step. Choose one of the 11 Ten Most Wanted Strategies for Shaping School Culture.

FINAL THOUGHT

The chapter ends as it began. The aquarium glows in a dimly lit room. What if a Thing 1 and a Thing 2 were to invade the aquarium? What impact would that have on the aquarium's culture? What if you are the Thing 1 or Thing 2? Thing 1 and Thing 2 are beings that can and will become a part of any organization. They have their own selfish personal vision and personal plan. Shaping culture and working with personnel is a never-ending responsibility for leaders. It's a quarter till eleven.

SORENSON-GOLDSMITH THING 1 & THING 2
SELF-ANALYSIS CHECKLIST

Instructions: Place a check in the box for each statement that describes you.

☐ I don't have time for the touchy-feely stuff.
☐ I keep school budget information from personnel.
☐ I use school resources to control personnel.
☐ I have not read a professional book in over a year.
☐ Site-based planning is a waste of my time.
☐ School improvement plans are never consulted after they are written or were never developed in the first place.
☐ Personnel are not to be trusted to do what is right.
☐ Personnel should not be treated as equals.
☐ Seeking input from personnel is usually a waste of time.
☐ Some personnel are more equal than others.
☐ Data analysis is not important; you can make data say whatever you want it to say.
☐ Personnel can only work to their innate ability or aptitude.
☐ Personnel can work if they choose to work. My responsibility is to give them the opportunity to work.

Scoring: Count the number of checks placed in the boxes. Write your score here: _____. Use the score analysis table below to analyze your score.

Number of Checks   Score Analysis

0   You are not Thing 1 or Thing 2.

1   Where's a net?

2   Get a box with a hook, now!

3+   You're a Thing 1 or a Thing 2.

DISCUSSION QUESTIONS

1. Find at least one illustration of how personnel and culture are evidenced in each of the six ISLLC standards at your school.

2. Use Figure 2.2, the Personnel Success Model, to illustrate your personal situation regarding school vision, personal vision, and personal skills. Recall that this model is not static. Arrange the three circles to represent how these factors overlap or do not overlap in your personal situation. Support your arrangement of the three circles.

3. Provide two examples of how you have observed Robbins's five functions of school culture where you have worked. What did you learn?

4. The authors compared understanding and changing culture and personnel to a journey. List five arguments to support the authors' assertion. If you disagree that understanding and changing culture and personnel is a journey, list five arguments to defend your position.

5. Which strategy from the 11 Ten Most Wanted Strategies for Shaping School Culture list would you use to effect change at your school? Why would the selected strategy be effective at your school?

6. Is there a strategy you would add to the 11 Ten Most Wanted Strategies for Shaping School Culture list? If so, what would it be and why would you add it?

7. Recount a time you *reacted* and a time you *reflected* in a situation. How were the outcomes different?

CASE STUDY APPLICATION

COMBES PUBLIC SCHOOLS

Earl Roloff Elementary School, located in the city of Combes, is one of nine elementary schools in Combes Public Schools (CPS). Combes, a suburban community of 80,000, was once *the* suburb for young upwardly mobile families. Fifty years ago the sleepy village of Combes was transformed almost overnight to a suburb of Mega City. Subdivisions were aggressively developed. Most people who moved to Combes commuted by automobile to work in Mega City. During its zenith, CPS opened a new school nearly every year. Enrollment was climbing and so was revenue. All the new buildings were state of the art—that is, for 50 years ago. In fact, CPS was a major reason families moved to Combes. Not only did CPS have a perceived superior academic program, they also had strong cocurricular and extracurricular programs. The Combes Mountaineer Stadium and its amenities were the envy of the state, as was the football team's winning tradition. The school's fine arts program was also superior. The strings program was unusually strong for a district of its size and received many state awards.

But 50 years later, things have changed in Combes. Combes has passed its zenith. Its population has remained somewhat constant at 80,000, but the demographics of the population have changed significantly. The upwardly mobile working professionals have for the most part left Combes for newer suburbs. As they

(Continued)

(Continued)

moved out, blue-collar and the working poor have moved in. At one time only 4% of the students in CPS qualified for free or reduced lunch. Today 89% qualify.

The racial composition of the school system has also changed. In the 1960s Combes was 85% Anglo, 3% African American, 8% Hispanic, and 4% other groups. Today, CPS is 38% Anglo, 26% African American, 30% Hispanic, and 6% Asian American. Interestingly, most of the Asian American students are first-generation Americans. Also a significant percentage of the African American population is made up of refugees from an assortment of African nations. Many of these families have French as a native tongue. Of the Anglo population, about a fifth is also first generation and many of them speak a Slavic language at home.

Wal-Mart is the single national employer in the town. CPS is the largest employer followed by the City of Combes. Cinco Systems, a janitorial service provider, is a major employer, as is St. John's Hospital, Jesse James Correctional Center, and Porky's Meat Processing and Packaging. Most of the employment opportunities are with fast food restaurants, aging motels, and small businesses such as Fatty's—a chain of convenience stores that decorate the town.

The tax base for CPS has eroded as the community continues its transformation from a premier suburb to an aging one. This process negatively impacts the local tax base, which shrinks the number of dollars available to CPS. The state funding formula for schools does not replace the lost local revenue. CPS is forever seeking creative solutions to stretch the declining revenue. The problem is further complicated because many of the original buildings were built in the 1960s and need to be replaced or substantially remodeled.

Currently a task force of local businessmen, the chamber of commerce, county and city officials, and the Combes Economic Development Corporation (CEDC) are collaborating with school officials and other community and parent groups to develop a recommendation for a major school bond proposal. The CEDC, which uses a pool of local tax money to provide incentives for businesses to relocate to Combes, is days away from announcing the relocation of a firm to Combes that will guarantee 100 new good-paying jobs and a promise to add 300 additional positions over the following five years. This anticipated announcement coupled with a possible bond election is creating more excitement than the community has seen in years.

Earl Roloff Elementary School

Earl Roloff Elementary School was built in 1961 and bears the name of a retired superintendent. The school's structure is the typical wing structure popularized in the '50s and '60s. When air-conditioning was added in 1973, the windows were covered to improve the heating and cooling factors. When the multipurpose room (gym) was constructed in 1993, the school's electrical system was upgraded to handle a larger presence of technology. Although this upgrade was very helpful, the school needs additional wiring.

Roloff (as it is called by its faculty and students) was built with little attention given to landscaping, and little has been given to it since, with one exception: The only outside improvement is the marquee that Mrs. Mary Beth Bodinsky provided in memory of her grandson, who was killed in an automobile accident.

Nearly all of the housing around Roloff consists of single-family, three-bedroom homes. Some homes have been well maintained and evidence owner pride, others do not. A few aging apartment complexes with subsidized rent exist. The Combes Housing Authority constructed the Orchid Apartments—known as the Projects—in 1980.

Roloff has had principals come and go. Many use Roloff as a way to get into administration and then leave at the first opportunity, a practice causing all aspects of Roloff to languish. Half the faculty are beginning teachers (less than 5 years' experience), while the others are veterans with 15 or more years of experience. The faculty generally ignore these short-term principals.

Other facts about Roloff:

- The PTA disbanded in 1996.
- Absenteeism for students is 50% higher than the district average.
- Personnel absenteeism is the lowest in the district.
- Head Start through fourth grade are served on campus.
- The secretary, Mona Chirac, has been at Roloff for 17 years. She is well liked and speaks French. She grew up in Africa, the daughter of American missionaries.
- The campus planning committee meets three times a year. Customarily the principal updates the campus plan and brings it to the committee in the spring to be adopted and then filed with the superintendent. A copy is kept in the principal's office should a teacher want to review it or discuss it with the principal. This seldom happens.
- The Big Brothers Big Sisters organization has expressed an interest in starting a program at the school for the last two years, but no one at the school has followed up on this interest.
- Big State University received a grant to develop a working relationship with a public school. The university expressed an interest in partnering with Roloff, but the principal has been stalling. He is not sure how wise it is to have university students and faculty on the campus.
- The test scores are low.
- There are low expectations of students.

The Challenge

Last year, Dr. Elena Cortez became CPS's first female, minority superintendent. She has finished her first year at Combes and is gaining the support of even her staunchest critics. The principal of Roloff for the past two years has resigned to take a management position at Porky's. Dr. Cortez created a principal interview team, the first in Roloff's history, to have input in the selection of the next principal.

(Continued)

(Continued)

The faculty, veteran and new alike, were surprised at the opportunity to provide input in the hiring process. The interview team took their assignment seriously. Congratulations! You are the new principal of Roloff. You were the first choice of the superintendent and the interview team. Dr. Cortez has given you the charge to be a visionary and a change agent. School starts in three weeks! Dr. Cortez also announced a grant for $150,000 for Roloff's campus planning committee to use as they transform Roloff into a model school.

Using strategies from the 11 Top Ten Most Wanted Strategies for Shaping School Culture list and additional resources, develop a plan to turn Roloff around. Give particular attention to culture and personnel. Include a rationale for the plan's implementation and how you would use each selected strategy.

OTHER RESOURCES

Barth, R. S. (2003). *Lessons learned.* Thousand Oaks, CA: Corwin Press.

Beaudoin, M., & Taylor, M. (2005). *Creating a positive school culture: How principals and teachers can solve problems together.* Thousand Oaks, CA: Corwin Press.

Deal, T. E., & Peterson, K. D. (1999). *Shaping school culture.* San Francisco: Jossey-Bass.

DuFour, R., DuFour, R., Eaker, R., & Karhanek, G. (2004). *Whatever it takes: How professional learning communities respond when kids don't learn.* Bloomington, IN: National Education Service.

Harris, S. (2005). *Best practices of award-winning elementary school principals.* Thousand Oaks, CA: Corwin Press.

Harris, S. (2006). *Best practices of award-winning secondary school principals.* Thousand Oaks, CA: Corwin Press.

Lindsey, R. B., Roberts, L. M., & CampbellJones, F. (2005). *The culturally proficient school: An implementation guide for school leaders.* Thousand Oaks, CA: Corwin Press.

Senge, P., Cambron-McCabe, N., Lucas, T., Smith, B., Dutton, J., & Kleiner, A. (2000). *Schools that learn: A fifth discipline fieldbook for educators, parents, and everyone who cares about education.* New York: Doubleday.

3

Personnel and the Principal

I don't want any yes men around me. I want everybody to tell me the truth, even if it costs them their jobs!

—Samuel Goldwyn

TRUTH IS STRANGER THAN FICTION

Samuel Goldwyn, long-time president and CEO of the most successful movie studio in the world, was frequently referred to as "the West Coast king of the malapropism" (Lazear, 1992, p. 116). While Goldwyn was terribly straightforward, if not brutally blunt, he was known to be honest in his assessment of personnel, and he most certainly left nothing to the imagination in his dealings with personnel at the Metro-Goldwyn-Mayer (MGM) studios. However, for most leaders, it is very difficult to be completely honest, especially when communicating with personnel. Naturally, it is only human to want to please, to be liked, and to be admired by subordinates. However, the little dishonesties we communicate to others do nothing to help those who need our honest assessment and only serve to diminish our reputations in the end.

By being truthful, leaders are able to take an even closer, if not a more discerning, look at themselves—at who they've become, and in truth, who they really want to be. However, with truth comes accountability, and with accountability comes responsibility. Covey (1992) stated, "Unless you regularly account for all your stakeholders, your organization will likely not survive" (p. 258). When accounting for school personnel, the campus principal must exhibit forthright and honest leadership actions and behaviors. Beckner (2004) reminds us that telling the truth is an accepted ethical practice. He further suggests that "most of us have little difficulty in accepting this standard, although we may have some difficulty in always following it" (p. 89). Only the truth can set you free when dealing with school personnel. However, when dealing with personnel, a school principal may find that "truth is stranger than fiction"!

Consider the following statements, as each one is a real "truth is stranger than fiction" account taken directly from the ranks of public school principals and campus personnel (Sorenson, 2004b). Each of these statements will be examined in greater detail later in this chapter.

Statement 1

"Yes, I asked two witches to come into my classroom to spread positive omens because I believe my principal is out to get me!"

Statement 2

"She needs to go. She is destroying my reputation. I know that the school perceives her to be the principal and not me. I want the superintendent to fire her!"

Statement 3

Interviewer: I couldn't help but notice that you did not list your previous principal as a reference on your résumé. Should that be of concern to me?
Applicant: Oh, absolutely not! Let me see that. I didn't realize that he was not listed. It must be a simple oversight. I can't believe that I left him off my résumé. He and I had a great working relationship. He's a good man!

These statements lead us to recognize the major responsibility and level of accountability a principal has in dealing with personnel issues. People-related problems are a part of a school leader's daily life. Confronting, handling, controlling, and solving personnel-related problems are critical aspects of the administrative role. In fact, the previously identified personnel incidents could each serve as defining moments in the development of an effective leader-personnel relationship.

THE EFFECTIVE SCHOOL LEADER
AND PERSONNEL RELATIONSHIP

Effective school leaders must quickly adopt some basic principles of appropriate, essential, truthful, and proactive communication while continually meeting higher standards of services (Sorenson, 2005b). One requirement of a principal is to be responsive to campus personnel. In the school setting, principals must be aware of the efforts of students, and the strivings of personnel. Webb and Norton (2003) remind school leaders that effective communication is essential in developing "a climate of trust, mutual respect, and clarity of function" (p. 107). Effective leadership is all about communicating. The principal who is committed to effective communication will be able to offer personnel recognition, praise, and professional regard, while establishing organizational expectations and developing a campus culture that benefits the entire learning community.

Jim Walsh, noted legal scholar and nationally recognized educational attorney with the law firm of Walsh, Anderson, Brown, Schulze and Aldridge, P.C., has stated that "no area within the scope of public school education generates more interest, more concern, and more legal disputes than personnel" (Walsh, Kemerer, & Maniotis, 2005, p. 180). Any individual who has spent even a limited amount of time in school administration would certainly agree with Walsh's assessment. Since school districts across the nation employ so many people and have to comply with scores of federal and state mandates, it is imperative that today's principal leaders understand the importance of the human resource function in school administration.

Young and Castetter (2004) noted that "individual performance is the core element fundamental to any organizational endeavor" (p. 17). This statement is testimony to the notion that school principals must provide considerable attention to the recruitment, selection, development, contentment, and retention of a school's second most precious commodity—its personnel. Employees new to any school system or even those employees transferring within a school district cannot be expected to fully integrate into a new campus setting without guidance and support.

When employees encounter new expectations, a different set of colleagues, or a new supervisor and are expected to meet evolving position demands, or find they are in the unfortunate situation of being simply ignored by school administration, the ideals of human dignity and worth may be diminished and the principal-personnel relationship becomes strained or broken. Successful school principals must lead with flexibility as demonstrated by challenging the status quo, embracing change, and communicating ideals that promote resiliency in personnel (Kaser, Mundry, Stiles, & Loucks-Horsley, 2002). Systematic-thinking principals who have a compelling vision, who cultivate high levels of interaction and visibility, and who empower personnel at all levels produce positive and productive results. These principals demonstrate their belief that all personnel are important. Principals who fail to anticipate and plan for the impact of personnel issues and considerations can expect less than fruitful results.

THE PRINCIPLED PERSONNEL MODEL

School business is big business. Many school districts are by far the largest enterprises in their communities in terms of revenues, expenditures, capital assets, and employment (Sorenson & Goldsmith, 2006). From the employment angle, Webb and Norton (2003) relate that personnel comprise 75 to 85% of a typical school district's budget. Personnel are essential to the success of a school system, and from a school administration perspective, it is essential that the best qualified personnel be recruited, selected, developed, motivated, and evaluated. The school principal plays a critical role in determining the professional satisfaction and performance of campus personnel.

Shapiro and Stefkovich (2005) remind us of the school leader's moral imperative to "serve the best interests of the student" (p. 25). No argument here! School leaders, particularly principals, must also serve the "best interests" of campus personnel. A school's faculty and staff are the critical link between student achievement goals and the achievement of the school's goals and objectives. Applying this assumption, the authors created the Principled Personnel Model (see Figure 3.1), which presents a process, from the principal's perspective, by which the school leader is viewed as the central cog in a revolving core of leadership skills necessary for ensuring the ultimate success of faculty and staff. In turn, school personnel advance the academic growth and overall achievement of the students served.

The Principled Personnel Model is not based on any ideological or theoretical strand of reasoning. Instead, the model emerged from the authors' interactions and experiences with school personnel. Logically, the model is based upon professional ethics and borrows concepts relative to practical leadership skills, which form fundamental elements related to the supervision of school personnel. Let's examine the six principles necessary for the growth and development of a school's faculty and staff.

Principle 1: Respect

"Respect is a guiding standard, even where there is disagreement" (Beckner, 2004, p. 138). Respect is probably the most important ingredient in the mixture of terms that define effective, principled leadership. When respect is shown, respect is earned. Respect is a key asset to any administrator, especially as related to the decision-making process. When a principal

Figure 3.1 The Principled Personnel Model for Effective Leader-Follower Relationships

1. Respect

Tolerant, accepting, appreciative, adjustable, flexible, sociable, listener, personable, positive, reflective, employee-centered, relationship-oriented, valued, legitimate, credible

2. Trust

Moral, ethical, rational, integrity, self-confident, trustworthy, experienced, professional, believable, confidential

3. Honesty

Truthful, integrity, honorable, candid, collaborative, genuine, sincere, direct, open, decent, scrupulous, policy-following, law-abiding

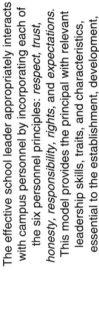

The effective school leader appropriately interacts with campus personnel by incorporating each of the six personnel principles: *respect, trust, honesty, responsibility, rights,* and *expectations.* This model provides the principal with relevant leadership skills, traits, and characteristics, essential to the establishment, development, enhancement, and maintenance of effective leader-follower relationships.

4. Responsibility

Competent, dependable, communicative, effective, decision-maker, self-directed, stress manager, task-driven, team-oriented, conflict-manager, responsible, influential, problem-solver, intelligent, reliable, motivational

6. Expectations

Creative, self-confident, energetic, achievement-oriented, assertive, directive, participative, quality-oriented, instructionally focused, goal-oriented, visionary, change-oriented, task-driven

5. Rights

Autonomy, authority, liberties, privileges, appropriate actions, reasonable behaviors, just, fair, moral, acceptable, justified, non-discriminatory, entitlement who is respected by the learning community makes a decision, it is viewed as authoritative and credible (Sergiovanni, Kelleher, McCarthy, & Wirt, 2004). Not only does respect help a principal earn support for a school, respect also increases a principal's legitimacy. Respect is synonymous with other important leadership traits, such as integrity, honesty, truth, honor, trust, and moral and ethical behavior.

Principle 2: Trust

Researchers House, Woycke, and Fodor (1988), Conger (1989), and Hilgert, Truesdell, and Lochhaas (2002) tell us that leaders who build trust in their followers by setting attainable organizational goals do so by exhibiting self-confidence, strength of moral conviction, personal example, and sacrifice. Effective school leaders also employ unconventional tactics or behaviors. Trustworthy principals exude vision, ability, knowledge, and experience and are committed to the well-being of individual faculty and staff members. Robbins (2004) suggests a lower level of trust often results in a higher level of illegitimate political behaviors, which frequently lead to conflict (see Figure 3.2). A high level of trust can only exist in a school where personnel understand that their needs, desires, and objectives are compatible with those of their principal. A school principal establishes trust through intimate, professional, and honest interaction with personnel (Lunenburg & Ornstein, 2004).

Principle 3: Honesty

Honesty has been described as the most fair and straightforward of actions that can be conducted by a school leader (Sorenson, 2004b). In fact, it was William Shakespeare who penned, "No legacy is so rich as honesty" (*The Columbia World of Quotations*, 1996). Honesty, much like respect, is tantamount to being honorable, trustworthy, and responsible. Honesty in school administration produces confidence, and when a principal is honest in dealings with campus personnel, a higher level of confidence is communicated to and from the various constituencies that make up a learning community. This high level of confidence enables the school leader to exhibit another important skill when working with personnel: assertiveness.

Assertiveness is neither acquiescence nor aggression; nor is it something in between. Assertiveness means being direct and making honest statements regarding expectations when working with personnel. Assertiveness is being strong in your convictions and actions. John MacArthur (2005), pastor, teacher, college president, syndicated radio host, and critically acclaimed author, states:

If you want to get stronger physically, what do you do? You put yourself through painful experiences. You go to the gym and work

Figure 3.2   The Relationship Between Trust and Political Behavior in Personnel

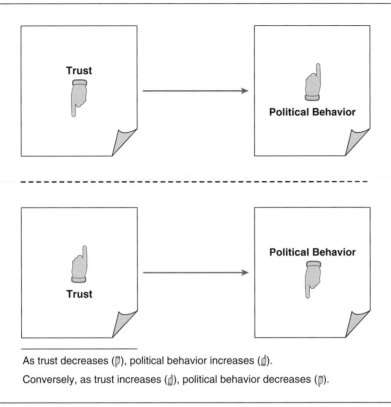

As trust decreases ([hand]), political behavior increases ([hand]).

Conversely, as trust increases ([hand]), political behavior decreases ([hand]).

and work. You do everything you can to strengthen your body, and you know that there will be pain involved, but you determine that the goal is worth the pain. In order to get strong, you have to be able to endure some pain and persevere in spite of it. (p. 36)

The same is true if you want to become stronger in your dealings with personnel. You will never mature as a leader unless you are assertive in your actions through honest behaviors, steadfast convictions, and persevering experiences.

Assertiveness equates to candid problem solving and is a prerequisite to open, honest, and collaborative decision making. A principal demonstrates assertiveness by willingly, honestly, and responsibly addressing and assessing the interests, concerns, and issues of all personnel.

Principle 4: Responsibility

Mosher (1968) declared, "Responsibility may well be the most important word in all the vocabulary of administration, public and private" (p. 7). Principals are frequently confronted with issues that demand prompt action. Let's return to a previous section of this chapter titled "Truth Is Stranger Than Fiction." Consider Statement 3: "It must be a simple over-sight. I can't believe that I left him off my résumé." The principal has a responsibility to follow through in this particular situation by making the necessary reference contact to ensure that the applicant is making a truth-ful assertion. Making contact with the principal who was conveniently omitted from the applicant's résumé actually allowed the interviewer to discover that the applicant was under investigation by the state's educator certification board and would later have all teacher certification credentials revoked. The applicant was a pedophile.

By identifying a problem, confronting an issue, and deciding on a response, a school principal defines his administrative responsibility. In this particular instance, making a decision to contact a previous employer when the applicant seemed so genuine, sincere, and most competent in filling the educational need not only served the best interest of the school district seeking an employee but, more important, saved a child from the solicitous, unsavory, and criminal behaviors of a pedophile. Additionally, the potential for certain legal entanglement was avoided.

Consider the following: How do you, as a school leader, balance your responsibility to provide for individual differences of personnel with your responsibility to maintain the highest standards and levels of expecta-tions? Cooper (1998) contends, "Responsibility is the key concept in devel-oping an ethic for the administrative role" (p. 65). Principals are responsible, from a personnel perspective, for the conduct of faculty and staff, as well as their own personal conduct. Principals must set organiza-tional expectations for personnel, direct the instructional activities of cam-pus personnel, provide appropriate resources (human, material, and fiscal) to the campus faculty and staff, and empower campus personnel with the authority to complete designated duties. Moreover, principals must monitor personnel performance and hold faculty and staff account-able for executing the instructional program. Fulfilling these administra-tive responsibilities in today's schools is a stressful and complex task for any principal. With responsibility comes conflict, especially when working with personnel. When conflict arises, a principal must be aware of the legal rights of all personnel.

Principle 5: Rights

Ottensmeyer and McCarthy (1996) wrote:

> When we say a person has a moral (or legal) right in a given situ-ation, we mean that it is ethically (or legally) permissible for him or her either to act in a certain way or to insist that he or she be treated in a certain way without obtaining anyone's permission to do so. (p. 15)

Beckner (2004) contends that individuals "tend to think of rights as something inherent and unquestionable" (p. 26).

While some rights are recognized as *absolute* (i.e., prevailing in all circumstances), most of our rights are *prima facie*. In other words, these rights can be overridden depending on the circumstance or situation. For example, consider Statement 2 from the Truth Is Stranger Than Fiction section: "She needs to go. She is destroying my reputation. I know that the school perceives her to be the principal and not me. I want the superintendent to fire her!" This statement refers to a school secretary who had garnered control of a campus, much to the dismay of the school principal. The secretary fell within a protected class: female over 40 years of age, a minority, and potentially a union member. Whether the secretary is a card-carrying member of a union or an "at-will" employee, some definitive level of protection from unwarranted termination is guaranteed by law (Alexander & Alexander, 2009; Dunklee & Shoop, 2006; Walsh et al., 2005). Whatever the secretary's rights might be in this situation, the principal bears the responsibility for ensuring that these rights are recognized and granted.

A principal is constantly challenged when conflicts arise from authority, rights, and autonomy issues. Does the campus secretary have the right to act as the school principal, to assume the role? Does the principal have the right to seek the termination of the secretary simply because she has exceeded her authority? Does the superintendent have the right to terminate the secretary? This situation and similar ones are not unusual in schools today and highlight the administrator's responsibility to establish work-related expectations, to properly interact with faculty and staff, and to understand the legal rights of school personnel.

Walsh et al. (2005) state, "An at-will employment arrangement is one in which there is no contractual commitment to a specified period of employment" (p. 125). Many noncertified employees in public schools do not have written contracts, and as a result, either the school district or the employee can terminate the relationship at any time, for any *legally permissible* reason. The operative terminology in this last statement is legally permissible. Therefore, it would be extremely difficult for a school district to prove that the termination of a secretary for allegedly assuming the role of a principal is legally permissible. Principals must remember that an at-will employee (in this case, the school secretary), while not under contract, enjoys every protection afforded by employment laws. The superintendent, in this situation, has no cause to terminate the secretary's employment simply because the principal does not have a good working relationship with or cannot manage the employee in question.

Principle 6: Expectations

Principals of effective schools have been described in the research (Bennis & Nanus, 1985; Burns, 1978; Heifetz, 1994; Sergiovanni, 1992; Sorenson, 2007;

Starratt, 1977) as possessing the ability to effectively work with personnel by securing their cooperation through the establishment of standards and levels of expectation. Effective principals exhibit pride in their faculty and staff and acknowledge these individuals as professional, dedicated, and competent people. Principals of effective schools instill confidence, interact cooperatively in group processes, listen carefully to their personnel, and show exceptional empathy for and understanding of their personnel (Becker et al., 1971). Such expectations inspire personnel to exert the necessary effort to gain the maximum results. Hughes, Ginnett, and Curphy (2002) assert that personnel will live up to the highest professional or positional expectations if three conditions are met: (1) the expectations are attainable, (2) efforts are recognized or rewarded, and (3) the recognition or reward is valued.

The Principled Personnel Model cannot be implemented overnight. A principal must be willing to initiate long-term levels of commitment, labor, and intensive leadership efforts in order to gain the trust, respect, and admiration of campus personnel.

LEADERSHIP TRAITS ESSENTIAL TO WORKING EFFECTIVELY WITH SCHOOL PERSONNEL

Stanley Gault, former chairman of the board and chief executive officer of Rubbermaid and the Goodyear Tire and Rubber Company, once made a critical assessment of the role of effective leaders and their working relationship with personnel. He stated, "You have to set the tone and pace, define objectives and strategies, and demonstrate through personal example what you expect from others" (*The Columbia World of Quotations*, 1996). Expectations are certainly one important key on the administrative ring of success to working effectively and appropriately with personnel. However, the following question begs an answer: What criteria, as related to effective leadership traits and skills, should be used to assess the overall success of a school principal in his interactions with campus personnel? Hughes et al. (2002) suggest three useful criteria to measure leadership effectiveness from a personnel perspective: (1) subordinates' ratings of satisfaction, (2) superiors' performance ratings, and (3) campus performance indices. Possibly the most important of these criteria is subordinates' ratings of satisfaction, because fostering a sense of cohesiveness and cooperation generally inspires the accomplishment of organizational goals (motivation) and establishes a school climate and culture (morale) conducive to learning (student achievement) and overall organizational success (Sashkin & Huddle, 1988).

Principals who work effectively with campus personnel typically exhibit one or more of the following leadership traits, depending on the situation (Hughes et al., 2002; Northouse, 2004; Sorenson, 2005a; Ubben, Hughes, & Norris, 2007; Yukl, 2001):

- Self-confidence
- Dependability
- Energy
- Intelligence
- Tolerance
- Flexibility and adjustability
- Sociability
- Temperament
- Assertiveness
- Ethical dimensions and moral values
- Quality expectations and orientations
- Communication (including active listening) skills

Personnel perceptions of principals can reveal effective leadership traits, even when the assessment is quite to the contrary.

Linda Garcia, recently retired principal leader at Connally Middle School in Northside Independent School District (San Antonio, Texas), is known to introduce beginning principal leaders, at the annual Texas Association of Secondary School Principals New Principals Academy, to a first evening session entitled "Tales From the Swamp." Over the years, the "Tales From the Swamp" stories have effectively served to relate differing and challenging principal experiences that Linda and her other invited principal guests have encountered. This first session makes for a great introduction into the principal role and readily sets the tone for the remainder of the conference. With this in mind, read the following teacher critique of a building principal. The description is revealing and relative to what effective leadership should be, most notably when viewed through a lens that identifies what effective leadership should not be.

A TALE FROM THE SWAMP

During a recent faculty meeting, our high school principal was sharing a new "zero-tolerance" policy. He suggested that the new policy would have minimal impact on our school since we did not have a drug or alcohol problem. Several of us looked at one another, rolled our eyes, and commented under our breaths that our principal should come out of his office more often and sniff (literally) around the student restrooms to get a whiff of weed!

Faculty meetings at our school were a rarity (three, maybe four a year), and department meetings were, for the most part, teacher-initiated and seldom monitored by campus administration. The principal's credo was simple, but did little to establish any level of instructional expectation: "Teachers know what's best for students!" While this

(Continued)

(Continued)

motto sounded good, it failed to increase student achievement, raise test scores, or promote ongoing professional development.

Our principal's interaction with campus staff was minimal, as he was frequently off campus at central office visiting with an old coaching buddy or over at the elementary school where his wife taught third grade. As a result of his low visibility and inattentiveness to faculty needs, our school's head football coach was indulging in an affair with one of the paraprofessionals, our agriculture teacher spent more time cooking barbeque than teaching animal husbandry, and one of our male mathematics teachers spent an inordinate amount of time tutoring a male student after school and at the teacher's apartment on weekends.

The campus counselors developed the faculty schedule, the clerk from the school's business office managed the campus budget, and the principal's secretary was known as the "real" principal because she had all the answers to questions frequently posed by faculty members, parents, and students. The secretary thus "ran the school" in the absence of any real leadership. Our librarian, the sweetest person you would ever wish to know, grew increasingly fragile and frail during her last year of service. She died of cancer during the month of March. Our principal never visited her in the hospital or at her home during her final days of life. He was "regrettably, out of town" at the time of her death and funeral. We found out later he was on a fishing trip.

School morale was at an all-time low, student disciplinary behaviors were typically ignored—unless dealt with by teachers—and new faculty were left to fend for themselves. For example, each school year our principal would announce at the new teacher orientation: "Being thrown to the wolves will make you a stronger teacher. Have a great year!"

Effective School Leadership

The research is clear: Effective schools are led by effective principals. Unfortunately, such was not the case in the previous scenario. Consider the following criteria of effective school leadership, which is reflective of research conducted by DuFour (2004), Tanner (1999), Sergiovanni (1994), Blase and Kirby (1991), and Blum, Butler, and Olson (1987); then respond to the question that follows.

The effective school principal exhibits the following leadership qualities:

- Establishes a visible presence in the school
- Monitors teachers and students
- Communicates a vision of school goals and objectives
- Fosters an open and positive school culture and climate
- Serves as an instructional expert available to faculty and staff

- Develops a safe and orderly learning environment
- Facilitates an instructional and curricular program that promotes student achievement
- Establishes high organizational expectations
- Collaborates regularly with school personnel
- Initiates a professional development program
- Implements ongoing evaluation of all personnel
- Aligns curricular and strategic plans to enhance teaching and learning

Question: Which of the effective leadership criteria listed above were reflected in A Tale From the Swamp?

May we surmise that you did not find any of the leadership criteria exhibited by the principal in the scenario? Research conducted by Sorenson (2007) reveals that lead teachers believe certain elements of a school's climate and culture are affected by campus principals and as a result do in fact impact personnel perceptions regarding the principalship. These elements include the following:

- High spirit of honesty, integrity, trust, and respect
- Safe and open communications
- Goal-oriented and student-centered learning environments
- Demanding, yet rewarding expectations
- Problem-solving efforts
- Meaningful collaboration

These elements strongly correlate with the research regarding behavior categories of effective school leaders (Bass, 1990; Bowers & Seashore, 1966; Hemphill & Coons, 1957; Likert, 1961; Stogdill, 1948). While this research may seem dated, each remains most applicable and relevant today.

So what's a principal to do? What serves to separate the good-to-better-to-best principals in our schools today, when assessing their leadership abilities as correlated with personnel perceptions of effective school leaders? Sharp and Walter (2003) write, "School principals are very much involved with personnel matters" (p. 99). They explain:

Superintendents seek principals who exemplify high moral values, and they want to hire administrators who are professional in their dealings with all stakeholders involved with the school: students, teachers, parents, and community members. Superintendents expect that successful principals should possess both leadership and personal skills in order to be the chief educational and chief executive officer of the building. . . . Principals must show the superintendent that they have a desire to serve the students, work professionally with the staff, and are willing to involve the learning community in the education of students. (p. 89)

Such an assessment identifies leadership traits and skills that are so essential to a principal's successful relationship with followers. To work effectively with personnel, a principal must possess traits such as involvement, high moral values, professionalism, personability, service orientation, and collaboration, as identified by Sharp and Walter (2003).

THE ADMINISTRATION AND SUPERVISION OF SCHOOL PERSONNEL

A priority for all principals is the development of a learning community that employs satisfied personnel. Developing a campus culture characterized by motivation, cohesiveness, cooperation, and positive morale must be a continuous focus for the effective school leader. The authors strongly suggest that principals critically evaluate, on a daily basis, the criteria they incorporate to assess their own effectiveness when working with school personnel. Principals are responsible for what Roberts (1990) believes are true measures of an effective leader's performance.

When supervising school personnel, the effective principal takes these steps:

- Establishes a positive, personnel-centered learning community
- Creates a culture where integrity, trust, and respect are organizational norms
- Develops high standards of performance and has no tolerance for incompetence
- Expects continual improvement from personnel
- Provides a wide array of professional development opportunities
- Regularly monitors and evaluates personnel

The administration and supervision of school personnel has become increasingly complex. Principals regularly face (1) personnel grievances, (2) legal challenges, (3) a less than loyal generation of employees, (4) union demands, and (5) a litany of complicated and multifaceted issues often accompanied by intricate questions and convoluted answers. Consider the following personnel-related questions that principals will confront during the course of a career, if not a school year:

- How do I handle a teacher who I suspect is using illicit drugs?
- How do I inform a high-achieving teacher that the school budget will not allocate funds to replace programmatic dollars once available from a now-expiring grant?

- How do I counsel a teacher who is burned out because of pressurized instructional expectations, irate parents, and increased accountability standards?
- How do I increase instructional expectations without decreasing staff morale?
- How do I work with a teacher who is "marginal" in terms of performance?
- How do I assist a teacher who is an instructional expert, but cannot manage students?
- How do I solve issues associated with increased employee absenteeism?

These questions beg for quick, serious, and appropriate solutions. Campus personnel deserve sound, objective, and fair advice from their campus leader. In fact, today's principals are obligated to provide the necessary answers and are expected to serve as decision makers who can offer innovative solutions to complex problems. This book is about finding the right answers at the right time in the right context to personnel issues and to seemingly insurmountable personnel problems—all depending on the situation.

Situational Leadership

While there is no simple formula for the effective administration and supervision of school personnel, the best campus leaders learn early in their careers to mentor and develop, monitor and assist, supervise and evaluate faculty and staff by assessing the individual as well as the situation. Hughes et al. (2002) tell us, "You cannot make an intelligent decision about the leader's actions by just looking at the behavior itself. You must always assess leadership in the context of the leader, the followers, and the situation" (p. 105). Maxwell (2003) writes, "Leadership is more art than science. The principles of leadership are constant, but the application changes with every leader and every situation" (p. 203). Furthermore, the school leader, when working with followers, must devise systematic approaches to solving personnel problems by making the most prudent decisions based on the situation at hand. Consider the following statements about the principal, the school personnel, and the situation, one from a sports-related perspective and one from an educational point of view:

- Principals may find it necessary to respond to the same faculty member differently, at different times—again, depending on the situation. Jerry Kramer, an all-pro guard for the Green Bay Packers for many years, was once asked by a reporter how he and his fellow players were treated by the legendary coach, Vince Lombardi. His response, while amusing, made a very interesting point: "He treats us all alike, he treats us all the same—like dogs!" (Kramer & Schaap, 2006, p. 207). Now, even those who have a limited knowledge of Vince Lombardi must understand that his ability to motivate and develop a winning attitude among his football players was not happenstance, nor did Lombardi treat them all the same. In fact, he never had a team that could even remotely be considered a loose collection of players. Lombardi was tenacious in his development of the team concept, which always began with his individualized treatment of players. One day Lombardi might scream, harass, and jump all over a certain player for a particular lack of effort—as a means of developing a superior level of mental toughness and excellence in that individual. However, the very next day, depending on the situation, he might greet the same player, still coaxing the very best from the individual, with a gentle and uplifting "Son, some day you're going to be one of the greatest players in football" (Lombardi, 2001, p. 312).

- Principals must recognize the needs of campus personnel, as the situation dictates. Karen Maxwell (2007), former principal, education service center consultant, and current university professor, relates a story about a former education service center executive director. Once when asked how the executive director was able to obtain so much from his employees, he responded by stating, "I find out what they need at the time and I give it to them!"

Yukl (2001) reveals that effective leaders have a strong regard for people, and this level of consideration is often increased, if not intensified, depending on the situation, problem, or issue affecting the progress of the individual in question and the overall success of an organization. Yukl further contends that the situation may be the primary reason why leadership traits, characteristics, and skills are less frequently related to leadership effectiveness than to leadership emergence. Many researchers believe that the situation, more than any trait or skill, is a determining factor in defining leadership success. This statement affirms the notion that leaders are made, not born. The more situational experiences a leader has, the more effective the leader will be. While certain cognitive abilities and personality traits are innate, individuals can grow as leaders, especially in the face of adversity and certainly through a variety of experiences (McGue & Bouchard, 1989). This accepted wisdom corresponds perfectly with an infamous quote by Abraham Lincoln: "I claim not to have controlled events, but confess plainly that events have controlled me" (*The Columbia World of Quotations*, 1996).

Hughes et al. (2002) remind us that organizations have unique cultures, which establish a framework for leadership. Thus, current as well as prospective school leaders must consider the following question: Given the complexities of situational leadership and followership, what should a leader be attuned to? The answer to this and other pertinent questions central to the effective principal and personnel relationship lies in understanding that exceptional school leaders, when working with personnel, build coalitions, think politically, reflect on their actions, monitor themselves, and maintain a positive attitude.

Humor, Leadership, and School Personnel

Having a sense of humor—especially when working with people—is a source of freedom and a form of leadership. Humor often allows a school principal to deal with important issues and people in a nonthreatening manner. Humor further enables a leader to better handle those aspects of school administration that are irritating, distasteful, and sometimes quite stressful, if not painful. Allen Elkin (1999a; 2004), noted clinical psychologist and founder of the Stress Management and Counseling Center in New York City, relates that humor can serve as an effective tool in helping others diffuse anger. Tense moments or difficult situations are less stressful and may be eliminated when a leader is able to find humor in a volatile circumstance. Naturally, it is important that a school leader know the individual involved well enough to predict a reaction, because the interjection of humor could negatively intensify the situation if the person perceives the humor to be demeaning. On the other hand, humor can allow personnel involved in a difficult matter to laugh, or at the very least smile, at the situation, thus alleviating a collision course that could possibly hurt all parties involved.

RAMONA EXPLODES

Ramona Wiley, an experienced sixth-grade science teacher, had worked diligently for weeks planning a student field trip to Seaside Kingdom, a marine and adventure park located several hundred miles southeast of Grand Pierce Elementary School. After much preparation, the sixth-grade team of teachers, parent chaperones, and school principal took nearly 150 students on what one parent deemed, "the trip of a lifetime!" Mrs. Wiley was almost as excited as the sixth graders, as they boarded the chartered buses and made the trip down the coast to where one exciting show after another would allow "inland" students to gain a better understanding of the natural marine attractions that inhabited some of the great oceans and waterways of the world. Two members of the sixth grade team of teachers included Ernest Teas and Charlene Briscoe. These two teachers spent most of the trip enjoying each other's company, often ignoring the needs of their students. Everything that could possibly have gone wrong on the field trip seemed to occur during the morning hours before lunch. Finally, Ramona Wiley's anger reached a boiling point at noon when the 150 students were all crammed into one of the park's small fast-food restaurants. While Mrs. Wiley and a couple of other teachers frantically worked the crowded room of students—most of whom were eager to get their "fun-pack" meals—Ernest and Charlene sat casually in a corner, chatting and paying no attention to the loud and

(Continued)

(Continued)

hungry kids. Ramona, having reached her "boiling point," grabbed Principal Andrew Taylor by his arm, exploding, "Look at those two—they're doing nothing to help out, but they certainly are having a great time in their own little world!" Mr. Taylor had spent most of the morning on another bus, oblivious to Mrs. Wiley's predicament. However, he replied in a most humorous tone, "Why, they look like an old married couple: They must be in love!" Ramona just burst out laughing and shouted, "Hey love birds, how about a little assistance over here?" The students overheard Mrs. Wiley and responded with the typical adolescent "o-o-o-o-o-o"! Embarrassed, Mr. Teas and Ms. Briscoe immediately jumped up from their table and began to work the crowded room of loud and lively students. Soon after the students had received their hamburgers and were quietly eating their meals, Ernest and Charlene approached Ramona Wiley and the principal. Both teachers apologized for being so neglectful. Principal Taylor jokingly responded: "Ah, don't worry about it. You know what they say about young folk who keep puttin' off getting married? They start getting distracted!" With that said, everyone let out a loud chuckle as the angry situation was now completely diffused, although the faces of Ernest and Charlene were a bit crimson. The remainder of the field trip to Seaside Kingdom was a tremendous success! By the way, Ernest and Charlene were married at the conclusion of the school year.

Humor as an anger and stress reducer has been clinically proven to relax the body, enhance immunity, and provide objectivity. Elkin (1999b) found a sense of humor to be one of the 10 habits of highly effective leaders. Humor, wit, laughter, and happiness are all synonymous terms and actually relate to a deeper level of emotional joy and intellectual engagement (Caulfield, Kidd, & Kocher, 2000). Glenn (2002b) notes that humor can increase learning, and there is no better time to gain insight and wisdom into a problem than when learning from the experience at hand.

Let's look back on Ramona Wiley's Seaside Kingdom predicament. While it is important for a school leader to understand the benefits of possessing a sense of humor, it is equally important for the leader to recognize that not all humor is funny based upon the setting, the situation, and the context. Laughing at Ernest and Charlene, while not intended, could very well be a form of disguised aggression, and while it may solve the problem at hand, it could also create a level of resentment. Such was not the case in the Ramona Explodes situation, as Principal Taylor knew Ernest and Charlene were engaged to be married, and he had developed a respectful rapport with both teachers. However, if you, as a school leader, are willing to laugh at someone's foibles and shortcomings, it is best to make that someone you. The school leader should be reminded of the old Chinese proverb: "He who learns to laugh at himself never ceases to be amused!"

A leader's humor is not only therapeutic; it is a process of self-disclosure, a reaction based on human need, and a reflection of self. Humor is actually quite serious because it permits a leader to relax, to let his or her guard down, and it even allows a school principal to ask those difficult questions that can plague the leader-follower relationship (Lazear, 1992). Consider in closing, the words of Samuel Clemens, great American writer and humorist: "Humor is mankind's greatest blessing. Genuine humor is replete with wisdom" (*The Columbia World of Quotations*, 1996).

FINAL THOUGHTS

Effective principals are forthright and honest in their leadership actions, interactions, and behaviors when interacting with school personnel. Effective principals are always responsive to the needs of campus personnel and adopt essential principles of appropriate, truthful, and proactive leadership behavior. Effective principals provide considerable attention to the recruitment, selection, development, contentment, and retention of campus personnel. When principals develop a compelling vision, interact with their employees, and empower campus personnel, the end result will be positive and productive.

Effective principals utilize respect, trust, honesty, responsibility, rights, and high expectations when leading personnel. These concepts embody the essence of meaningful leader-follower relationships. These concepts are highlighted in the Principled Personnel Model (see Figure 3.1). Each concept is based on the ethical standards of the education profession. Furthermore, each concept is critical to the successful administration and supervision of school personnel.

Effective principals interact regularly and appropriately with campus personnel. They exhibit leadership traits such as self-confidence, dependability, intelligence, tolerance, flexibility, assertiveness, and humor. Effective principals uphold ethical and moral values and develop a learning community in which satisfied personnel are committed to a student-centered and instructionally focused learning environment. Today, more than ever, principals must exercise a strong regard for all personnel and must be willing to solve problems, make decisions, and lead with confidence in all situations. Personnel should never have to speculate about the vision, values, or leadership capabilities of a principal. Unless effective school leadership provides clear direction for all personnel, excellence will languish and mediocrity will flourish.

DISCUSSION QUESTIONS

1. Consider the statement from this chapter, "only the truth can set you free when dealing with school personnel." Beckner (2004) makes an interesting point when he relates, "To get around strict adherence to truth telling, . . . we may come up with statements such as 'you should tell the truth, but you don't have to tell *all* the truth'" (p. 90). Should a principal "tell *all* the truth" when working with school personnel? Explain your answer. How does this question interrelate with the Principled Personnel Model? Which of the principles (see Figure 3.1) best correlate with your answer?

2. Utilize the Principled Personnel Model to identify which principles best relate to this concept: Principals who cultivate a high level of interaction and visibility with their employees effectively lead in producing end results that are positive and productive. Explain your answer.

3. Which of the leadership traits presented within this chapter relate to what the Northwest Regional Educational Laboratory (1984) describes as effective school leadership?

    Leaders expect all staff to meet high instructional standards; classroom visits for the purpose of observing instruction are frequent; personnel supervision focuses on instructional improvement. Leaders involve personnel in planning; they set and enforce expectations. Leaders rally support from all personnel. (p. 114)

    How do the leadership traits you identified correlate with the principles noted within the Principled Personnel Model?

4. Consider, from a principal's perspective, the following question as previously posed within this chapter: How do I increase instructional expectations without decreasing staff morale? When supervising personnel, which of Roberts (1990) measurements of effective leadership performance (see p. 60) relate to this question? Support your answer by incorporating principles from the Principled Personnel Model.

5. Situational leadership has been defined by Northouse (2004) as the demand for different types of leadership in differing situations. Effective leaders adapt differing leadership styles, all depending on the situation. Consider this chapter's insight: The effective principal and campus personnel have a relationship. How does situational leadership connect with this insight? Support your response.

6. Which one of the six principles identified within the Principled Personnel Model is considered more important than the others? Explain.

CASE STUDY APPLICATION

TRUTH CAN BE STRANGER THAN
FICTION IN PERSONNEL ISSUES

You Do Voodoo?

Dr. Clarence Davenport was working in his office one morning, completing a teacher appraisal, when head custodian, Paula Lopez, unexpectedly appeared at his door and abruptly entered, white as a ghost and trembling. Dr. Davenport immediately stopped the task at hand and invited Miss Paula to sit down, asking, "Paula, are you all right?" Miss Paula responded, after catching her breath, that there were two witches in Mrs. Agnes Whitworth's first-grade classroom. Dr. Davenport, puzzled and not quite understanding Miss Paula's pronouncement, responded by asking, "What did you say?" The custodian reiterated that there were two witches in Mrs. Whitworth's room and further stated, "Dr. Davenport, I'm not going back in there—I'm scared!" Dr. Davenport by this time had gotten up from behind his desk and was comforting Miss Paula. He suggested that she stay in his office and gain her composure while he walked down to the first-grade wing of the building to check in with Mrs. Whitworth and her students.

Upon entering the first-grade classroom, Dr. Davenport noticed that the students were working quietly, completing some independent seatwork, while Mrs. Whitworth and two nicely attired ladies were sitting at the "kidney-shaped" reading table near the front of the classroom. Dr. Davenport, much to the surprise of Mrs. Whitworth, greeted the ladies and then introduced himself. He asked Mrs. Whitworth—who remained quite taken aback—what was the purpose of the two visitors, and if they had checked in and received visitor's passes at the front office. One of the ladies responded by stating, "No, we are just friends of Mrs. Whitworth, and we entered the building from the side street." Dr. Davenport recommended that the ladies come to the administrative office and sign the visitor sheet and obtain a visitor badge. The ladies, not exactly knowing how to respond to the principal's suggestion, reluctantly agreed and walked to the office.

Once the ladies had arrived at the receptionist's office and signed in, Dr. Davenport invited them into his office where he asked their purpose for being in the first-grade classroom. The ladies, in a matter-of-fact response, stated that they were assisting Mrs. Whitworth with a problem. Dr. Davenport asked what the problem might be, and they responded, "Mrs. Whitworth is a friend of ours, and we came by to spread positive omens in her classroom." Dr. Davenport was now even more intrigued and questioned what credentials the ladies possessed that granted them the expertise to spread positive omens. Each lady then presented Dr. Davenport with a business card indicating she was a high priestess in the Wicca religion. Following a brief interaction with the two "witches," Dr. Davenport escorted the two ladies out of the office, reminding them that in the future, they were to seek permission from his office before coming onto campus. Otherwise, campus security would have the ladies arrested for trespassing.

(Continued)

(Continued)

After the departure of the two ladies, Dr. Davenport immediately called the superintendent of schools and related the situation. Dr. James Tillman, district superintendent, recommended that campus security be put on alert immediately and noted that he was coming directly to the campus. Dr. Tillman also suggested that Dr. Davenport get a paraprofessional to cover Mrs. Whitworth's classroom and then personally escort Mrs. Whitworth to the principal's office, where the campus leader and the superintendent would meet with her as soon as Dr. Tillman arrived.

Mrs. Whitworth had no sooner arrived in the principal's office when Dr. Tillman came in, and all three individuals sat down for a conversation at the principal's round table. Dr. Tillman asked Mrs. Whitworth if she knew why she was asked to come into the office and visit with the superintendent and the principal. Mrs. Whitworth responded, "Yes, I asked two witches to come into my classroom to spread positive omens because I believe my principal is out to get me!"

Application Questions

1. What possible repercussions will Agnes Whitworth face as a result of her actions? Explain the "risk factors" associated with this particular situation.
2. Can controversial individuals be prohibited from public schools by a principal or a school district? Would members of Wicca be considered controversial at a public school? Support your answers.
3. Could Mrs. Whitworth be terminated for her actions? On what particular basis? Explain your answer.
4. How does religion in public schools relate to this case study? Consider the issues of secular humanism, welfare of students, clergy in schools, and religious accommodations. Support your response from an educational and personnel law perspective.
5. Which of the Principled Personnel Model principles, from the perspective of Principal Clarence Davenport, relate to or are applicable to the situation in the case study presented? Explain your answer.
6. What legal and moral obligations does a principal have in protecting members of the learning community? In this case study, which members of the learning community should be protected and why?

OTHER RESOURCES

Beaudoin, M., & Taylor, M. (2005). *Creating a positive school culture: How principals and teachers can solve problems together*. Thousand Oaks, CA: Corwin Press.
Tate, J. S., & Dunklee, D. R. (2005). *Strategic listening for school leaders*. Thousand Oaks, CA: Corwin Press.

4

Personnel and
Communication

What we got here is failure to communicate.

—The Captain in *Cool Hand Luke*

Paul Newman's Cool Hand Luke was a nonconformist character in the 1967 movie with the same name. Luke, imprisoned for minor offenses, meets the Captain, who becomes an authoritarian force in Luke's life. The Captain believes Luke needs additional disciplinary rehabilitation. In addressing Luke's defiant behavior, the Captain utters what becomes the most famous line from the film, "What we got here is failure to communicate" (Dirks, 2007).

Like the Captain and Luke, principals and personnel face communication challenges. Commitment and trust require open communication. Principals typically supervise more people than their private sector counterparts. This increased supervisor-to-personnel ratio requires principals to conduct more personnel meetings. Scheduling meetings and consulting with individuals is a challenge, given crowded schedules. As a result many principals tend to limit leadership participation to an inner circle of advisors at the expense of excluding others (Heller & Yukl, 1969). A principal at a large high school often communicates to faculty and staff through associate principals and department chairs.

Supervising larger numbers of employees increases principals' administrative workloads, which in turn decreases principals' opportunities to interact with individuals. Ford (1981) noted the administrative workloads also limited principals' opportunities to maintain effective relationships with their faculty. Larger personnel groups increase the likelihood of cliques and competition. This pressures principals to dedicate more time to team building and conflict management, which competes against the added administrative responsibilities of supervising large personnel groups. The fact that teachers primarily work independently further ripens the opportunity for communication challenges.

Consider this scenario. Mr. Wagstaff teaches for 25 years, has a 95% attendance rate, and teaches six lessons a day. During the course of his career, Mr. Wagstaff teaches 25,650 lessons. If Mr. Wagstaff's principal observes one complete lesson each year, he would observe 1 out of every 1,026 lessons per year, or 25 out of 25,650 lessons during Mr. Wagstaff's teaching career. This is less than 0.001% direct observation of Mr. Wagstaff's teaching. The Wagstaff scenario illustrates the challenge principals face in having meaningful communication with teachers about the heart of their work: learning. Add to this the communication required with other school stakeholders such as students, staff, parents, and community members, and the obvious quickly becomes apparent: Effective communication is challenging to say the least.

Communication problems have existed between humans since the beginning of time. When problems arise, whether in the family, at work, or in the public arena, the first cry heard is, "What we got here is failure to communicate." We all hear it. Successful principals are effective communicators (Halawah, 2005; Schneider & Hollenczer, 2006). In this chapter, we narrow our examination of communication to that between the principal and campus personnel. The next chapter will address communication in conflict resolution.

The transformation of the U.S. economy from an industrial to an information to a knowledge economy has only heightened the importance of communication (Friedman, 2005). No longer is news received in a neatly packaged 30-minute evening format. News is now disseminated 24–7 or, as Fox News touts on its Web site (www.foxnews.com/foxreport), "the speed of live." Like the news, the speed and avenues of communication have changed. The landline telephone is rapidly giving away to cell phone technology. Ask someone under the age of 18 about long distance calls and you receive a confused stare. Gone is the solitary black phone attached to the kitchen wall servicing the entire family. The formal printed memorandum is competing with the informal e-mail message, which is ceding to newer technology such as text messaging or instant messaging. School Web sites, Listservs, and telephone messaging are now essential communication tools for two-way communication with parents (Neely, 2005). Despite the changes in how humans communicate, our social nature causes the basic need for meaningful communication to remain constant.

Principals must be effective communicators. When problems arise, the principal's communication skills are tested, and "what we got here is failure to communicate" echoes throughout the school. Principals cannot afford to ignore communication matters. They must hone their communication skills. Poor communication causes relationships to deteriorate as time passes.

BASICS OF COMMUNICATION

Principals interact with personnel through written, verbal, and nonverbal communication. Written communication includes text messaging, instant messaging, e-mails, memoranda, letters, and faxes. Verbal communication includes face-to-face conversations and telephone calls. Nonverbal communication involves touch, body language, voice, and proximity.

A Basic Communication Model

Basic building blocks exist in all communication. Krone, Jablin, and Putnam (1987) developed a general communication process model that is widely accepted by educators. Figure 4.1 illustrates this model.

Figure 4.1   The Communication Process Model

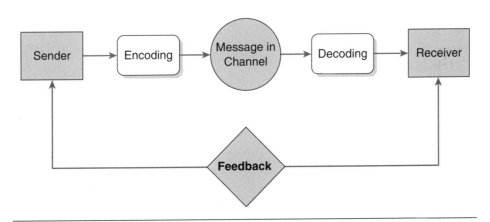

Source: Krone et al. (1987).

Krone et al.'s Communication Process Model is used to analyze Principal Pepper's e-mail (Figure 4.2) to Claude Fingers, a teacher. Principal Pepper, the sender, encoded her thoughts when she typed the e-mail. When she hit the *send* button, and until Claude hit the *open* button, the message was in the channel. Decoding occurred when Claude, the receiver, read the e-mail. Given the information provided, we could only speculate about the feedback, which could include a return e-mail, a meeting after school, or no response at all.

Figure 4.2   An E-mail From a Principal to a Teacher

From: Dr. Cheyenne Pepper, principal
To: Mr. Claude Fingers, teacher

Stop by my office before you
leave for the day!

CP

Feedback is the tricky part of written communication, because verbal and nonverbal clues are missing. Receivers need these important clues to accurately decode the sender's message. Feedback to Principal Pepper's e-mail could take several different directions depending on Claude's interpretation of the e-mail's written text. Interpretation is further clouded by Claude's emotional state at the time he reads the e-mail. If Claude is upset with a student when he decodes Principal Pepper's e-mail, he might decode it in a "direct order" voice and believe the principal is upset with him. If he decodes the e-mail after reading a complimentary note from a parent, he might decode Principal Pepper's e-mail in a friendly "drop by and see me" voice. The state of one's mind strongly influences how messages are received and decoded. Similar situations have happened to you. You decoded or read a written message one way, but once feedback was received from the sender, you realized you read the message totally wrong and missed its intent.

When writing to personnel, keep the following in mind:

- Be concise
- Proofread
- Use simple language
- Have a purpose
- Provide adequate time when a response is requested

The multiple ways Claude might decode Principal Pepper's e-mail bring to light another dimension of communication: richness. Richness of a communication is determined by which verbal and nonverbal clues are used. Ambiguity in the transfer of information decreases as the richness of the media increases (Daft & Lengel, 1984, 1986). Figure 4.3 illustrates

Figure 4.3   Communication Media and Richness

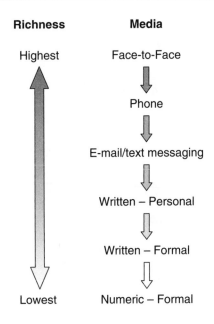

Richness	Media
Highest	Face-to-Face
	Phone
	E-mail/text messaging
	Written – Personal
	Written – Formal
Lowest	Numeric – Formal

Source: Adapted from Daft and Lengel (1986).

this relationship. The authors updated Daft and Lengel's model to include electronic messages that were not common when the richness scale was developed.

Rich media offer quick feedback, multiple clues, variety of language, and tailoring of messages to individual situations (Huber & Daft, 1987). Principals should use rich media such as face-to-face conversation as much as possible when conveying qualitative information such as praise or encouragement, because it lessens the ambiguity in interpreting the message (Glenn, 2002a). Rich media are best for praise, encouragement, and those difficult conversations. Least rich media are best for conveying quantitative data such as test scores and budget information.

Principal Pepper's e-mail is in the center of the richness scale (Figure 4.3). This location means Principal Pepper's e-mail is subject to multiple interpretations. Because e-mails do not offer verbal or nonverbal clues, the receiver must guess at the messenger's voice and body language. This absence of nonverbal clues is a likely reason those yellow faces with a variety of expressions and the more basic ":)" and ":(" are so popular in electronic correspondence. These facial expressions are the sender's effort to provide verbal and nonverbal clues to the receiver.

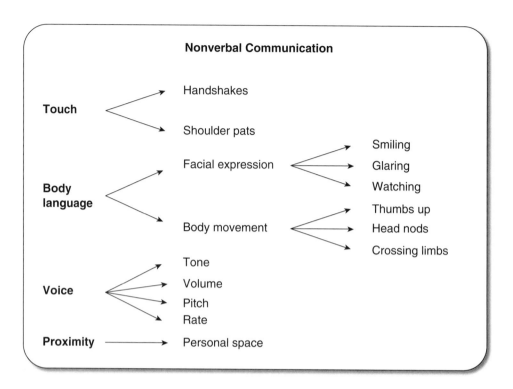

Nonverbal Communication

Touch — Handshakes / Shoulder pats

Body language — Facial expression — Smiling / Glaring / Watching

Body movement — Thumbs up / Head nods / Crossing limbs

Voice — Tone / Volume / Pitch / Rate

Proximity — Personal space

"You Better Be Careful"

A mother just made this statement to her child.

1. Read this statement in a voice conveying a loving reminder to be safe.

2. Read the statement as a warning to someone who is crossing the line of what is appropriate.

Lack of visual and context clues leads to misinterpretation in written communication.

Had Principal Pepper conveyed her e-mail message to Claude face-to-face in the hallway with a quick, "Stop by my office before you leave today," Claude could have picked up on the tone and pitch of Principal Pepper's voice along with other body language and more accurately interpreted the message's tone. On the other hand, how would Claude have interpreted this message if it had been delivered in a sealed envelope?

For the record, Principal Pepper wanted to advise Claude about a student's family problem. Although an e-mail was appropriate for this situation, Principal Pepper ran the risk of Claude interpreting her message in multiple ways. A quick verbal message in the hallway would significantly reduce the chance of a miscommunication. While rich media are the most desirable, they are also the most time intensive, and the reality of the principal's workload limits their use. Principals must make quick decisions in choosing their communication style. The quality of the principal's relationship to the personnel receiving the message as well as the message itself should influence the richness level of the media selected.

Another communication example between Principal Pepper and Claude involved the campus attendance report. At the end of each grading period, Principal Pepper provides the faculty with a student attendance report on an Excel spreadsheet. The current year's attendance rate is compared with the previous year's attendance rate as well as the five-year average. Using Figure 4.3 to analyze this communication's richness, it is apparent that spreadsheets are numeric-formal, placing them at the least rich end of the richness scale. Since Principal Pepper's message consisted primarily of *quantitative* data (an Excel spreadsheet), her communication avenue choice was appropriate. Receiving these data is straightforward. Analyzing these data is a different matter, requiring the use of richer media.

Active Listening

Active listening is an art achieved by practice (Davis, Hellervik, & Sheard, 2001). Active listeners focus on understanding the individual who is speaking and avoid distracting nonverbal behaviors (e.g., looking at a watch, avoiding eye contact, multitasking). Active listeners don't interrupt the speaker or respond in an uninterested or disparaging manner. They withhold judgments about a speaker's message by carefully listening until the entire message is delivered.

Principals exhibit active listening when they allow others to speak their piece. Rather than interrupt the speaker, they ask clarifying questions at the appropriate time. They watch the speaker and nod. They avoid negative body language such as crossed arms and scowling. When personnel come to the principal with a concern, they must be received in an open manner regardless of the principal's emotional stake in the message being communicated (Eagan, 2002). Even the best principals are challenged to actively listen when a conversation is emotionally intense.

Difficult Conversations

Difficult conversations require courage from at least one, if not all, of the parties involved. Those involved must be able to speak in such a way that others can hear the message. After all, the purpose of a difficult conversation is to "clear the air and to find resolutions to situations that are bothersome to you" (Sanderson, 2005, p. 5).

Most of us try to avoid difficult conversations. When we have them, we often handle them poorly. Stone, Patton, and Heen (1999) in their book, *Difficult Conversations: How to Discuss What Matters Most,* compare a difficult conversation to a hand grenade: "Coated with sugar, thrown hard or soft, . . . it is still going to damage" (p. xvii). Principals become stronger leaders when they deal successfully with frustrating and painful difficult conversations.

Stone et al. (1999) assert that every difficult conversation is really comprised of three conversations:

- *The "What Happened" Conversation,* which explores what happened or should have happened
- *The Feelings Conversation,* which explores feelings
- *The Identity Conversation,* which explores possible interpretations of the situation (pp. 7–8)

The remainder of their book provides advice not only on how to develop the necessary stance of mind and heart but also on the necessary expressive skills needed to communicate effectively when bridging significant differences in beliefs, emotions, and experience.

Difficult conversations associated with conflict resolution are discussed in greater detail in the next chapter.

Story

Some people marginalize the importance of stories as a form of communication. They liken them to the old professor most of us had in graduate school who told "war stories" from his or her personal experiences. However, well-told stories teach us values and lessons. Bolman and Deal (1997) assert that "stories keep traditions alive and provide examples to guide everyday behavior" in high performing organizations such as schools (p. 255). Principals can use stories to capture their schools' visions and remind personnel about "us" and "our" school.

Robert McKee (1997), trainer of many of Hollywood's most successful screenwriters, writes, "Story is about principles, not rules" (p. 3). Rules tell us we must do things a particular way. Principles tell us that something over time has proven that it works. Story is never out of style because story is eternal. Even in our data-driven education environment, peppered with endless acronyms and ever-changing policies, people still connect with story. Good storytellers communicate messages in rich and voluminous language while respecting and understanding their audience. Good stories possess important social and psychological meaning that connects the audience with the human side of the school.

SOPHIA'S STORY

Sophia was a master elementary school teacher. Parents frequently requested to have their children assigned to her classroom. Her classroom organization was highly structured. Her classroom was one from which you could "eat off the floor"—which is quite something to say about an elementary classroom. Even her trash can was neat. Students had assigned cubbies, each student had organized assignment folders, and all had a place in the room to display the work they chose to display.

Sophia knew her students. She utilized diagnostic testing data to identify and target each student's instructional needs. She then meticulously designed lessons that could be customized to meet those needs. Seldom did a student fail to master the state's criterion-referenced assessment test, no matter how challenging.

Sophia possessed the knack of doing all of this while maintaining her professional appearance. She could be around scissors, glue, markers, and nine-year-olds and go unscathed. On a hot, windy day when returning from recess duty, she would enter the building with every hair in place and no apparent sweat. How she was able to accomplish this was a mystery to the school's somewhat envious faculty.

She seldom found a need to send a student to the office for disciplinary issues despite the fact she had several significantly challenging students each year. Even those wiggly, squirmy, rough-around-the-edges little boys connected with Sophia and her classroom management style. Sophia brought structure to many a boy's life without the use of medication.

Sophia's life changed the day the doctor located a suspicious lump in her left breast. The identification led to additional testing, which led to a referral to a prominent regional hospital, which led to a visit to the principal's office.

Sophia shared her diagnosis and the pending out-of-town hospital visit with the principal. She was scared, but as usual she had everything under control—at least on the outside.

Several weeks later, Sophia returned to the principal's office and informed him that her appointment at the regional hospital would be in three weeks and she would need a substitute for several days. The principal asked if there was anything he could do to help her. Sophia replied she needed only the substitute and prayers.

Two days before the hospital visit, Sophia came to the principal's office to finalize her substitute arrangement. As she was leaving the principal's office, she stopped at the door and turned to the principal and said, "I know you are a man of faith. Would you lead the faculty in prayer for me?"

The principal told Sophia he could not call such a meeting. Sophia replied that the next day at 4:10 p.m. (after the official school day) many of the school's personnel were meeting in the library to pray for her before she left the next day for the hospital. She invited the principal to come. He did.

(Continued)

(Continued)

Most of the faculty and staff gathered in the library. They formed a circle and held hands. Then, in an unplanned moment, all turned and looked at the principal. After a moment of awkward silence, the principal prayed a prayer of healing and safe travel for Sophia and her family. When the short prayer was over and everyone raised their heads, a sense of unity filled the room. One of the teachers broke the extended silence and said, "Look at us! We are all from different religious heritages, and some of us have no religious heritage, but we're all here together."

The principal remarked, "Isn't it interesting how a crisis reminds us what is important in life. Things that we let divide us immediately become unimportant."

The meeting ended with lots of hugs and positive support.

Reflecting on Sophia's Story

Deal and Peterson (1994) assert that in most schools certain personnel become the unofficial priests or priestesses. "They hear confessions, preside over rituals and ceremonies and link the school to the ways of the past" (p. 29). This appears to be what happened to the principal in Sophia's story. This one brief event forever altered the faculty and staff of Sophia's school. Sophia's story became a part of the school's story.

From that day forward, the personnel at Sophia's school were closer to each other. Of course, Sophia's story did not end here. She eventually had a variety of medical procedures and taught four more years before retiring. She is now a 10-year breast cancer survivor.

Attributes of a Good Story

- Conveys a message
- Creates memories
- Engages emotions
- Feels intimate
- Is real and genuine
- Is honest
- Leaves a lasting and positive impression

Aquarium Story 2: A Fishy Story of a Fowl Whose Life Had Gone Afoul

Aquarium Story 2 in Chapter 1 is a story from one of the authors' schools. It is a story about bringing multiple generations together for a community cause. It is a story about teaching children values that cannot be quartiled or stanined or disaggregated into endless subpopulations. Rather, it is a story that resides in the hearts of hundreds of students, parents, grandparents, personnel, and community members, most of whom cannot recall the school's state academic accountability exam scores. As stories like this one are told and retold, they become written on the hearts of not only the personnel but also the school's stakeholders. While we can remember neither the test scores nor the state campus rating that year, Diablo's bake sale, replete with its sights, sounds, and aromas are vividly etched in our memories.

Some might be skeptical of story as an important communication skill for principals. It seems so "folksy," so lacking in sophistication. Aesop used fables, Jesus used parables, and American cowboys used ballads to tell their stories. In an age where technology

Stories are the elixir that fills the faculty and staff with the school's vision and mission.

spews endless data and we attempt to place a numerical value on every aspect of schools, principals and personnel would do well to reconnect with the low-tech, highly personal communication skill of storytelling.

THE COMPLETED PERSONNEL SUCCESS MODEL

The Personnel Success Model, introduced in the first chapter (Figure 1.2), graphically represents the relationship between school vision, personal vision, and personal skills. Aligning these three factors creates the personnel success zone. The model, as expanded in Chapter 2 (Figure 2.2), classifies school vision as a culture factor and classifies personal vision and personal skills as personnel factors.

The Personnel Success Model is expanded a final time to include communication (Figure 4.4). An ellipse representing communication surrounds the original model, emphasizing that school vision, personal vision, and personal skills cannot flourish without rich communication.

THE PRINCIPLED PERSONNEL MODEL AND COMMUNICATION

The Principled Personnel Model for Effective Leader-Follower Relationships, introduced in Chapter 3, like the Personnel Success Model, requires excellent communication to function optimally. The Principled Personnel Model is based upon respect, trust, honesty, responsibility, rights, and expectations, all of which are underpinnings of effective communication. Respect is demonstrated when people

Figure 4.4   The Personnel Success Model

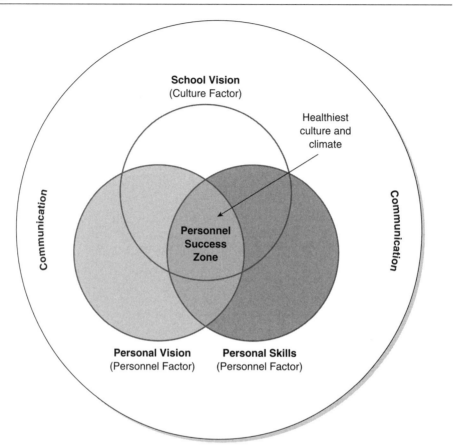

value each other. People cannot hear each other's message when respect does not exist. Respect requires trust, which is earned when the communicator is believable and honors confidentiality. Honesty must be present for trust to exist. People do not have to agree with each other for honesty to exist, but they must be open, direct, and genuine. Responsible communicators have the difficult conversations and face the hard issues. Responsible communicators ensure confidentiality and honor privacy. They see that laws are obeyed, and they set high standards for communication and teamwork. Effective communicators exhibit fair and reasonable behaviors, and they expect the same from the people around them.

Effective principals possess impressive communication skills. A leader can be persuasive and lack vision, but a leader cannot be a visionary and lack persuasiveness. Personnel do not make a poorly communicated vision their own. Successful principals must be good communicators.

EFFECTIVE COMMUNICATION BEHAVIORS

The following behaviors can be used to enhance a principal's communication skills.

- *Be frequent.* Make frequent contact with personnel. Contacts can be brief and still be effective. A nonverbal acknowledgement such as a nod, a wave, or a smile as you walk down a hallway is a positive communication. A brief text message (c u l8r ☺) also encourages personnel.
- *Be positive.* Job responsibilities can be stressful. People become overwhelmed and feel underappreciated. Trite as it may sound, a short, positive communication does wonders to lift someone's spirit and improve morale. For example, when passing a janitor, saying, "The floors are so shiny! You do so much to make our school look great!" brings validation to the janitor's effort. If you can't be sincere with a compliment, silence is probably better. Remember what your grandmother used to say, "You catch more flies with honey than you do with vinegar." Grandma knew something.
- *Be honest.* Principals must be diligent in building a reputation of honesty. Don't think you can pull one over on your personnel. Most people will know it immediately. Those who don't catch it immediately will eventually do so, and relationships will be forever damaged.
- *Be prepared.* Know what needs to be communicated, know to whom it needs to be communicated, and have others proofread written messages before they are distributed.
- *Be online.* The Web is always open. Unlike humans, it never tires. Leaders must take advantage of this communication tool. The Web site must be maintained and current if it is to attract repeat traffic. Although the principal is not the person to maintain it, the principal needs to ensure it happens. Online faculty handbooks and other resources make it easier for personnel to access information.
- *Be humorous.* Humor made our 11 Ten Most Wanted Strategies for Shaping School Culture list. Humor releases tension and helps settle problems that emerge from daily routines as well as unexpected crises (Boleman & Deal, 1997). Principals with a sense of humor make humor acceptable in the school. Good-natured joking when someone makes a mistake can put people at ease. When principals joke about their own mistakes, they motivate others to take chances (Jonas, 2004). Humor can also be used to help personnel remember important information. It can encourage personnel to complete the trivial and to do the tedious. Like all behaviors, humor must be used judiciously. Principals should not turn their schools into 30-minute sitcoms with a laugh track. A final caution: Completely avoid put-down humor. People live real lives, not 30-minute sitcoms.

- *Be appreciative.* People want and need to be appreciated when they do their jobs well. How principals manifest appreciation is limited only by their imaginations. What works well at one school might not work as well at another school. Likewise what works well with one individual might not work as well with another one. Appreciation shows itself in a sincere compliment or recognition. Calling attention to personnel in appropriate ways shows appreciation. One principal places a note and a carnation on the desk of every teacher on Valentine's Day; another principal hands out Payday® candy bars with the paychecks. Find your personal way to show your appreciation.
- *Be empathetic.* You can't fake this one. Just like you, people know when empathy is synthetic. Communicate your care for personnel in your own way. Send a get-well card, attend a funeral, be a good listener.
- *Be clear and concise.* School personnel are extremely busy. Principals must respect their time. It is easy to ramble, but it is difficult to be concise. Newsletters, e-mails, memos, and so forth must be written so they can be quickly read and comprehended. The adage used to be "a memo in the faculty box should be able to be read between the mailbox and the trash can." The electronic version is, "communication must be read between when it is opened in the inbox and the *delete* button is hit." Faculty meetings should be organized, well paced, and agenda driven.
- *Be truthful.* If you are truthful, you don't have to try to remember what you said to whom. Sometimes we struggle with this, particularly when difficult topics need to be discussed. No one respects a liar—and truth eventually comes out.

FINAL THOUGHTS

The way principals and personnel communicate with each other significantly impacts their schools' cultures and climates. Everyone must constantly work on improving communication, and all must be prepared to extend and accept apologies when communication goes awry.

Principals can use story to make their schools come alive. Through strategic use of story, schools become more than some government agency's or special interest group's subject for analysis and classification based on agenda-driven data analysis. Principals must tell their schools' stories. Write it on the hearts of personnel and other school stakeholders.

ONE MORE FINAL THOUGHT

Luke and the Captain never did communicate effectively. Luke escaped from the prison and ironically holed up in a church. The Captain and the guards tracked down Luke and surrounded the church. Luke opened a window and in a cocky but cool-handed manner yelled, "What we got here is *a* failure to communicate." At that moment, the Captain shot and killed him (Dirks, 2007).

Principals must communicate effectively.

DISCUSSION QUESTIONS

1. As principal you want the faculty to consider an integrated math-science curriculum structure you have been exploring. Develop a communication strategy for broaching this topic with the faculty so that it will receive due and fair consideration. Defend the steps of your communication plan.

2. List three ways the Personnel Success Model and the Principled Personnel Model for Effective Leader-Follower Relationships depend on the principal being an effective communicator. What impact does a principal with poor communication skills have on a school using both of these models? Explain.

3. Use the You Better Be Careful box on page 74 to respond to this question. Use circle 1 to draw a face to convey the voice of speaker one for message one in the You Better Be Careful box. Repeat for speaker two using circle 2.

1

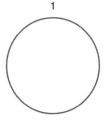

2

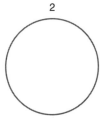

4. Describe times when you either used or witnessed humor that (1) made a person who had made a mistake feel more at ease, (2) helped personnel remember important information, (3) motivated personnel to complete a tedious job, and (4) inadvertently hurt someone. What factors made the last situation different from the other three?

5. Describe a time when you were challenged to remain an active listener. What made it difficult to remain an active listener? How was your nonverbal communication impacted? What personal strategies work for you in remaining an active listener?

(Continued)

(Continued)

6. Describe a time you witnessed a leader lie to or purposefully mislead personnel. What were the results of this behavior on the leader-personnel relationship? How did it impact the organization?

7. Recall a story from your school or one from a school you attended as a student. Write this story or tell it to someone. Describe why your story is important to you and what it communicates to others.

CASE STUDY APPLICATIONS

SATLEWHITE CASE

Mrs. Satlewhite is the mother of Kaiesha, a student in Claude Fingers's shop class. She advised Principal Pepper about a personal problem that happened at home over the weekend that might affect Kaiesha emotionally. Principal Pepper needs to make Claude aware of the situation. She knows Claude doesn't have a conference period for another three hours. Which would be the best way to share this information with him: (1) Leave him a voice mail on his classroom phone; (2) ask him to drop by and see her as she passes him in the hallway next period on her way to the gym; (3) walk to his room and talk with him; (4) put the parent's concerns in writing in an informal personal note; or (5) other? Refer back to Figure 4.3 for assistance. Defend your response.

LEI CHAN CASE

During a campus planning meeting, Principal Pepper is making a brief status report on the campus budget. She expresses concern that some higher than anticipated expenses require the committee to amend the budget by deleting $2,000 in expenditures. Principal Pepper notices Claude Fingers look at Lei Chan, a biology teacher, and roll his eyes. Lei rolls her eyes back at Claude, who smiles. The exchange happens in about two seconds. Using the Communication Process Model in Figure 4.1, identify the components of this nonverbal communication. Analyze the richness of the communication using Figure 4.3.

OTHER RESOURCES

Cerra, C., & Jacoby, R. (2004). *Principal talk! The art of effective communication in successful school leadership*. San Francisco: Jossey-Bass.

Sanderson, B. E. (2005). *Talk it out! The educator's guide to successful difficult conversations*. Larchmont, NY: Eye on Education.

Schneider, E. J., & Hollenczer, L. L. (2006). *The principal's guide to managing communication*. Thousand Oaks, CA: Corwin Press.

Stone, D., Patton, B. M., & Heen, S. (1999). *Difficult conversations: How to discuss what matters most*. London: Penguin Books.

5

Personnel and Conflict Resolution

Joe L. Cope

Things alter for the worse spontaneously, if they be not altered for the better designedly.

—Francis Bacon (*The Columbia World of Quotations,* 1996)

WHO MADE YOU BOSS?

Her hands gripped the mug with a force ordinarily reserved for clutching life rings in an open sea.

"What was I thinking? I really thought that I wanted to be in charge. I have been looking forward to being a school principal since I was in my principal prep program."

The surface of her coffee began to quiver and then exaggerated ripples threatened to splash the hot liquid on the conference table.

"It's my first day. I don't feel like I'm in control of things. The boys who were hanging out by the gym took off when they saw me coming. According to the truant officer, they were located at the theater in the mall around noon. The sophomore counselor made me late to a parent conference with his tirade over the district's new policy on excused absences for college visits. The parent who was waiting for the conference threatened to call the superintendent—her neighbor—to report my tardiness. Her call list expanded to include everyone on the school board when I told her that I wouldn't be able to transfer her son out of his English class. The football coach sat in the back of our first weekly faculty meeting and made wise-cracks. Then he refused to stay after the meeting to talk to me about it. Right after lunch, I was called to the fine arts wing where two teachers had gotten into a shoving match over a LCD projector. With the help of the janitor, I was able to separate them. I took the projector into custody and scheduled appointments with each of them for tomorrow.

"Our on-campus police officer made three arrests for drug possession in the parking lot after school. That wasn't the only problem in the parking lot. Evidently, one of the teachers involved in the altercation over the projector had the other guy's car towed away.

"I just finished a meeting with the assistant principal. The new, auto-mated student records system malfunctioned today. No class rolls were available to teachers. He also reported that there was a mix-up in class-room assignments. The calculus teacher shared his room with the modern dance instructor for four of the seven periods. Neither was amused. Oh, and the vice principal just wanted me to know that he had no hard feelings over the fact that I was named principal instead of him—despite his considerable experience and ability.

"I've got a stack of phone messages." Her right hand left the security of the mug momentarily to fan the pink slips of paper across the table. "Superintendent, board member, parent, superintendent again, lawyer for one of the teachers, football coach calling to tell me he won't be able to return my call, another board member, superintendent one more time, and that parent calling to tell me her son would have to miss English tomorrow because of a sudden illness that apparently will strike just prior to second period . . .

"What in the world was I thinking? I'm no leader. All I want is a little peace and quiet. And maybe an unlisted office telephone number."

This chapter was written because we believe Sir Francis Bacon was right. Conflict, if not approached with a healthy design in place, will only get worse.

EFFECTIVE SCHOOL LEADERSHIP
IN THE MIDST OF CONFLICT

Strange, isn't it? We often think effective school leadership produces a calm and reasonable environment where students, faculty, staff, parents, superintendents, and board members glide serenely to their proper places with smiles on their faces. Problems will occasionally surface. But those will be dispatched with a well-discerned command from you, the principal.

Instead, you feel barricaded in your office with the hope that somehow, some way, peace is going to break out all around you. In the meantime, the better part of valor seems to be to play defense, develop no-nonsense policies, and to speak with intense volume and great authority in the hope that those around you will either rally to your side or cower in your presence.

It doesn't have to be like that. And often it isn't when you're able to get a clear view of what conflict is and how it can be managed. To get started, it may be a little easier to define "peace." Peace is what we really want in our lives.

> Peace is not an absence of war, it is a virtue, a state of mind, a disposition for benevolence, confidence, justice. (Baruch Spinoza, *The Columbia World of Quotations*, 1996)

What!?! Benevolence, confidence, and justice!?! No, we want *real* peace. Serenity, calm, paradise. People doing what they are supposed to and leaving us and each other alone. That's peace, right?

Actually, Dutch philosopher Baruch Spinoza had it right when he noted that peace was not the absence of war or conflict. Peace occurs in the midst of conflict.

The truth be told, the effective school leader *needs* conflict.

The Negative Things About Conflict

At your next faculty meeting, ask the assembled academic warriors, "How many of you *like* conflict?"

If your crowd is typical, you'll see only a few, if any, hands go up. Most of those who respond affirmatively will be either your campus clowns or individuals no one else really cares for all that much. The campus clown just wants attention. In all likelihood, when confronted with conflict, the jokester is the first one to offer a glib remark and then disappear. The final group is composed of those who could best be called troublemakers. They feel they have power. When we were young, we called them bullies.

Most people don't raise their hands because they share negative views of conflict. Wilmot and Hocker (2007) propose a list that resonates with all of us (see Table 5.1).

Actually, there is one more group that will admit a "liking" for conflict. In fact, it's a group that we hope you'll join. Once in a great while, a hand will float upward attached to someone who believes that conflict can be positive. Wilmot and Hocker (2007) also have a list of positive approaches to conflict (see Table 5.2).

For those who choose to manage conflict in a positive way, these approaches set the stage for using disagreement and difficulty as a way to

Table 5.1   Negative Views of Conflict

---

1. Harmony is normal and conflict is abnormal.

2. Conflicts and disagreements are the same phenomenon.

3. Conflict is a result of personal pathology.

4. Conflict should never be escalated.

5. Conflict interaction should be polite and orderly.

6. Anger is the predominant emotion in conflict interaction.

7. There is one right way to resolve differences.

Source: Wilmot and Hocker (2007, pp. 34–36).

Table 5.2   Positive Approaches to Conflict

---

1. Conflict is inevitable; therefore the constructive way to approach conflict is as "a fact of life."

2. Conflict serves the function of "bringing problems to the table."

3. Conflict often helps people join together and clarify their goals.

4. Conflict can function to clear out resentments and help people understand each other.

Source: Wilmot and Hocker (2007, pp. 37–38).

transform problems and people. An analogy of how conflict can build up your school and those who work and study there is seen in physical exercise and its benefit to the body.

Let's concentrate on strength training. Did you know that weight lifting does not build muscle? If done properly, a result of weight lifting is strong muscles. But the initial effect of lifting a heavy object is the depletion of muscle fiber. In fact, if exercise is overdone, muscle fiber can be seriously injured or destroyed.

Strong muscles result from three interlocking causes. First, there is the exercise that challenges the targeted muscle or muscle groups. Second, the muscle must enter into a time of rest. During the respite from extreme exercise, the fibers have the opportunity to rebuild at a greater capacity. Finally, the body must have proper nutrition to rebuild the muscle.

Conflict resolution works in the same way. First, a problem arises that challenges those involved. This initial event is necessary because it draws attention to the problem and sets in motion a rebuilding process.

Second, a conflict should be *rested*. Note that *resting* and *avoiding* aren't the same things. In this context, resting refers to a conscious effort to separate people from the problem and to deal with the problem (Fisher, Ury, & Patton, 1991). In other words, we must work to attain and maintain a proper perspective. When we concentrate on people instead of the problem, we lose objectivity and our edge for problem solving. Finally, conflict requires proper nutrition—an appetite for mutual benefit and a penchant for understanding.

Just as in bodybuilding, conflict resolution requires the participant to be open to conflict (exercise), perspective (rest), and a desire to bring mutual benefit whenever possible (nutrition). Skipping any of these elements leads to disaster. Even though the conflict experience may be distasteful, an effective school principal will embrace the conflict and do everything possible to bring perspective and mutual benefit to all parties.

"Yeah, right," you're saying. "That won't work with my crowd."

No, it doesn't work out that easily all of the time. Sometimes you just have to be the boss and make hard decisions. It comes with the territory. Yet if that's the only way you deal with conflict, you won't be viewed as an effective leader. Dictators can be extremely efficient, but in the long term, they are rarely effective. Nowhere is this more apparent than in the school. You're an educator. Just because the sign on your door says "Principal" doesn't mean you've been stripped of your teaching credentials.

Problems are opportunities for teaching. If you really want to have a lasting impact on your students, your faculty, and your community, handle conflict in a way that builds understanding and teaches others to do the same.

THE PRINCIPAL'S PEACE PRIMER

Remember, peace can always be present—even in the presence of conflict. Through the rest of this chapter, we'll be looking at eight platforms that will assist in bringing peace to your campus. While these are presented in sequential order, remember that peace is an environment where conflict surfaces and stirs constantly. You'll need to develop an ability to flow toward conflict from any of these platforms, a concept personal management guru David Allen (2001) calls "mind like water" readiness (pp. 10–11). The key is appropriate response to what is happening around you.

Here they are, 8 platforms (with 16 "Ps") to guide you and your school to peace:

- Preserve Purpose
- Protect Process
- Practice Patience
- Promote People
- Prize Perceptions

- Praise Progress
- Produce a Plan
- Perfect Peace

These same platforms are useful in any conflict situation. Since this is a book on school personnel, our case study will be focused on dealing with teachers.

CASE STUDY: REMEMBERING HANK

Henry J. "Hank" Wallace was a remarkable man. He was a fixture in the North Plains Independent School District (NPISD). Very few townspeople could remember a time when Mr. Wallace wasn't on duty at Elmwood Middle School. After almost 50 years of teaching and administration, Mr. Wallace retired to Florida. In his absence, trouble began to boil at Elmwood.

Mr. Wallace had a unique management style. He was able to turn away most problems just because of who he was. He was Mr. Wallace. And for most people in North Plains, he was "Mr. Wallace, my second grade teacher" or "Mr. Wallace, my grade school principal."

At his retirement, the local paper, *The North Plains Picayune*, devoted a whole section to his career. Actually, that amounted to about two pages of actual stories and pictures and two more to advertising from local merchants wishing Mr. Wallace a happy retirement. In a small sidebar, the paper noted a remarkable circumstance: It seemed that every teacher and staff person working at Elmwood on Mr. Wallace's last day was a former student of his.

Mr. Wallace's retirement coincided with the last day of school. Throughout the summer, the community contemplated Labor Day and the opening of school without him. The majority of the conversation was on who his replacement might be. The most likely candidates appeared to be the two vice principals, Lauraine Oldenburg and Garrison Passmere. In a surprise announcement at the town's Fourth of July picnic, Sam Stirple, NPISD superintendent, named Patsy Nuñez to lead Elmwood Middle School.

Ms. Nuñez had been an elementary principal in the South River School District. Her school, Greenville Elementary, had been an "exemplary school" noted for its strong involvement of parents and community leaders in its ongoing programs. *State Teacher* magazine touted Ms. Nuñez as a "school leader for the 21st century" and the "kind of principal who makes things happen." Anticipation of her arrival stirred many lively conversations in the North Plains town square.

One week before school was to open, Elmwood teachers made their way into the multipurpose room for their first official faculty meeting with Ms. Nuñez. All were seated, and a hush fell over the group as their new principal burst through the door with a large box.

"Good morning! If we haven't had the opportunity to meet, I'm Patsy Nuñez and I'm looking forward to being part of the North Plains community. We are going to build on the excellence that Mr. Wallace and all of you have established at Elmwood. But there will be some changes."

Mrs. Oldenburg and Mr. Passmere exchanged pained expressions—an action that was not lost on the faculty or Ms. Nuñez. Ignoring the reaction, Ms. Nuñez dug into her box and began distributing materials—an events calendar, an article reprinted from the Journal of Educational Administration, and a small bound booklet titled, *Guide to Professional Educators: A Handbook for the Faculty of Elmwood Middle School.*

The calendar and the article were introduced and explained in a few moments.

"I'd like to spend the rest of our time today going through the professional guide," Ms. Nuñez explained. And then she did. For the next two hours, the teachers fought equal feelings of boredom and indignation as new policies and procedures were detailed and emphasized. The group broke for lunch with Ms. Nuñez's promise that, in the afternoon session, an equal amount of time would be spent exploring her plan for intensive peer evaluations of every teacher.

Ms. Nuñez was the first one out of the room at noon—hurrying to a luncheon with Superintendent Stirple and the other principals from around the district. The teachers didn't move as quickly. A number of them gathered around Mrs. Oldenburg and Mr. Passmere.

"What are you two going to do about this?" Coach Swift demanded. "We're going to spend all of our time doing paperwork and in meetings. I can't—I won't—be treated this way!"

"That's right!" Tina Simmons, the diminutive music teacher, inserted. "This isn't the way that Hank took care of things. This Nuñez woman is a nuisance. Do something and do it soon. If you don't, I vote we should all call in sick for the first week of school. That'll get the attention of the administration."

Others echoed these feelings. The sentiment grew and the teachers of Elmwood Middle School coalesced into a very surly group. At 1:15 p.m., Ms. Nuñez faced an angry crowd and the vocal opposition of its appointed spokespersons, Mrs. Oldenburg and Mr. Passmere. Taken aback by the reaction, Ms. Nuñez's first emotion was one of anger. But taking a moment to think, she announced a short recess and asked her assistant principals to join her for a conference.

When Ms. Nuñez shut the door to her office behind them, Mr. Passmere blurted, "Well, I suppose you called us in here to fire us. But I guarantee that won't be the last of it. A lot of people in this town don't want you here and you will lose the war!"

Mrs. Oldenburg blinked, her eyes watering slightly, and then nodded her agreement.

(Continued)

(Continued)

"I've not called you in here to fire you," said Ms. Nuñez, "although I could, and after hearing Superintendent Stirple's mandate at lunch for improving this school district, I don't think I would lose anything—not a skirmish or a major battle or even the war. No, I've called you in here because we are going to work through this problem, and we're going to walk out of here with a solution we can all live with."

"How do you suppose we're going to do that?" Mr. Passmere asked.

Platform 1: Preserve Purpose

When dealing with conflict, the effective school leader must keep purpose as the center of all actions and conversations. "What are we trying to accomplish? Is it important? Is my idea of our purpose unique or does the other side share my ideals?"

Conflict resolution professionals, the people who deal with the problems of others on a daily basis, know that the most intense conflict happens between and among individuals who share, to some extent, common purposes and values. Think about it. Why would you argue and fight over something you didn't care about?

Preserving purpose allows the effective principal to sidestep petty behavior and to call all parties back to a solid place.

Ms. Nuñez smiled. "We're going to do that because we're going to find our common ground and we're going to make certain that we keep our discussions centered there. So let me ask you, 'What are we doing here? Why have we chosen to be at Elmwood Middle School?'"

"We're here for the children," Mrs. Oldenburg offered. "We're doing all of this for them and to make sure they get the best education."

"I can agree with that," Ms. Nuñez said. "Mr. Passmere?"

"Agreed," he mumbled.

"So," Ms. Nuñez continued, "I will make sure that, over and above everything else, our discussions preserve this overall purpose."

By setting a standard for the discussion, Ms. Nuñez has provided a touch point that she and the others can use to keep the conversation on task. If conversation breaks down, becomes heated, or loses focus, any one participant can call the group back to the purpose.

Preserving purpose is important as an internal guide for school leaders as well. Keeping your purpose in the forefront assists you in judging your own motives and assessing your own behavior. Words chosen with a purpose in mind are rarely words regretted.

Platform 2: Protect Process

The effective school leader manages conflict by drawing others into a process that ensures fairness. We often think about process as a mechanical function—a checklist of things to do. That's what it is. Yet it is much, much more.

Process enables trust. It accomplishes that by assuring the participants that, as long as they act within the boundaries of process, they will be protected from arbitrary actions and judgments.

"With our purpose agreed on, I want to talk about the problem that surfaced in the faculty meeting a little while ago." Ms. Nuñez looked from Mrs. Oldenburg to Mr. Passmere. "I saw the way the two of you reacted this morning when I mentioned that we would be making some changes, and I think you need to tell me what caused your behavior."

"Here we go!" said Mr. Passmere. "I can see where this is headed."

"And where is that, Mr. Passmere?"

"You're setting us up," he answered. "You're going to trick us into saying things you don't want to hear, and then you're going to fire us."

The only sound for a few seconds was the ticking of the apple-shaped clock on the principal's desk. Mrs. Oldenburg looked down. Mr. Passmere glared directly at Ms. Nuñez.

"Okay, that's a legitimate concern," Ms. Nuñez agreed. "Let me start by saying that I will not use this conversation as a basis for dismissing you. I really need to know what you think. You've been here longer than I have. I have much to learn. The only way I can do that is to listen and observe.

"So, here's a rule that I will follow. I pledge to listen to you—even if I disagree with your position. Further, I agree to make no decisions regarding your employment based on what is said in here. Please note that these are internal rules that apply to the handling of our conflict. Insubordinate behavior outside this room may require other consequences."

"What does that mean?" Mrs. Oldenburg said softly.

Ms. Nuñez settled back in her chair. "That means that either of you or both of you or anyone who works at Elmwood Middle School can come to me and talk about anything. I promise to listen, to try to understand, and, if I can, to come to agreement. If I can't agree, I will do my best to explain why. And I will never use the conversation to punish you."

"But you said something about consequences," Mr. Passmere stated. "What's that about?"

(Continued)

(Continued)

"I am suggesting a process that allows you or anyone else to talk to me about anything without fear of reprisal. That goes for conversations in this office and will, most often, extend to appropriate public meetings, like our faculty meetings. My hope is that those discussions will allow us to collaborate on solutions to problems. Yet there will be times when consensus cannot be reached and someone will have to make a decision. When that decision is mine to make, I must have your cooperation."

"That's certainly understandable," said Mrs. Oldenburg. "But how can we be sure that you're going to honor your promise not to punish us for what we say to you?"

"I hope to earn your trust in that regard. And if I violate my agreement to honor the process, I feel certain that you will tell the rest of the faculty—and probably Superintendent Stirple, the school board, and the newspaper," Ms. Nuñez caught Mr. Passmere nodding with a sideways glance. "You see, if I really want to honor our purpose—to provide a great education for our students—I must protect this process. I must earn the trust of everybody."

Platform 3: Practice Patience

One of the most difficult principles in conflict resolution is that of persevering in patience. The effective school principal must, in order to preserve purpose and protect process, exercise considerable restraint in dealing with people. Remember, most individuals aren't accustomed to dealing with conflict in a healthy way. As a result, their anxiety or other emotions may cause them to act out in frustration. Patience requires the effective leader, whenever possible, to pause and to forgive another party's indiscretion. Karl Slaikeu (1996) notes that there is more to forgiveness than theological aspirations. Whenever people are working together and one offends another, forgiveness is a way of saying "I agree to stop holding this conflict over our heads as we work together toward the future" (p. 37).

When you are in conflict or you are working with those who are, patience is the key to the future. By allowing someone a little room to err, we have created significant territory for trust building and the nurture of relationships. But remember that patience isn't blind acquiescence. Patience demands accountability.

"I still think you're going to use what we say against us," Mr. Passmere injected.

"I understand," Ms. Nuñez said smoothly. "I only ask you to trust me to whatever extent you can. I promise to do my best to earn that trust."

Another benefit of patience is that those to whom patience is extended will often return the favor. Effective principals have a lot of wonderful traits going for them. Being absolutely perfect, unfortunately, isn't one of them.

Platform 4: Promote People

Whenever individuals become embroiled in conflict, their most common response is one of defensiveness and caution. They believe that they are personally under attack and that their very survival is dependent on "winning." As a result, conflicted people begin to lose sight of the problem and its underlying causes and assign the whole package (issues, interests, symptoms of the problem, anxiety, anger, fear, frustration, etc.) to the person who is at the focal point. This transference of problem to a person is unhealthy and at the root of most unresolved conflict.

We really have only two choices in how to deal with someone in conflict. We can exclude the other person, or we can embrace them. When we exclude the other, we attempt to differentiate ourselves from them. Further, because that person is different and thus an enemy, everything that is wrong in this situation is personified in our opponent. On the other hand, if we embrace our opponent, we begin to see how he or she is like us (Dunn, 1999, pp. 42–43). That recognition leads to better understanding and an increased capacity for patience. After all, if the one we excluded (our enemy) is now embraced, we begin to see and understand how someone could disagree with us (p. 44).

"So you're not angry with us?" asked Mrs. Oldenburg.

"No, I value your experience and your support. I would hope that we could be friends and colleagues for years to come. My job is not to control you. I'm in a supervisory role, but I really want you to excel," Ms. Nuñez explained. "I don't believe you are trying to cause trouble. I think that all three of us are trying to get back to our common reason for being here—the students."

"You're saying that you are glad that things flared up in the faculty meeting?" Mr. Passmere questioned.

"Absolutely," Ms. Nuñez replied. "I value the professional judgment of you and of all of my teachers. What I really need is for you to tell me what your perceptions are."

Platform 5: Prize Perceptions

Have you ever noticed that two people can witness the same event, from the same location, and then tell two distinct stories? If you've ever been a juror in a court trial, you also would note that those two versions, even where many facts agree, can assign blame to totally different parties.

What's going on? Are the witnesses lying?

Maybe. Some people have a pathological or moral problem with being truthful. However, most people are honest. They report their perceptions of what happened, because that is all they have to work with. Perception really is reality—until you challenge it. And before you start challenging someone else's perception, begin to test your own.

Patterson, Grenny, McMillan, and Switzler (2002) have asserted that testing perception is really an exercise in developing a "pool of shared meaning" (p. 21). When we attempt to understand the perceptions of others (and the accompanying judgments and assumptions they carry), we build on our ability to understand the concerns they have. Thus we are able to better communicate our positions and perceptions. The first step in deepening that pool of shared meanings is to prize the perceptions of others.

Develop the ability to welcome and explore the perceptions of others.

Ms. Nuñez sat and looked expectantly...first at Mrs. Oldenburg and then at Mr. Passmere. Finally, Mr. Passmere broke the silence.

"Look, I'm not sure what you want, Ms. Nuñez. You've talked about talking. What do you want me to talk about?"

Ms. Nuñez smiled, "I'll tell you what I want, Mr. Passmere. I want you to call me Patsy. I want you to tell me, face-to-face, what is going on here at Elmwood Middle School and with you. And if you feel qualified, I want you to tell me what the other teachers are feeling." She drummed the desk with her fingers. "That's what I want."

His mouth opened, just slightly. Then closed again.

"And that's what I want from you, too." Patsy was looking at Mrs. Oldenburg.

"You can call me Lauraine—no, make that Laurie," Laurie said. "How about it, Gary?"

"You go first, Laurie," he said and then whispered toward Laurie, "I want to see how this goes for awhile."

For the next half hour, Laurie began to tell Patsy how things had been done at Elmwood, how Hank—Mr. Wallace—had run his operation. He was never questioned. After all, he had been the teacher or the principal for every employee in the building. And he didn't change anything. Each new school year brought only new children. Teachers received the same classroom assignments, Hank wasn't interested in new curriculum, and the school administration didn't dare ask him to do anything different.

By that time, Gary was feeling more confident. He told Patsy how the faculty at Elmwood felt really comfortable with the way Hank did things. "We didn't have any conflict because he didn't expect us to do anything different. Things were very settled here. And Hank protected us. No one ever poked their nose in our business."

"I'm beginning to hear that my introduction of new things and new ideas is bothersome to you—to all of the teachers here," Patsy said.

"It's not just the new ideas," Laurie inserted. "You just waltzed in and told us things were going to change. You're acting like a lot of things need to be fixed around here. I can't speak for everyone, but I don't think much of anything is broken."

"You're new, too," said Gary, almost imperceptibly.

"Excuse me?" Patsy said.

Gary cleared his throat. "Well, some of us just haven't really gotten used to the idea that an outsider would be running Elmwood." He shifted uneasily in his chair. "I don't mean any offense by that."

"And there's none taken," Patsy assured him. "I think I'm beginning to understand your perspective on all of this. That's very helpful. Why don't we go back to the faculty meeting? I'm sure that everyone is wondering what has happened to us."

"I'm kind of wondering that myself," Gary whispered to Laurie as they followed Patsy back down the hall.

Platform 6: Praise Progress

Conflict resolution professionals often talk about their success. Accomplishment is measured by some as how many deals were made or agreements reached. Yet if you looked at what conflict really is, you would apply a different standard.

Conflict occurs when two or more people get stuck. They take positions, and they spend their energy trying to get the other party to move. By concentrating on moving someone else, they lose sight of their real purpose. And they grow weary of the struggle.

The effective school principal measures success by whether the parties to conflict move. While movement isn't always in a positive direction, a leader who listens and tries to understand can usually make the most of even the slightest leaning. And once movement is detected, praise should be poured out to fuel the momentum of change.

"Ladies and gentlemen, please take your seats. I apologize for the delay. Laurie, Gary, and I needed to discuss a few things that I believe will be very important to all of us. I regret that I had not talked with them before now." Patsy's voice was firm and unwavering.

The faculty looked anxiously at Laurie and Gary. What had this woman done or said to them? Were they okay? What is going on?

"I want to commend the two of them. In our meeting this morning, I made some assumptions and I wasn't thinking of you. They confronted me in a professional and

(Continued)

(Continued)

courteous way. I'm not sure they were comfortable in doing that. However, their willingness to talk with me should be an example to you and to me."

Laurie and Gary nodded reassuringly to their colleagues. Gary even managed a thumbs-up to Coach Swift.

"I have some very specific things I want us to accomplish here at Elmwood in the next year. I don't apologize for that," Patsy paused, looking around the room. "I do apologize for failing to talk to each of you to learn of your dreams and your vision. We are—or at least we will be—a team. I pledge to you my loyalty. And I promise to honor your investment in our students.

"Thanks again to Gary and Laurie. Their leadership has moved us a long way down the road to success."

Platform 7: Produce a Plan

Conversation is essential in dealing with conflict. But if you simply talk the talk and you don't walk the walk, conflict will continue to surface. Unfortunately, it won't just surface. It will escalate.

An effective school principal will make the construction of a plan an important part of the conflict resolution process. Building a plan furnishes a number of opportunities to build peace.

First, building a plan helps ensure that the parties understand both the positions and perceptions of all involved. A plan is a road map to some desired location and it always begins with an honest look at where you are.

Second, planning is a work in progress. While all parties to a conflict are concerned with substantive issues to some extent, each shares a common and intense interest in the process that will be used to move past the problem. Let's rewind that and play it at a different speed. While we all care about how things work out, a deeper concern is that the process used was fair. With few exceptions, people within an organization will rally if they believe that their voices were heard and that the decisions made, even if they weren't exactly what they wanted, were delivered with respect to the opinions and feelings of all.

Third, a plan provides a way to measure future progress. Once again, because of the importance of process, it is important that progress be compared to an agreed standard. The well-considered plan provides that standard.

Finally, accomplishing a plan—or even accomplishing pieces of a plan—brings a feeling of satisfaction and fulfillment to a group.

Effective leaders are planners. But more important, they are planners who are willing to involve others—particularly those who have a different perspective—in the process.

Patsy began to move around the room, picking up the *Guide to Professional Educators*. The teachers fell silent as she took the booklets and placed them back in the box.

"This guide should be a joint effort. I would benefit from your input. In reflecting on my conversations with Laurie and Gary, I'm thinking that we should spend a little time this afternoon putting together a committee to write *our* guide. Gary, why don't you lead the discussion?"

Gary took the marker that Patsy was offering and made his way to the white board. "Okay, let's start with an understanding of what our purpose is . . ."

Platform 8: Perfect Peace

Peace exists in the face of conflict. It balances on a thin edge between justice and mercy. It feeds on understanding and conversation. While conflict rages, peace can be perfected. Perfecting peace requires preserving common purpose, protecting the process, practicing patience, promoting people (over personal gain), prizing the perceptions of all involved, praising the progress made, and producing (and reproducing) plans that bring people together—and back to the common purpose.

Effective school principals will constantly hone their peace skills. Conversation will be encouraged. Understanding will be insisted upon. And patience will bring all to a sense of community.

Application Questions

1. When Ms. Nuñez was confronted by her faculty, she immediately called a conference with Mrs. Oldenburg and Mr. Passmere. What would be the advantages of meeting with the entire faculty to talk through the issues and interests? What would be the disadvantages?

2. Because of the importance of process, committing the details of a conflict resolution process to writing can add credibility. What do think the three most important principles for such a process would be?

3. Capturing the perceptions of others can be difficult. What standard questions could you ask to help others share their perceptions and provide insight to a deeper understanding?

4. Conflict exists in many forms and intensity levels. Some conflicts emerge as common, everyday issues. What platforms from the Principal's Peace Primer could you use in solving simple problems?

FINAL THOUGHTS

Conflict resolution is a work-intensive activity. In the interest of full dis-closure, an absolute dictatorship is easier and in many ways more efficient. The problem with top-down control is keeping people at the bottom. And while the exercise of power seems to work at first, over time the revolution will surface. Revolutions in schools manifest themselves in a number of ways—a breakdown in school discipline due to a disinterested faculty, a significant drop in student learning outcomes, an exodus of talented teachers, or an uprising of parents (usually closely followed by an upris-ing of school board members). Like it or not, any system designed to sup-press people fails eventually.

Looking through the lens of the ISLLC standards, the school leader's role as a conflict resolution advocate and expert is apparent. In fact, you might say the role is glaring—shiny and bright and ever so clear.

Standard 1—bringing about a vision of learning shared and supported by the school community—is the beginning point for collaboration of purpose. And where parents are involved and their children's futures are at stake, collaboration is the key. By definition, conflict nests around collaboration.

Standard 2—ensuring a school culture and instructional program con-ducive to student learning and staff professional growth—touches the strength of conflict resolution. Culture is a societal invention that pro-tects the status quo. Change upsets and disrupts that culture. Conflict must be engaged and resolved so that essential change can be utilized in an effective and timely way.

Standard 3—ensuring management of organization, operations, and resources—ensures that conflict and its resolution cycle in an orderly manner. Conflict presents problems and opportunities, with resolution hatching answers and plans that take advantage of scarce resources.

Standard 4—collaborating with families and community members in a context of diversity in order to meet needs—speaks to the social impor-tance of conflict resolution. Not only are collaborative decisions made, the effective school leader teaches faculty, students, parents, and com-munity leaders the power of working together. Schools attract diver-sity. The principal stands as a central figure in bringing together all aspects of the community.

Standard 5—acting with integrity, fairness, and in an ethical manner—bolsters the underlying beauty of conflict resolution. The peacemaker in the school continually points to the value of all persons involved and heightens the worth of mutual gain.

Standard 6—taking part in the larger world around us—is an appeal to the absolute necessity of conflict resolution and reconciliation. If school leaders are able to model for students, parents, and community leaders appropriate avenues to discuss ideas and solve problems, all of the pieces of our world move closer together.

It's all about conflict. Rather, it's all about how you *handle* conflict. That's why they made you the boss.

DISCUSSION QUESTIONS

1. This chapter emphasizes the need for effective school leaders to collaborate and promote peace on their campuses. When would collaboration not be an appropriate approach?

2. An effective school leader is instructed to practice patience as part of the conflict resolution process. How does one practice patience without appearing weak?

3. If perception is reality, what hope does a principal have in winning over an obstinate faculty?

4. Conflict resolution takes a large investment of time and energy. What results would justify the investment?

5. If peace exists in the presence of conflict, what are the benefits of resolving the conflict?

CASE STUDY APPLICATION

Unlike the other chapters, where there is a case study at the end of the chapter, Chapter 5 itself was the case study.

6

Personnel and Recruitment and Selection

The first method for estimating the intelligence of a ruler is to look at the men he has around him!

—Niccolò Machiavelli (*The Columbia World of Quotations,* 1996)

FINDING MR. OR MS. RIGHT

Not so long ago in a graduate class, the professor—while standing in a hallway during a much needed break—couldn't help but overhear a student state to a fellow classmate: "I just keep looking for 'Mr. Right'!" In love and marriage, finding Mr. (or Ms.) Right is often analogous to finding the right person to fill a needed position in the school business. Many a principal has been confounded by the prospect of seeking the right person for the right position. Accomplishing this goal is not an easy task, especially when the principal is less than adept in the recruitment and selection process.

Effective principals recognize and incorporate into practice the truism found in the introductory quote by Niccolò Machiavelli. This truism reveals that everyone matters, and everyone wins, when the school leader seriously utilizes effective recruiting methods and techniques, which are so essential to the appropriate selection of campus personnel. When the principal, working in collaboration with the site-based decision-making team, selects the best possible candidate for the position available, there is a greater likelihood that the varied needs of all constituencies within the school community will be met and addressed. That said, it is important to note that finding Mr. or Ms. Right is no simple matter when it comes to the recruitment of personnel.

RECRUITMENT OF PERSONNEL

The most significant factor influencing the quality of any instructional program, from a principal's perspective, is the recruitment and ultimate selection of capable, talented, and skilled personnel. Some years ago, yet so relevant today, Harris, McIntyre, Littleton, and Long (1985) suggested that "a mutt cannot be transformed into a show dog, regardless of the training, grooming, and love that are lavished upon it, and neither can basically weak personnel be [professionally developed] out of their ineptitude" (p. 103). If such an analysis is correct, the recruitment of competent personnel by principals today must incorporate opportunities for revealed leadership—leadership for meeting the issues and problems of the modern educational setting, especially when the school leader is attempting to identify potential candidates for employment who will meet and exceed the job-related behaviors and performance outcomes associated with a school (Norton, 2005).

School administrators would agree with the age-old adage, "You hire a problem, you'll fire a problem." Principals must understand they are not just recruiting a person for their particular school; they are recruiting for their school district. Before hiring a problem, a principal would be well advised to take appropriate actions in the recruitment process. The first aspect of this process involves the development of an overall campus vision.

Campus Vision

Principals are responsible for developing and articulating a guiding vision for their schools. This vision must be reflective of and based upon several key factors and questions. Factors include culture and climate, as previously examined in Chapter 2. Recall, school culture is defined as a set of important traditions, beliefs, assumptions, values, and attitudes that members of a learning community share. Climate, on the other hand, is simply the collective personality of a school. Both the climate and culture of a school can be positively or negatively affected by a leader's vision for the campus. Furthermore, Norton (2005) suggests that the visionary process is initiated when the campus principal answers three basic questions: (1) What has been the purpose or perspective of the school, both traditionally and historically? (2) What clientele is currently being served and, just as important, not served? (3) What will potentially define student, teacher, principal, and organizational success in the future?

After these questions are addressed, the effective principal seeks answers to the following four questions: (1) What type of school organization is presently in place? (2) What is the current purpose of the school and its personnel? (3) How is campus success presently defined and measured? (4) What guides the current organizational approach to reach greater levels of student achievement and personnel success? These questions can be further realized, if not visualized, when associated with the creation of a campus vision (see Table 6.1). Principals acquire this realization when they develop a campus vision from a *traditional perspective*, a *current perspective*, a *potential perspective*, and an *evaluative perspective*.

Table 6.1   A Seven-Step Approach to Creating a Campus Vision

Traditional Perspective

Step 1	The school principal, in collaboration with the campus team, seeks to identify what has been the traditional or historical purpose of the organization. This process is facilitated by an analysis of data, a review of assessment measures, an investigation into the stakeholder selection processes, and an evaluation of goal-setting and performance objective utilization (see Sorenson & Goldsmith, 2006, pp. 69–74).

Current Perspective

Step 2	The school principal, in collaboration with the campus team, conducts an in-depth analysis of the current campus culture and climate, focusing on how the leadership team can bring about incremental change to the organization, thus leading to the transformation of the campus from a level of maintaining the status quo to one of purposeful adjustment and direction.

Potential Perspective

Step 3	The school principal, in collaboration with the campus team, conducts a critical examination into what the school, as an organization of leaders and learners, should become and achieve.
Step 4	The school principal, in collaboration with the campus team, assesses the organizational strengths of the campus and moreover identifies areas targeted for potential growth, development, and achievement.

(Continued)

Table 6.1 (Continued)

Step 5	The school principal, in collaboration with the campus team, identifies campus problems and other inhibiting factors that interfere with organizational progress, student achievement, and personnel development.

Evaluative Perspective

Step 6	The school principal, in collaboration with the campus team, develops a visionary plan of action focusing on best practices, effective instructional techniques, and alternative approaches that support personnel in their quest to increase student achievement and organizational success.
Step 7	The school principal, in collaboration with the campus team, continuously monitors, evaluates, and adjusts the campus visionary plan of action through frequent meetings and brainstorming sessions with various members of the learning community.

No matter how perfect the vision is on paper, programmatic improvement, personnel development, and visionary enhancement will have little chance to succeed in an environment that fails to elicit from personnel an intrinsic personal motivation and a purpose-driven enthusiasm for coming to work. Research conducted by Buell (1992), Hallinger and Leithwood (1998), Pawlas (1997), and Scoolis (1998) has revealed that school principals who develop an ongoing visionary process through collaboration and cooperation with personnel will lay a solid foundation for personnel achievement, for personnel commitment, for personnel communication, for personnel contentment, and for personnel recruitment, selection, and retention.

Attracting the Right Applicant

Rebore (2007) suggests recruitment is the process of discovering potential applicants for anticipated vacancies. Principals have an ethical, if not a moral, obligation to attract the very best candidates to fill the personnel positions within their schools. Attracting the right applicant for the right position in any school is by far the most challenging and time-consuming responsibility of a principal. Placing the right person in the right position is critical to assuring the effectiveness of individuals in maintaining a school's vision, mission, and goals. New recruits must be identified, screened, interviewed, and ultimately selected based on policy guidelines, application processes, formal interview techniques, evaluative procedures, and designated staff involvement in the personnel selection process. These practices involve position analysis, staff diversity considerations, background checks, and the frequent need for "on-the-spot" hiring procedures. In far too many instances, a quality applicant is lost to another school or school system because a principal did not understand the recruitment game or the craft of selecting qualified personnel.

SELECTION OF PERSONNEL

The selection process represents one of the best methods for initiating change and ensuring instructional improvement in any school (Webb & Norton, 2003). In fact, a well-planned and carefully executed screening and selection process can breathe new life into a school where ineffective visioning and planning, low morale, teacher absenteeism, low test scores, and overall tedium are the norm. Effective screening and selection processes and procedures begin with the principal. Appropriate personnel selection identifies the qualified as well as the quality candidate and places the right person in the right position while considering staff diversity, balance, and teaching load. Correctly implemented, the selection process also enhances the school's academic and other educationally centered goals, positively affects the quality of teaching and learning, promotes a positive organizational climate, and develops constructive peer relationships.

Procedures in the Selection Process

Employee selection is a major expense for any school district (Rebore, 2007). Recall from Chapter 3 that school districts expend up to 85% of their total budget for personnel costs. Rebore estimates that the minimum cost of hiring a new school employee can be $1,000; the maximum may exceed $25,000. The objective of the selection process is hiring school personnel who bring competence and excellence to the school system, as the cost factor is a high-stakes proposition. Important considerations include academic criteria (appropriate university course work, degree(s) or certification, grade point average); personal characteristics and qualifications (appearance, presentation, voice projection, pleasant personality, leadership traits, flexibility); professional characteristics and expertise (knowledge of subject or skill area, student-centeredness, enthusiasm for teaching, instructional strategies and methodologies, classroom management techniques); and relevant experience and professional development (previous teaching experience, appropriate student teaching practicum, participation in relevant professional development activities, membership in professional organizations). Additionally, 12 selection processes and procedures are identified in Table 6.2.

Finally, DeCenzo and Robbins (2005) suggest selection processes and procedures must reflect the vision, goals, and objectives of a school, as any

Table 6.2   The 12 Stages of the Personnel Selection Process

The personnel selection process is typically implemented through a variety of stages to ensure quality selection and the subsequent hiring of the most qualified candidate. The stage sequence identified below is generally initiated in the order listed.

Stage 1	Conduct a position analysis
Stage 2	Write a position description
Stage 3	Develop selection procedures and establish appropriate practices
Stage 4	Post a vacancy announcement
Stage 5	Advertise the vacant position in appropriate media
Stage 6	Construct, disseminate, and collect application form(s)
Stage 7	Interview potential candidates for position opening
Stage 8	Conduct criminal history and reference checks
Stage 9	Select the most qualified applicant
Stage 10	Issue a position offer to the best applicant
Stage 11	Receive a position acceptance from the applicant selected
Stage 12	Notify the unsuccessful applicant(s) by telephone, e-mail, or in writing

Source: Adapted from Sorenson (2007, pp. 33–44); Carrell, Kuzmits, and Elbert (1992, pp. 196–197); Rebore (2007, pp. 123–140).

decision related to the selection of campus personnel can bring about the following four possible outcomes, two positive and two negative.

Positive Personnel Selection-Related Decisions

1. The individual selected proves to be successful in the position.

2. The individual rejected would have proven inadequate in the position.

Negative Personnel Selection-Related Decisions

1. The individual rejected would have proven successful in the position.

2. The individual selected proves to be inadequate in the position.

The implications for properly following procedures associated with the selection process are obvious: The right person for the right position is essential to a school's success. The same can be said of the principal, another insight into understanding that leadership effectiveness is a significant attribute when correlated with the personnel selection process.

Developing a Position Analysis

The first procedure in the selection process involves a review and analysis of the vacant position relative to the minimum educational qualifications and certification requirements. Such an analysis is useful in the recruitment and selection process because the identification of competency-competence-task relationships is crucial in recruiting and selecting the right person for the right position. A position analysis is simply a review of a position including the examination of existing job descriptions, position qualifications, job functions, recruitment criteria, and selection procedures. Conducting a position analysis permits a principal to systematically investigate the tasks, duties, and responsibilities of a particular campus level position. This process, according to Carrell, Kuzmits, and Elbert (1992), includes investigating the level of decision making of personnel in a particular position, the skills necessary to meet task criteria associated with the position (such as effectively communicating in the first language of students in a bilingual program), and the mental and emotional abilities essential to the appropriate and effective performance of personnel in the position. According to Bolton (1997), a position analysis should be designed to achieve any one or all of the following objectives:

- Clarify the details of a particular position for which a candidate is being recruited
- Provide detailed information for the development or revision of a job description
- Stipulate indicators for which personnel performance can be monitored and measured
- Identify how the position relates to the school vision, goals, and overall organizational structure
- Define specific role responsibilities as related to a particular position

Webb and Norton (2003) suggest that the "process of collecting, organizing, and evaluating information relating to the responsibilities and tasks associated with the successful performance of a specific job" (p. 437) begins with the development of a position analysis. The position analysis serves to identify the instructional relevance of a position, the quality factors associated with a position, organizational expectations related to a position, services provided by personnel in a particular position, and personnel behaviors relative to the practical integration of a position within a school. These criteria are identified in Table 6.3 and further relate to the situation presented in the That's Not My Job Case Study.

Table 6.3   Criteria for Conducting a Position Analysis

I. Prerequisite Criteria

A. *Instructional Relevance*

1. What is the mission of the school and how does the position relate?
2. How does the position relate to campus programmatic goals and objectives?
3. How will the position enhance current learning conditions?

B. *Quality Control*

1. How will the position ensure the continuity or creation of research-based practices?
2. How will the position complement current educational programs and further facilitate programmatic growth and change?
3. How will the position coordinate with the current campus/grade-level/departmental structure?

II. Strategic Criteria

A. *Organizational Expectations*

1. What knowledge bases and academic skills are essential to the position?
2. What time frame is associated with performance acquisition and demonstration of position knowledge and skills?
3. How will the position serve to meet student acquisition and mastery of learning knowledge and skills?

III. Position Criteria

A. *Related Services*

1. What services at the position level will be provided?
2. To whom shall the services be provided?
3. How will the designated services improve the instructional program?
4. How will the services increase student achievement?
5. How will the services facilitate appropriate change?

IV. Personnel Behaviors Criteria

A. *Relative to School Site*

1. What specific personnel behaviors are required of personnel serving in the campus position?

2. How will the stipulated personnel behaviors impact students, parents, colleagues, and administration?

B. *Relative to Members of the Learning Community*

1. What interpersonal skills are required in relation to the position?

2. What specific communication skills are required?

THAT'S NOT MY JOB

Teresa Cortinas was a paraprofessional at Ridgetop Middle School where she was employed to serve students in the school's computer lab. Because she spoke Spanish, she was frequently interrupted and pulled from her lab responsibilities by the campus principal and office staff so she could communicate with non-English-speaking parents who were either calling the school or were in the office needing assistance. Since neither the principal nor the office staff spoke or understood Spanish, Teresa possessed a valuable skill to effectively translate between parents and office and principal, which took up a good portion of the time she needed to be working in the technology setting.

Teresa had been hired neither as a translator nor for her bilingual communication skills, nor was her bilingual ability identified as a requirement in her job description. Additionally, she was not being compensated for this additional duty. Teresa actually believed that she was being penalized for her ability to communicate in Spanish and thus filed a grievance against her principal, stating "that's not my job!"

This isolated incident quickly escalated beyond the grievance level into actual charges brought by the Equal Employment Opportunity Commission against the school district, noting that the campus principal and district were violating the Civil Rights Act of 1964 by requiring Teresa to speak and translate Spanish without additional compensation.

Application Questions

1. How might a position analysis have served to avert the problem identified in this case study?
2. Which of the relevant criteria identified in Table 6.3 relates to the case study, yet was not considered when hiring Teresa Cortinas?
3. What specific questions, as related to the criteria for conducting a position analysis, should Teresa's principal have considered prior to hiring her as a computer lab paraprofessional?
4. Which of the criteria-related questions, as noted in Table 6.3, might the principal in the case study consider when determining office personnel changes necessary to provide for better communication with the Spanish-speaking members of the school's learning community?

Selection Criteria

Criteria for the selection of school personnel must be established by the principal in collaboration with the site-based decision-making team prior to the interview process. Such criteria facilitate the development of organizational goals, position design, position performance measurements, position skills relative to performance success, and the appropriate selection instruments necessary in determining desired traits, skills, and characteristics (see Figure 6.1). These criteria are typically associated with a candidate's academic background, personal characteristics, and relevant experiences in the field of education (see Table 6.4). Selection criteria are often used to delineate between those individual applicants with ideal characteristics (equating to successful position performance) and those with less than suitable characteristics (equating to unsuccessful position performance).

Reviewing Résumés

Résumés, while varying in style, substance, and format, continue to be the most popular and appropriate professional source of communicating applicant qualifications. School district personnel officers and principals still prefer to incorporate the résumé review process during the initial screening stages of screening applicants. Young (2008) relates that many applicants are beginning to utilize electronic portfolios, with résumé inclusions, to market their skills to school districts. Electronic résumés are provided to potential school district employers by means of a CD-ROM or through Web site postings. While the electronic résumé is a new professional communication medium, recent studies conducted by Young and Chounte (2004) suggest that principals continue to prefer to receive and review candidate résumés through the traditional medium of paper copies. This particular study further indicated that applicants utilizing electronic portfolios and résumés were at a distinct disadvantage at the screening stage of the selection process when compared to those applicants who simply mailed in their portfolios and résumés in a hard copy format, even though all candidates had identical qualifications.

Reference Checks

Today, more than any other time in the school business, social conditions and safety concerns require thorough background checks of prospective employees. Reference checks, even more so than the review of the application form and résumé, can be both an energy-saving procedure and cost-effective method for screening out unacceptable applicants.

Figure 6.1   Selection Criteria Relative to the School Setting

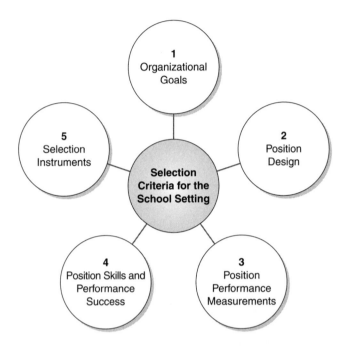

1 *Organizational Goals*—What specific goals have been established relative to hiring policies and practices, as well as the selection process? Organizational goals are generally dictated by board policy or administrative regulation and reflect how a school system values its employees.

2 *Position Design*—What campus-level expectations and responsibilities have been assigned to a specified position? Position design is typically determined by the school's selection committee and reflects specified tasks and duties that can affect the motivation and enthusiasm of selected personnel relative to their performance level and standards of excellence.

3 *Position Performance Measurements*—How is position performance measured? Position performance measurements help to determine what kind of applicant should be selected for the current position as well as future position openings. These measurements may be developed by the district human resource department or by the school's selection committee.
   Examples of position performance measurements include the applicant's resume, letters of recommendation, visual screenings, and initial screening devices such as "knock-out" questions (Fear & Chiron, 2002; Within, 1980), which promptly identify whether an applicant is qualified (e.g., Do you have a specialized degree? Do you hold certification required in this position? Will you be willing to participate in a six-month professional development program to become "highly qualified" as defined by the No Child Left Behind Act?).

4 *Position Skills and Performance Success*—What traits, skills, and qualifications are essential for successful position performance? Elements related to these particular criteria include the development and utilization of the position analysis as well as the position description.

5 *Selection Instruments*—What instruments have been identified or developed to assess desired traits, skills, and characteristics that will facilitate the selection of the best candidate available? Instruments include applications, tests, work samples, electronic portfolios, interview questions and scenarios, and other devices such as the Myers-Briggs Type Indicator (MBTI), which measures preferences (e.g., extrovert or introvert). While there is no single instrument that will guarantee the selection of the very best candidate, the implementation and utilization of several instruments can better ensure a quality selection.

Source: Adapted from Sorenson (2007, pp. 33–43); Fear and Chiron (2002, pp. 61–69); Within (1980, pp. 573–575).

Table 6.4   Selection Criteria: Background, Characteristics, and Experiences

Selection criteria may be developed by the human resource department, school administrative personnel, or site-based selection committee members, all in accordance with the acceptable standards of a school district.

Academic Background

- Degree(s)
- Grade point average (GPA)
- Certification(s)
- Verbal and written skills
- Understanding or knowledge of specified school/district/state-mandated curriculum
- Appropriate teaching skills relative to the position
- Professional development

Personal Characteristics

- Healthy, considerate, and mature attitudes
- Interpersonal and communication skills
- Appropriate attire
- Socially acceptable standards of hygiene
- Patient, flexible, creative, organized
- Problem-solving capacity
- Open to new ideas and change
- Interest in career advancement (i.e., desire to seek administrative role)
- Willingness to abide by ethical standards of conduct as well as district policies and administrative regulations

Relevant Experiences

- Student teaching practicum
- Previous teaching experience
- Scope of previous teaching experience
- Classroom/student management experience
- Relationship with students, parents, previous administrators, colleagues
- Professional development experiences (i.e., participation in professional seminars, educational workshops/conferences, lifelong learning initiatives such as graduate coursework)
- Membership in pertinent professional organizations

Interestingly, between 10 and 15% of all applicants falsify information on the application form (Baehr, 2005; Camden & Wallace, 1983), and as a result, school district administrators are continually conducting confidential investigations of applicants' backgrounds before proceeding through the selection process. Campus principals in many districts have been empowered to conduct background checks of applicants, most notably through telephone calls to previous supervisors. Principals are more likely to provide complete information regarding a candidate's background in telephone discussions, which continue to be the most common form of determining a candidate's viability as a future employee. Stanton (1988) identifies four advantages to conducting telephone reference checks:

- *Immediate clarification* as related to important information and issues can be accessed and assessed.
- *Additional information* can be obtained over the telephone as compared with the return of mailed reference forms or electronic reference responses.
- *Specific responses* are likely to surface during a telephone conversation, especially when the "familiarity factor" is initiated by the caller making a reference check (i.e., Principal A calling Principal B: "How are you handling the new accountability standards?" or "I used to work with [insert name] from your school district. How is he/she doing these days?" or "We've just completed the budget planning and development process. How did it go with you and your team?" or "You all had a great football season. What are the prospects for next year's team?").
- *Structured telephone questions* gain insightful information, and provide quick and efficient documentation of the telephone conversation findings.

While school principals continue the time-honored practice of conducting telephone reference checks, it is important that principals know how to answer reference checks. Few legal entanglements arise in reference-checking practices when principals respond to inquiries with accurate, verifiable information about previous personnel employed. Such information includes dates of employment; job progression; position titles, duties, and responsibilities; performance records by the employees' appraisers; and other objective, factual measures of employee performance, such as absenteeism. Because personnel are increasingly filing lawsuits against former principals and districts, contending that they have been defamed in a reference check (see Case Study Application: The Hekawi Students Threaten to Walk Out), many school districts are releasing former employees' verifiable work records and dates of employment information only. Listed below are 10 guidelines, as suggested by Bell, Castagnera, and Young (1984) and Sorenson (2004a) to consider when answering reference checks over the telephone.

1. Never volunteer information. Respond only to specific organizational inquiries and requests. However, before responding, telephone the inquirer to verify the validity of the person calling and the request.

2. Direct all communication to those individuals who have a real and specific request. Be aware of whom you are talking to, and more important, whom you are *not* talking to over the telephone.

3. State in any reference response that the information you are disclosing is confidential, using qualifying statements such as the following:

    - "I am providing information that was requested."
    - "I am relating this information only because it was requested."
    - "I am providing reference information that is to be used for professional purposes only."

    Sentences such as these imply that the reference information was not released for the purpose of damaging an individual's reputation or chance for employment elsewhere.

4. Obtain written consent from the former employee, if possible, before releasing reference information.

5. Provide only reference information that relates to the position and to the position performance in question. Some school districts advise that the "sending" principal say nothing about a teacher's performance. If such is the case in your school district, then the "receiving" principal can simply ask the teacher being considered to provide copies of previous performance evaluations.

6. Avoid vague or opinionated statements such as the following:

    - "He was an average teacher."
    - "She was careless at times."
    - "He displayed an inability to work with others."

    Be specific, factual, and communicate only verifiable data and information.

7. Document all released reference information.

8. Avoid subjective statements such as the following:

    - "I think she's an alcoholic."
    - "In my opinion, he's a womanizer."
    - "Believe me, she's a worthless employee."

9. When providing a negative, yet factual, reference, add the following phrase: "This is documented fact."

10. Avoid answering questions that are asked "off the record" as nothing is ever "off the record." Finally, never answer trap questions such as, "Would you rehire this person?" Answer such a question with the following statement: "We seriously consider all applicants."

While the reference checking process may be time-consuming, and possibly frustrating to the school administrator, consider the wise advice of Mark Goulet (2005), attorney at law with the firm of Walsh, Anderson, Brown, Schulze and Aldridge, P.C.:

> Hiring employees is a process that presents legal risks. Attention to detail during the application and interview process and applying preventative techniques will ensure fewer instances of legal liability and more productive working relationships in the long run. The more time and effort expended on checking references, the fewer problematic employees will be hired. (p. 2)

LEADING BY INTERVIEWING

The most frequently utilized job predictor continues to be the selection interview (Arvey & Faley, 1992; Lunenburg & Ornstein, 2004; Sorenson, 2007; Young & Castetter, 2004). Interestingly, interview formats and techniques vary from one organization to another, and as a result, many interviews are nothing more than freewheeling discussions that neglect to isolate specific and relatable topics and thus serve as extremely poor position performance predictors (Bretz & Judge, 1998). While the interview remains the most relevant process by which information about an applicant can be obtained, the effective school principal recognizes that the interview process is much more than exploring an applicant's qualifications, skills, and experiences. The interview must be utilized as a means of leading the selection process.

Today, interviews must incorporate opportunities for revealed leadership—leadership for meeting the issues and problems regularly faced by principals, especially in the area of identifying potential candidates for employment who meet and exceed the position-related behaviors and performance outcomes associated with a school or school system (Norton, 2005). Recall the earlier reference to the age-old adage: "You hire a problem, you'll fire a problem." Before hiring a problematic employee, a principal would be well advised to take appropriate action by interviewing for a solution to the personnel needs, as opposed to simply filling a position. Effective interviewing requires effective leadership. Listed in Table 6.5 are several leadership skills and traits that ensure the appropriate selection of personnel and the successful development of a school organization.

Interview Process

Today, school principals must do the preliminary work necessary to laying the foundation for an effective interview process. Fear and Chiron (2002) suggest initial interview functions should include the following:

Table 6.5   Assessing Leadership Skills and Traits

The effective school leader as an interviewer:

Communicates a vision of the school's goals and priorities

Provides assurance of leadership support and commitment

Establishes a climate and spirit of trust, which is conducive to teaching and learning

Attaches value to high standards of employee performance

Identifies expectations for continual school and personal improvement that are based on the concept of lifelong learning

Provides assurance that the leadership team within the organization will make necessary sacrifices for the good of the learning community

Provides a clear understanding of the leader-follower relationship within the organization

Establishes the idea or concept of individual contributions as well as team-oriented performances

Communicates position responsibilities

Disseminates useful and necessary information about the organization

Recognizes, praises, and reinforces previous performance efforts

Acts friendly, reveals consideration, and is supportive of the applicant's personal and career-oriented accomplishments

Source: Adapted from Yukl (2001, pp. 252–277); Hogan (1992, pp. 3–5); Hughes, Ginnett, and Curphy (2002, pp. 193–199); Sashkin and Huddle (1988, pp. 8–15); and Sorenson (2007, pp. 33–43).

1. A careful examination of the application file

2. The elimination of those individuals in the applicant pool who do not meet the position profile or fail to possess the appropriate qualifications

3. Meticulous consideration of potential interview questions

By incorporating these functions into the interview process, the effective principal expects to competently continue the selection process by utilizing appropriate interviewing techniques that enhance leadership effectiveness and better facilitate appropriate personnel selection decisions (Sorenson, 2007).

Planning the Interview

Planning for any interview should always include a careful review of all pertinent materials within the applicant's personnel file. Attention should focus on clearly defined criteria that will identify the applicant's areas of personal strengths, areas to be targeted for professional growth, along with the identification of specified needs for organizational improvement. Recording of this information can be completed by listing in short phrases, bulleted comments, or condensed statements any specified dimensions of strength, such as having effective interpersonal skills that reveal, for example, that an applicant is caring, rational, flexible, organized, and cooperative.

Targeted growth dimensions might note that the applicant is working on being less impatient with colleagues and becoming a better listener when interacting with others. School improvement components might focus on increased productivity, enhanced communication, improved decision making, curricular design and development, individualized performance expectations, effective teaching and learning strategies, autonomy with accountability, and sustainable leadership.

During this phase, planning for the interview involves a factual analysis, not an evaluative review. The preinterview process assists the school leader and the site-based selection committee in determining what relevant and position-related interview questions need to be developed. In fact, many school districts utilize preinterview planning forms to record applicable criteria and questions for consideration prior to the interview itself (Sorenson, 2007).

Conducting the Interview

The structured interview has been found to be a format that eliminates the problem of information incomparability, as this type of interview utilizes a set of prescribed questions that measure the knowledge and skill components associated with position performance (Dipboye, 1992). Additionally, all applicants are assessed utilizing an interview matrix. This process can be completed in either a dyadic or committee design. In dyadic interviews, one interviewer assesses the applicant; in committee interviews, multiple contributors to the interview are involved. The committee design or structure is often associated with the site-based decision-making process.

The physical setting of any interview strongly correlates with the quality of information obtained from an applicant. The face-to-face interview process continues to be the most common and preferred form of conducting an interview. The interview should always be held in a private location (preferably a quiet office or conference room) where distractions will not interfere. Additionally, the private area supports the idea of confidentiality and open communication. Principals often inquire as to where an applicant should sit in relation to the interview committee. Generally, having the applicant and the selection committee seated around a conference table in comfortable chairs is a recommended interview practice. If the interview is conducted solely by the campus principal, sitting side-by-side on an office sofa is not recommended for obvious ethical, if not moral, reasons, since the slightest suggestion of any inappropriate action or less than impeccable business behavior could bring a quick end to what was once thought to be a very promising career in school administration (Martin, 1993; Sorenson, 2002). Sitting across the desk from the applicant may be the only manner, for logistical reasons, in which an interview can be conducted; however, at a table and at a right angle to the applicant is an appropriate one-on-one interview practice.

The Dos and Don'ts of Interviewing

Leadership behaviors and interpersonal indicators of both the school principal and the interview committee can affect the quality of the interview and, just as important, the quality of information gained during the interview process. Several *dos and don'ts* have been identified to better ensure quality control during an interview (Sorenson, 2007).

The Dos

- Minimize the applicant's stress level by being open, friendly, and nonjudgmental.
- Place the applicant at ease with a smile and a relaxed manner. Typically the applicant will respond accordingly, and generally offer more honest and forthright responses during the interview.
- Reveal understanding and show attentiveness during the interview by observing and by listening. This includes regular eye contact, concentrating on the answers provided by the applicant to the questions posed, listening until the entire response is delivered, and negating nonverbal behaviors such as the crossing of the arms, checking the clock, or yawning during the interview.
- Take quality notes that can be referred to at a later time when assessing the applicant's responses. Allot time immediately after the interview to evaluate the applicant. Too often, especially when several candidates are being interviewed during the course of a day, the interviewer(s) can easily confuse one applicant's answers with those of another.
- Utilize effective questions that are position-related and ensure consistency and fairness in the questioning process. (This interview procedure will be examined in more detail in the subsequent section titled *Questioning Techniques*.)
- Strive to ensure that the experience for the applicant is both positive and nonthreatening, yet at the same time an opportunity for the applicant to realize that the interview process provides for both personal and professional development.

The Don'ts

- Avoid frowning and exhibiting an authoritative manner.
- Avoid glancing at a wristwatch or clock, looking out of a window, or examining papers—even when a negative decision is obvious.

- Avoid cutting off an applicant's speech by anticipating what is being said. Be an active and purposeful listener by not intruding upon the applicant's responses.
- Avoid interpreting questions for the applicant. Webb and Norton (2003) suggest it is the candidate's own interpretation of any question that is most important.
- Avoid making assumptions during the interview. Always probe with diligence and directness by asking for clarification, and by asking the applicant to share educationally related accomplishments and contributions relative to work-oriented projects and experiences.
- Avoid "leading" the candidate to believe that the position is his or hers—especially if such is not the case, or if the offering of the position is not yours to make.

Questioning Techniques

During the interview session, the school principal and team members should utilize effective questioning techniques to ensure consistency and fairness in the questioning process, and to further ensure that the best possible answers are obtained from the interviewing candidate. Such a technique will better facilitate the selection of the right person for the right position. Carrell, Kuzmits, and Elbert (1992) identify four question types that should be asked during any interview:

Situational: "How will you respond to class work assignment requests from two different parents, one whose child will be out of school for a week due to a tonsillectomy, and one whose child will be out for a week on a fun-filled trip to Disney World?"

Position knowledge: "What areas of basic and fundamental skills would you expect a student to have when entering [identify grade-level assignment]? What skills would you expect the student to possess when exiting [identify grade-level assignment]?"

Simulation oriented: "What steps or techniques would you employ to motivate student learning in your history class?" or "Here's a book: Teach me to read."

Employee required: "Are you willing to participate every other Saturday in a three-month professional development program to become 'highly qualified' as defined by the No Child Left Behind Act?"

Remember to ask questions that are open-ended and reflective. Always seek to ask the "tough" questions, such as those presented in Table 6.6. Finally, the manner in which a question is presented will affect the answer provided, for example, "You don't have any trouble with classroom management, do you?"

Table 6.6   Personnel Selection: Asking the "Tough" Questions

General questions

1. What four words would students use to describe you, your teaching style, technique, or strategies?

2. What is your greatest professional challenge?

3. What rules or expectations do you have for your students?

4. What teaching experiences have angered you?

5. You've been with your current school district for a very short time. Is this an indication that you will be frequently moving during your teaching career?

Dismissed-terminated

1. Have you ever had your contract nonrenewed?

2. Have you ever resigned and received a settlement agreement?

3. Why did you leave your last teaching experience?

Performance evaluations

1. How were you evaluated in your last teaching experience?

2. What were the results of your last performance appraisal?

3. What was the worst mistake you made at work? How did that mistake affect the school organization?

Interpersonal skills/collegial relationships

1. How do you expect your departmental colleagues to assist you in this teaching assignment?

2. What do you expect from your principal?

3. What kind of colleagues/principals do you find difficult to work with?

4. Have you ever had a communication problem with a colleague?

5. How do you deal with coworkers who disagree with you?

6. What types of individuals do you have difficulty working with?

Teacher/student relationships

1. You make an assignment. A student ridicules the assignment, saying it doesn't make sense and it's not interesting or it's irrelevant. What would you do?

2. How would you individualize instruction for students?

3. How would you differentiate instruction for students?

4. How would you challenge the slow learner and the advanced learner within the same class?

Teacher/parent relationships

1. A parent walks into your classroom before the school day begins, yelling and complaining about something to which you are not privy or just simply don't understand. The parent is obviously very upset. What would you do?

2. What do you sense, believe, or know is the most effective manner to communicate with parents? Describe how you have used this/these technique(s).

3. Describe the reasons you should contact or communicate with parents.

Targeted areas for professional development

1. Of what area(s) of your teaching performance was your previous principal most critical?

2. What would your colleagues consider your weaknesses?

3. What school-related responsibilities do you find the most troublesome?

4. What are the problematic areas you have found in your teaching experience(s)?

5. What is something in your last teaching experience that you are not proud of?

6. What are your plans for continuing your professional development?

Source: Adapted from HR-Guide.com (1999); Pawlas (1995, pp. 62, 65); and Sorenson (2007, pp. 33–43).

Evaluating the Interview

The complete interview process should be regularly evaluated to determine methods and techniques for improving candidate selection. A useful technique, readily available for accomplishing the important task of evaluating the interview, is the comparison of performance appraisals of candidates employed with the interview or screening evaluations and matrices to determine degrees of alignment and agreement. Principals have an administrative responsibility and organizational obligation to conduct a careful analysis of the screening process to determine how interviews lead to selection problems. Principals must learn from their past experiences in order to make the necessary adjustments critical to the elimination of recurring interview and selection errors.

Lead by Interviewing

Recruiting and selecting the most appropriate individual for employment in a school is a complex task requiring the implementation of a consistent method of interviewing, which allows applicants the opportunity to demonstrate what they can offer to the learning community. This process goes beyond simply confirming employment or job-related expectations. The interview process involves effective principal leadership that focuses on the real needs of the school. To lead by interviewing, Payne (n.d.) suggests a principal must practice the following:

- Have interview questions prepared in advance
- Ensure consistency and fairness in questioning
- Focus on the dictates of the position analysis
- Ask relevant questions to gain information essential to employee, school, and student success
- Focus on the selection criteria
- Assess all information (application form, resume, and references)
- Identify essential employment criteria (e.g., those that will aid in completing the task relative to the position)
- Provide constructive and justifiable feedback to unsuccessful applicants as related to their performance in the interview

Position Simulations

The selection of quality personnel can be greatly enhanced with the incorporation of work samples, position simulations, and the utilization of assessment measures (Maurer, 2002; Schmitt, Noe, Meritt, & Fitzgerald, 1984). Work samples include portfolio presentations, the development of written lesson plans based on some aspect of a curriculum guide that is provided to an applicant, or an actual teaching demonstration. Assessment measures may include an in-basket exercise whereby a candidate is provided certain skill-oriented tasks to complete, or the candidate is administered a particular test (keyboarding, for example) to measure a necessary skill. Finally, position simulations are usually presented in the form of situational case studies, decision-making activities, or problem-solving exercises. Position simulations are typically utilized when selecting campus administrators such as principals or assistant principals.

Final Selection and Notification of Candidates

Once all relevant information and data have been collected and analyzed regarding a particular vacancy and the appropriate candidates, a rank ordering of candidates by individual scores calculated on an interview matrix (see Figure 6.2) should serve to identify the most qualified candidate as a result of the interview process. This analysis, in conjunction with other verifiable data including credential scrutiny, the examination of

Figure 6.2   Teacher Interview Matrix

Name of Candidate_____   Date_____

Rating Scale
5 = Excellent   **4** = Satisfactory   **3** = Average   **2** = Below Average   **1** = Unsatisfactory

Interview Questions	Scale Score	Notes and Comments
1. Tell us about yourself and your educational experiences as they relate to the position for which you are applying.		
2. How do you plan to meet the needs of students with varying abilities without lowering standards?		
3. What do you believe are the critical attributes that make for a positive, student-centered learning environment?		
4. How do you plan to incorporate technology into your instructional plan?		
5. Describe something at which you tried and failed and what did you learn from that experience?		
6. What do you believe is the most effective method to use when supervising students?		
7. What are some effective methods of communicating with parents that you would incorporate as a teacher?		
8. Describe in as much detail as possible what a truly effective classroom looks like.		
9. Describe your teaching style(s).		
10. Describe how you would effectively involve parents and other community members in the education of the students you serve.		
11. How do you help students experience success?		
12. What procedures do you utilize to evaluate student progress besides tests?		
13. What quality or qualities do you possess that would enhance the teaching staff at our school?		
14. Parents come to speak to you about their child. They are convinced that their child is performing poorly because of you. How would you react to this situation and how would you resolve the issue?		
15. How do you address the issue of student discipline in your classroom?		
16. What needs and expectations do you have of the school administration team?		
17. Why did you choose to become a teacher?		
18. Describe a typical lesson in your classroom. What would we see you and your students doing?		
19. Is there anything you would like to add?		
Total Score =		

reference letters, reflection upon reference contacts, as well as the review of application forms and criminal history checks, will serve to identify the best qualified candidate.

Once the selection process has concluded, a formal position offer can be made. If the candidate selected accepts the offer, and it is a professional position, a contract will need to be signed by the new employee as well as the superintendent of schools or an official designee. Then a recommendation of employment will be made by the superintendent to the local school board, who will then approve or disapprove the selection.

Only after the position has been filled by the approved candidate should other candidates be notified that the position has been offered to and accepted by the most qualified candidate. Notification of unsuccessful candidates is generally the responsibility of a school district human resource administrator. However, this may be one of the assigned duties of the principal. If so, it is important that principals make prompt contact with the unsuccessful candidates informing them of the decision, as this allows the unsuccessful candidates the chance to seek other positions, and it permits the school leader an opportunity to express appreciation to the applicants for their active participation in the interview and selection process, which in turn serves to build excellent public relations.

FINAL THOUGHTS

Effective principals utilize appropriate selection, recruitment, orientation, and mentoring processes to collaboratively and successfully lead school personnel. Effective principals incorporate best-practice recruitment processes to develop a campus vision and mission whereby a positive climate and an open culture serve to create intrinsic motivational factors and personal enthusiasms for personnel, which in turn drive programmatic improvement, professional development, and thus lead to organizational progress and achievement. These factors increase the commitment, contentment, and likely retention of school personnel.

Effective principals seek the right personnel for the right positions by incorporating selection procedures such as conducting a position analysis, utilizing application forms and résumés, interviewing potential candidates, and conducting reference checks through collaborative leadership. Effective principals utilize selection criteria that develop and augment organizational goals relative to appropriate hiring policies and practices and further establish the expectations and responsibilities of campus personnel by implementing position performance measures to better determine the type of candidates necessary to ensure programmatic success. Effective principals, during the selection process, identify position traits, skills, and qualifications essential to organizational improvement and personnel professional development by utilizing selection instruments such as application forms, work samples, interview questions, scenarios, and other position simulations, all in an effort to better guarantee the selection of the very best candidates, as the students of a school deserve nothing less.

Finally, effective principals lead by developing a relationship between recruitment, selection, induction, and retention. Such a leadership model permits the campus principal to communicate the school's goals and priorities; establish a climate of trust where all personnel are valued; develop an organizational concept of individual contributions that enhance team-oriented performances; and recognize, praise, and reinforce personnel efforts and accomplishments. To quote William P. Foster (1984), professor of education at Indiana University:

> Leadership, in the final analysis, is the ability of humans to relate deeply to each other in the search for a more perfect union. Leadership is a consensual task, a sharing of ideas and a sharing of responsibilities, where a "leader" is a leader for the moment only, where the leadership exerted must be validated by the consent of followers, and where leadership lies in the struggles of a community to find meaning for itself. (p. 114)

DISCUSSION QUESTIONS

1. Reflect upon the following statements taken directly from the chapter, relative to the recruitment of school personnel:

    "The recruitment of appropriate, competent, and instructionally focused personnel is undoubtedly the most critical aspect of the school leadership role."

    "Attracting the right applicant for the right position in any school is by far the most challenging and time-consuming responsibility of a principal."

    How do these statements relate to one another, and what do they suggest regarding personnel recruitment, the role of the principalship in the recruitment process, and the recruiting of personnel in general?

2. Consider Figure 6.1, Selection Criteria Relative to the School Setting, and identify which of the five selection criteria were not incorporated into the selection and utilization of Teresa Cortinas, the paraprofessional depicted in the That's Not My Job scenario found on page 111. Explain how the incorporation of those particular criteria identified would have helped avert the lawsuit brought against the school district by the Equal Employment Opportunity Commission?

3. Think about a recent interview in which you participated as either an interviewer or a candidate. During the interview process, which of the *dos and don'ts* listed on pages 120–121 of the chapter were incorporated? Now reflect on

(Continued)

(Continued)

Table 6.5, Assessing Leadership Skills and Traits, and identify which specific traits and skills were utilized by the school leader as an interviewer. Which were not and what could be the potential implications?

4. Develop and share with your colleagues at least one *situational*, *position knowledge*, *situation oriented*, and *employee required* question. Next, examine Table 6.6, Personnel Selection: Asking the "Tough" Questions, and then contemplate the following question: Which of the "Question Categories" (i.e., General Questions, Dismissed-Terminated Questions, Interpersonal Skills/Collegial Relationships, and so forth) would each of the questions you developed best relate?

5. John C. Maxwell (2003), in his book *Leadership: Promises for Every Day*, writes, "One of the mistakes leaders make is that they focus too much attention on their dream and too little on their team" (p. 50). Reflect upon the *campus vision* aspect of this chapter and then consider the following: How does developing a campus vision correlate with the adage, "The team holds the dream"?

CASE STUDY APPLICATION

THE HEKAWI STUDENTS THREATEN TO WALK OUT

Dr. Morgan O'Rourke, principal at Hekawi High School, recognized that Randolph Agarn was a frustrated teacher struggling during the second semester of his third year with senior honor students in his Advanced Calculus II course. Principal O'Rourke sensed that the situation in the classroom was quickly deteriorating as students were coming into his office and complaining about Mr. Agarn. Listening to complaints about teachers was nothing new to Dr. O'Rourke, but this was a first for him at Hekawi High School, as the loudest complaint from the students related to a lack of academic rigor in Mr. Agarn's calculus course. The students demanded that Mr. Agarn be fired.

The students, led by class president, Nash Vanderbilt, threatened, in Vanderbilt's words "to go on the warpath" by staging a walkout unless action was taken by Dr. O'Rourke against Mr. Agarn. Additionally, parents were making calls to the principal's office stating that their children were not receiving the necessary academic instruction in calculus, especially as they prepared for their upcoming university endeavors.

Principal O'Rourke had made numerous efforts to assist Mr. Agarn by offering nonthreatening meetings in which the issues of course rigor and student motivation were discussed. The principal conducted numerous formal walk-throughs, along with additional teacher observations, in an attempt to bring structure and instructional effectiveness into Mr. Agarn's classroom. Furthermore, Dr. O'Rourke reviewed the lesson plans prepared by Mr. Agarn and offered suggestions. He discussed teaching techniques and strategies with Mr. Agarn and frequently identified areas to target for professional growth. Dr. O'Rourke even sent Mr. Agarn to several workshops aimed at improving the teacher's instructional ability. Dr. O'Rourke actually assigned a mentor to assist Mr. Agarn with his daily teaching duties. None of these instructional leadership efforts proved effective in changing Mr. Agarn's performance. He failed to make the required improvements and generally ignored the advice and written directives provided by Principal O'Rourke.

All the while, Mr. Agarn filed several grievances against Dr. O'Rourke, claiming his principal was harassing him. Each grievance was heard, thus providing Mr. Agarn with due process as was required and deserved. At the conclusion of the semester, Mr. Agarn abruptly submitted his resignation by marching into the principal's office and throwing his room key and written resignation on the principal's desk, stating: "You want my key, you've got it! I'm out of here!"

Following his resignation, Mr. Agarn had difficulty securing employment in neighboring school districts. He then decided he would contact his brother, Wilton, who was a branch manager at the Parmenter State Bank. The brother then contacted Principal O'Rourke by telephone, claiming to be a school principal and thus asking for a reference regarding Mr. Agarn. Brother Wilton quickly learned that Principal O'Rourke would not provide a positive reference, in part because of the tendency of Mr. Agarn to regularly file grievances. O'Rourke proclaimed over the telephone, "Mr. Agarn couldn't teach, but he sure could file a grievance. He's not missed around here!" Next, the teacher's cousin, Hannibal Dobbs, a small claims court lawyer, called Hekawi High School, posing as a human resource director from an upstate school district. He too talked with Dr. O'Rourke, who stated when asked if he would rehire Mr. Agarn, "Not on your life, he's completely incompetent! I not only had students regularly complaining about him, but their parents were constantly on my case! I've got enough problems without bringing him back onto campus!"

Ultimately, Mr. Agarn filed a complaint with the State Commissioner of Education claiming that Principal O'Rourke had penalized him for exercising his right to file a grievance, which resulted in his inability to obtain work as a teacher. When the case of *Agarn v. O'Rourke* was heard, the commissioner ruled in favor of Randolph Agarn and revoked Dr. Morgan O'Rourke's principal's certificate (to review the actual case, see *Sitzler v. Babers* [1992], grievances and employment recommendations).

Application Questions

1. The commissioner of education wrote in his dicta, "This practice cannot be tolerated. It threatens to undermine the right of teachers to file grievances against their employers." What implications are associated with the commissioner's ruling?

(Continued)

(Continued)

2. With your colleagues, conduct mock reference calls related to past professionals whom you genuinely liked and whom you passionately disliked. Practice the art of receiving a reference call as well as placing a reference call.

3. How could Principal O'Rourke have better handled the reference calls he received regarding Randolph Agarn? Explain your answer by providing examples.

4. Examine Table 6.1, A Seven-Step Approach to Creating a Campus Vision. Which of the seven steps did Principal O'Rourke incorporate relative to the case study presented? Just as important, which steps were not effectively incorporated? After identifying the steps that were not effectively incorporated, explain how you as a school leader would ensure the creation of a vision that would help avoid the circumstances associated with Randolph Agarn, the teacher in the case study.

5. Consider the old adage: "You hire a problem, you'll fire a problem." In this case study, Morgan O'Rourke had a personnel problem. What selection criteria, as identified in the chapter (see, e.g., Tables 6.3 and 6.4), would have assisted Principal O'Rourke in avoiding the complications associated with Randolph Agarn?

OTHER RESOURCES

Brock, B. L., & Grady, M. L. (2007). *From first-year to first-rate: Principals guiding beginning teachers*. Thousand Oaks, CA: Corwin Press.

Elbot, C. F., & Fulton, D. (2008). *Building an intentional school culture: Excellence in academics and character*. Thousand Oaks, CA: Corwin Press.

7

Personnel and Induction and Mentoring Programs

Until we recognize that we have a teacher retention problem, we will continue to engage in a costly annual recruitment and hiring cycle, pouring more and more teachers into our nation's classrooms only to lose them at a faster and faster rate. This will continue to drain our public tax dollars, it will undermine teaching quality, and it will most certainly hinder our ability to close student achievement gaps.

—National Commission on Teaching and America's Future (2008)

HOW PRINCIPALS FAIL PERSONNEL

Recall from Chapter 6 the case study titled The Hekawi Students Threaten to Walk Out, which involved Dr. Morgan O'Rourke, the principal at Hekawi High School, and Randolph Agarn, the frustrated third year advanced calculus teacher. Principal O'Rourke made numerous efforts to assist the struggling teacher by offering meetings, conducting formal walk-throughs and teacher observations, reviewing lesson plans, and even sending Mr. Agarn to several workshops aimed at improving the teacher's instructional abilities—all to no avail. Mr. Agarn failed to improve and ultimately resigned his high school mathematics position, convinced that teaching was a profession beset by too many administrative directives, unattainable expectations, and instructional leaders that were unfocused, ill prepared, and vindictive in assisting beginning teachers. Whether these perceptions were real or imaginary, it becomes obvious that one of the more important details of being a school principal when working with personnel is to properly and effectively help teachers in need of assistance by providing them with necessary resources, personal attention, and professional development (Hoy & Hoy, 2006). This is exactly what Principal O'Rourke did. So what went wrong? Did the Hekawi High School principal fail to help Randolph Agarn, or did Mr. Agarn fail to help himself? Were the leadership efforts made by Principal O'Rourke typical of what instructional leaders do or don't do in our schools today, and do we ultimately neglect the effective mentoring of our new and beginning teachers?

The National Commission on Teaching and America's Future (2003), in extensive research, found that far too many principals fail to provide faculty with comprehensive induction and mentoring programs, which can serve to reduce personnel attrition rates by 50%. Note that the operative term in the previous sentence is *comprehensive*. In other words, to comprehensively help teachers in need of assistance, principals must initiate and implement induction and mentoring programs that embrace the following elements: (1) high quality mentors, (2) realistic and rewarding instructional expectations, (3) socialization and team-building processes, (4) pertinent professional development extending beyond the standard "drive-through" workshop approach, and (5) effective mentoring responsibilities for the instructional leader, which serve to help retain new and beginning teachers (Morgan & Kritsonis, 2008). The development of effective induction and mentoring programs for school personnel is a difficult chore for even the most seasoned of principals. In some school districts, as much as 70% of first-year teachers abandon the profession. Astounding as it may seem, in some schools and districts, the teacher attrition rate is significantly higher than the student dropout rate (U.S. Department of Education, 2005). So what's a principal to do?

THE INDUCTION AND MENTORING OF PERSONNEL

Closely related to the discussion of recruitment, selection, and retention processes, as detailed in Chapter 6, is the induction and mentoring of personnel. The purpose of staff induction and mentoring programs, especially as related to new personnel, is to create positive first impressions, relieve any individual anxieties associated with joining a new team, establish high levels of professional and instructional expectations, provide opportunities for campus socialization and team building, and retain highly qualified personnel in the profession. Induction activities should be ongoing throughout the careers of all personnel, as effective principals provide opportunities for faculty and staff to participate in lifelong learning experiences through relevant, practical, and relatable professional development.

Induction

While the No Child Left Behind Act of 2001 created requirements that included our schools being staffed by personnel that are "highly qualified," the recruitment of new teachers alone can never begin to solve the current teacher shortage facing our nation. School districts have long recognized the necessity of retaining professionally skilled personnel as a means of subverting the national teacher shortage. In fact, Webb and Norton (2009) reveal that 44 states now mandate induction programs for new teachers in an effort to not only select the best, but retain the best by properly welcoming, orienting, training, and investing in our future highly skilled professionals.

Characteristics of Effective Induction Programs

Research conducted by the National Commission on Teaching and America's Future (2008) and the Alliance for Excellent Education (2005) and the works of Kapadia, Coca, and Easton (2007) and Wayne, Youngs, and Fleischman (2005) clearly reveal that effective induction programs incorporate the following criteria:

- The program is designed in collaboration with campus teachers and administrative staff, district support personnel, and new and beginning teachers.
- The values and expectations of the school and district are integrated within the induction program and are clearly communicated to the participants.
- New employee participation is required.
- Principal support and active participation is crucial.
- The promotion of research-based and student-centered best practices is critical.
- Reduced teaching loads for first-year teachers are required so mentoring interactions and teacher-to-teacher observations can occur.
- The assignment of highly qualified mentors in the same grade level or subject area is essential.
- Teacher-to-teacher observations, where best teaching practices are modeled, are required.
- Professional development opportunities and ongoing training over a three-year period is necessary.

It is important to recognize that induction is not mentoring. Induction is defined by the Institute for Teacher Renewal and Growth (2003) as a highly structured training process for all teachers new to a school district. Such a program instructs and models the values and expectations of a school and school system beginning with a series of induction sessions that include *preemployment, preorientation, orientation,* and *postorientation* activities.

Preemployment Session

This first session in an induction program can occur at either the district or campus level. Personnel seeking employment are provided with an overview of the school or school system and the learning community, professional expectations and responsibilities, information relative to student achievement and demographics, and professional opportunities within the school district or at the campus level. This session typically occurs during the interview process.

Preorientation Session

This second session in an induction program will occur once again at either the campus or district level. The preorientation session is held concurrently with the hiring of new personnel and generally allows for the dissemination of a district or campus orientation packet. This packet can very well include inserts such as (1) dates and agendas for an upcoming orientation program, (2) a school district calendar, (3) a copy of the personnel handbook with relevant district personnel policies, (4) upcoming professional development opportunities for the school year, (5) salary schedule and pay periods, (6) a district map, (7) insurance and other district benefit packages, and (8) a welcoming letter from the superintendent or principal (Hays Consolidated Independent School District, 2008).

Orientation Session

The third session in an induction program typically occurs at the campus level and involves the principal, the new employee, as well as other important campus personnel (see Table 7.1). This induction session is an important opportunity for the principal to share district and campus policies and regulations relevant to the teaching position. Examples include homework policy, required record and report submissions, policies and procedures as related to parental communication, student grading and absences, student promotion and retention, student discipline, and parent conferences. Additionally, the orientation session serves as a time to review job descriptions and faculty handbooks. Finally, campus tours are generally held during the orientation session.

Table 7.1   T. M. Clark Elementary School Orientation Agenda

8:00–8:15 a.m.	Welcome and Introductions Dr. Tom T. Riffick, Principal
8:15–9:00 a.m.	Campus Policies, Procedures, and Regulations Dr. Tom T. Riffick, Principal
9:00–10:00 a.m.	Faculty Handbook Review Dr. Tom T. Riffick, Principal and Ms. Ima Helpper, Assistant Principal
10:00–10:30 a.m.	Record Keeping and Teacher Reports Ms. Kit Monami, Secretary
10:30–10:45 a.m.	B-R-E-A-K!
10:45–11:30 a.m.	Parental Communication and Conferencing Ms. Suzan Rowland, Parent Liaison
11:30 a.m.–1:00 p.m.	L-U-N-C-H!
1:00–1:30 p.m.	Student Grading and Attendance Procedures Ms. Melissa Alworth, FEIMS Clerk
1:30–2:30 p.m.	Student Discipline and Promotion/Retention Policy Ms. Ima Helpper, Assistant Principal
2:30–2:45 p.m.	B-R-E-A-K!
2:45–3:00 p.m.	Custodial Operations Ms. Paula Leon, Head Custodian
3:00–3:15 p.m.	Homework Policy Ms. Polly Wihour, Team Leader
3:15–3:45 p.m.	Counseling and Diagnostic Services Ms. Diane Channing, School Counselor Mr. John Steven Miller, Diagnostician
3:45–4:30 p.m.	Campus Tour: Instructional Resource Center, Technology Center, Library, Clinic, Cafeteria, Gymnasium, Music Room, and Playground Ms. Flo Cortez, Instructional Assistant

Postorientation Session

The fourth and final session in an induction program occurs at the campus level and focuses on transitioning new personnel into their various professional roles. This particular session serves as the capstone experience relative to the induction process and introduces new personnel to the campus mentoring program.

Mentoring

An additional aspect of the induction process is a personnel mentoring program. Mentoring builds effective communication, allows for continuous professional growth and development, provides personal support services, extends insights into the campus vision and mission, and most important, ensures a working relationship with a master teacher/mentor who can serve as a role model for appropriate educational practices and procedures. Regrettably, the mentoring of school personnel in most schools is truly in an embryonic state. Mentoring is something many school professionals, most notably principals, talk about publicly, but privately fail to implement appropriately, effectively, or enthusiastically. In fact, Kelley (2004) asserts that the education profession has historically ignored the support needs of its new recruits. Listed below is an example of a induction/mentoring program as described on a district Web site:

> Each new teacher to _____ Independent School District will be assigned a trained mentor during their first year in our district. This is done to promote the personal and professional well-being of incoming teachers and to ensure that they have a rewarding and successful year.

This description of a real school district's induction/mentoring program exemplifies what the authors refer to as a "public lip service, private dismissal" program.

Now carefully consider the following 10 key questions and associated responses essential to the development of a truly effective mentoring program.

What Is Mentoring?

Mentoring has been defined as a means of support from a more experienced and qualified colleague who has agreed to help a new or beginning teacher perform at a higher level in order to promote job performance and self-reflection (Villani, 2006). Webb and Norton (2009) describe mentoring as a method of identifying "an experienced professional who guides the personal development of a less experienced individual by serving as a role model; a wise and faithful advisor or tutor" (p. 357). Rebore (2007) notes that mentoring is the "practice of pairing newly employed teachers with experienced colleagues to provide support and encouragement" (p. 372). Whatever definition or description is applied, the authors of this text characterize the mentoring of school personnel as a necessary building block or foundation for true individual achievement and professional success at the campus level.

What Is the Potential of Mentoring as Part of New Teacher Development?

Mentoring has at least two potential applications relative to improving new teacher development. First, mentoring is the basis for ensuring that a new teacher understands the procedures, policies, and practices of a school. Mentoring is the most effective means of providing feedback to the new or beginning teacher as it relates to the mastery of technical and instructional skills so essential to effective performance in the teaching role.

Second, effective mentoring goes beyond the technical and instructional skill development of a new employee. Effective mentoring also addresses the practical preparation of the new or beginning teacher. For example, Annette Breaux (2002), in her book, *101 "Answers" for New Teachers & Their Mentors: Effective Teaching Tips for Daily Classroom Use*, and Paula Rutherford (2005), in her *21st Century Mentor's Handbook: Creating a Culture for Learning*, assert that an effective mentor can readily assist new personnel in understanding how to handle discipline problems, manage classroom concerns, develop lesson plans, learn campus norms and expectations, utilize socialization skills, develop techniques for conferencing with parents, and overcome other challenges and concerns facing new teachers.

What Are Characteristics of Effective Mentors?

Effective mentors have been described by Sorenson and Goldsmith (in press) as possessing 10 characteristics essential to the development of exceptional teachers. These characteristics reveal that effective mentors

1. should have substantial experience in the role of teaching and instruction, and they should be regarded by their principal and peers as being organized and skilled in teaching methods, strategies, and techniques;

2. exhibit positive instructional skills to include intelligence, good communication, and well-developed interpersonal sensitivities;

3. ask the "right" questions and provide the "right" answers;

4. accept alternative "ways of doing things," and avoid instructing beginning teachers to do something because "it's the way I do it";

5. model principles of lifelong learning, along with appropriate moral and ethical conduct;

6. exude an enthusiasm for teaching that is sincere, convincing, and is constantly conveyed to their protégés;

7. ensure sensitivity when communicating constructive criticism that is necessary for a new teacher's professional development;

8. serve as active listeners and exhibit a caring attitude and belief regarding the potential of a new teacher;

9. exhibit flexibility and demonstrate a healthy sense of humor; and

10. incorporate a restrained sense of guidance and direction in order that the new or beginning teacher can develop as independently as possible.

What Are Essential Responsibilities of Mentors?

Essential responsibilities of mentors include advising, communicating, counseling, guiding, modeling, protecting, promoting, and developing teachers new to the profession. The effective mentor never fails to recognize a beginning teacher's need for additional information (advising), regularly provides needed emotional support (counseling) by being open and available (communicating), orients the new teacher to the formal and informal "rules" of the school (guiding), exhibits professional behavior and demonstrates competent performance (modeling), serves as a buffer when others attempt to interfere or speak detrimentally about a beginning teacher's performance (protecting), speaks up for and showcases the beginning teacher in front of other professionals, including the principal (promoting), and assists the beginning teacher in acquiring necessary skills to be successful in the instructional role (developing).

From a principal perspective, consider the sound advice of Morgan and Kritsonis (2008) regarding the mentoring of beginning teachers:

> The campus principal must take a hands-on approach to teacher mentoring. Too often, the responsibility of acclimating new teachers falls to the assistant principal or a lead teacher, creating a disconnect between the principal and his newest/most impressionable employees. The principal must set aside time regularly (weekly is ideal) to debrief and interact with new teachers. Time with new teachers is far too critical for a principal to delegate, and should remain a priority on a principal's agenda for the entire academic year. (p. 5)

No truer words could have been written!

What Are the Benefits of Mentoring Teachers?

The Center for Teaching Quality (2006) examines three important benefits of mentoring new or beginning teachers: (1) improved job satisfaction, (2) increased peer recognition, and (3) the potential for career advancement. Consider how Webb and Norton (2009) describe the benefits of mentoring new and beginning teachers:

Mentoring programs benefit not only the mentee, but the mentor and the school district. The new teacher gains access to an experienced member of the staff for purposes of learning about the school system, its policies and procedures, and effective instructional practices. The mentee also develops a system of personal support and increased self-confidence, develops insight into district purposes, and develops a relationship with a master teacher who can serve as a role model for teaching. The mentor benefits through increased personal self-esteem and recognition as a successful teacher and contributor to the school's program. (p. 162)

This quote is extremely relevant to the practice of effective mentoring and serves to validate the three important benefits of mentoring new or beginning teachers as detailed by the Center for Teaching Quality (2006). It also readily relates to the principal advice previously provided by Morgan and Kritsonis (2008).

How Does a Mentoring Program Get Started?

Mentoring programs can be implemented at the campus level when principals find it important to develop specialized training activities to assist new and beginning teachers. Sorenson and Goldsmith (2006) suggest that principals must exhibit a high spirit of honesty, integrity, trust, and respect. They also allow for safe and open communications. Principals who desire to develop an effective mentoring program must be viewed by members of the learning community as being hard workers, producing goal-oriented and student-centered learning environments where demanding yet rewarding expectations are the norm. Effective principals engage in meaningful collaboration with the campus team when developing a mentoring program, and these same principals are willing to seek out successful mentoring programs along with sufficient funds to replicate said programs.

What Skills Are Necessary for Effective Mentoring?

Breaux (2002) believes three skills are necessary for effective mentoring: (1) problem-solving skills, (2) conferencing skills, and (3) observation skills. Effective mentors define the issue, concern, or problem at hand and decide on a plan of action to solve the problem in an effort to help the protégé. Effective mentors are able to appropriately confer with a protégé by sharing ideas, relating experiences, seeking solutions, providing encouragement, and developing a positive climate of trust and mutual respect and support. Effective mentors also carefully monitor and watch what the new or beginning teacher is doing instructionally, often dropping in during instructional time to quickly and positively observe what is happening or, just as important, not happening in the beginning teacher's classroom. For the "drop-in" observations to be non-threatening, a significant level of trust and respect must be developed between the mentor and the protégé.

How Does a Principal Develop an Effective Model for Training Mentors?

To develop an effective model for training mentors, principals must follow the effective school research, which dates back to the 1980s. For example, effective principals lead mentor training programs by developing a vision or mission, by building strong, confident, and positive leadership, by frequently monitoring mentor and protégé performance, by developing a positive school climate, and by providing sufficient opportunities for professional development. Additionally, an effective model for the training of mentors must be based on 10 measures that have proven successful for the authors while serving as principals in state-recognized schools:

1. Gain approval and acceptance for the training model from district central administration.

2. Follow established school board policies regarding mentor training.

3. Work collaboratively with members of the campus learning community in the development of the training program.

4. Provide for a needs assessment to best understand what mentoring needs and directions are essential for the school.

5. Develop a budget that includes funding allocations for the mentor training program.

6. Design the program by setting appropriate goals, objectives, strategies, and actions to ensure programmatic success.

7. Select the most "highly qualified" staff members to serve as mentors-in-training.

8. Initially implement the mentor training program on a "pilot" basis.

9. Regularly evaluate the program for successes and moreover identify areas to target for growth and improvement.

10. Seek out other mentor training programs in neighboring schools or districts and learn from their successes and failures.

Do Campus Personnel Really Have Time for Mentoring?

What a question! We all know the answer to this one. We never have enough time to implement anything on campus. However, we must make the time! Recall the words of the famous German writer and thinker, Wolfgang von Goethe (1749–1832):

> The day is of infinite length for those who know how to appreciate and use it. (*The Columbia World of Quotations*, 1996)

Where Can a Principal Find Models of
Induction and Mentoring for New Personnel?

Consider the following models and sources for the development of effective induction and mentoring programs:

- The New Teacher Center (California)—Read about effective induction and mentoring in Ellen Moir's and Janet Gless's (2003) article "Meeting the Challenges of Recruitment and Retention."
- The Flowing Wells School District (Arizona)—See the Institute for Teacher Renewal and Growth (2003) article, *Staff development, induction, mentoring.*
- Center for Teaching Quality—See the 2006 article, "Why Mentoring and Induction Matters and What Must Be Done for New Teachers," in *Teaching Quality Across the Nation: Best Practices and Policies.*
- The Clark County School District (Nevada)—Examine this "fixing the hole in the bucket" account of induction and mentoring as related by the National Commission on Teaching and America's Future and cited in the 2008 Policy Brief titled "The High Cost of Teacher Turnover."
- Chicago Public Schools (Illinois)—Review the research conducted by Kavita Kapadia and Vanessa Coca (2007) in *Keeping New Teachers: A First Look at the Influences of Induction in Chicago Public Schools.*
- Freeport Intermediate School (Brazosport ISD-Texas)—Read "An Exemplary Middle School" and how mentoring has been incorporated at this school in one hour of "team time" each day, as described in *Whatever It Takes: How Professional Learning Communities Respond When Kids Don't Learn,* by Richard DuFour, Rebecca DuFour, Robert Eaker, and Gayle Karhanek (2004, pp. 86–91).
- The Benwood Initiative (Hamilton County, Tennessee)—See the Public Education Foundation (2006) account of induction and mentoring in *Lessons Learned: A Report on the Benwood Initiative.*
- The Dayton City School District (Ohio)—Read the research conducted by William R. Drury in his 1988 article "Entry-Year Administrator Induction: A State and Local School District Model." While this induction/mentoring account is administrator-related, the research conclusions also serve to support effective teacher induction and mentoring programs.
- Consider seeking information related to mentoring programs as detailed on your state education agency's Web site. State education agencies can provide a wealth of information to interested school principals who desire to initiate, implement, and even improve beginning teacher mentoring programs.
- Examine the additional key questions and related descriptors detailing the mentoring process as identified in Table 7.2 as a means of developing an effective model for mentoring new personnel.

Table 7.2   Criteria for Mentoring New Personnel

Key Questions	Relevant Considerations
Who is the mentor?	
1. What are the criteria for serving as a mentor?	• Experience, expertise, collegiality
2. Who serves as a mentor?	• Current or retired employees
3. How are mentors selected?	• By district or campus administration
4. How are mentors and protégés matched?	• Like positions, needs, and teaching/learning styles
What are the expectations for mentors?	
1. What are mentor responsibilities?	• Meet daily in person with the protégé
2. When do mentors meet with protégés?	• Predetermined and mutually acceptable times
3. How often do mentors work with protégés?	• One year minimum
4. What are the coaching/observation requirements of mentors?	• Protégés should have opportunities for regular observations of mentors
What support systems are in place for mentors and protégés?	
1. Who trains the mentors?	• Campus administrator or district facilitator
2. What professional development opportunities are available for mentors and protégés?	• At least two training sessions per semester with one follow-up session
3. What resources (fiscal/human/material) are available for mentors and protégés?	• Budgeted funding along with professional readings and instructional materials
4. Who supervises the mentors?	• Campus principal or district facilitators
What are the expectations for protégés?	
1. Which individuals are available to mentor and support protégés?	• Principal, facilitators, and other designated support teams

Key Questions	Relevant Considerations
2. What formative and summative assessments are required?	• Determined/designed by district or campus teams
3. Should protégés be required to maintain a portfolio?	• Portfolio preparation serves to facilitate professional growth
4. Should protégés meet regularly with their campus principal?	• Meetings with campus principal should be at least once every week to every three weeks
How is the mentoring program evaluated?	
1. Do formative and summative assessments of the program occur? Who is responsible for program evaluation?	• Campus principal and district facilitators, in collaboration with mentors and protégés, should meet at least two times per semester to elicit input, feedback, and assessment information
2. What data is collected and how does it correlate with programmatic success?	• Data collected from surveys and appropriate assessment instruments should be utilized
3. Who views the evaluative results?	• Campus principal, district facilitator, and other district administrative team members
4. What are the indicators of programmatic success?	• Favorable mentor and protégé comments and relationships • Improved teaching techniques and instructional strategies • Regular exchange of ideas • Increased student achievement • Improved mentor, protégé, and administrator communication

FINAL THOUGHTS

The appropriate implementation of induction and mentoring programs serves as an important step in the maximization of school personnel and can establish a lasting foundation that ensures the retention of outstanding educators. Some years ago, while serving as school principals, the authors were asked four relevant and thought-provoking questions related to personnel induction and mentoring. These four questions were posed by the district's personnel director. These questions are still relevant and applicable today for principals who wish to develop effective induction and mentoring programs at their schools.

- How much do you currently know about induction and mentoring?
- How committed are you to personnel induction and mentoring programs?
- How much do you expect your school to benefit from an induction and mentoring program?
- How willing are you to advance the professional development of your campus personnel and the achievement of the students you serve?

Beginning teachers need assistance. They need your help today. By seriously considering these important questions, along with others raised in this chapter, the effective principal can create a school environment that ensures that everyone matters!

DISCUSSION QUESTIONS

1. L. M. Kelley (2004) in his article, "Why Induction Matters," as noted earlier in the chapter, suggests that educators have historically ignored the need to mentor beginning teachers. One school district's induction/mentoring program is described as follows:

   > Each new teacher to _____ Independent School District will be assigned a trained mentor during their first year in our district. This is done to promote the personal and professional well-being of incoming teachers and to ensure that they have a rewarding and successful year.

   Might the name of your school district readily fit into the blank noted above? If yes, what might you, the new or prospective school administrator, do to ensure the adoption and implementation of a more effective induction and mentoring program for beginning teachers? Provide specifics as you explain your answer.

2. Which one of the characteristics of effective induction programs, as described in this chapter, is the most important consideration when designing an induction program for beginning teachers?

3. Albert Schweitzer once stated, "I don't know what your destiny will be, but one thing I know: The ones among you who will be really happy are those who have sought and found how to serve" (*The Columbia World of Quotations*, 1996). Mentoring others is truly a form of service. Which of the 10 characteristics of effective mentors exemplify servant leadership? Explain your answer.

4. Essential responsibilities of mentors include advising, communicating, counseling, guiding, modeling, protecting, promoting, and developing teachers new to the profession. Identify one additional essential responsibility that a principal mentor must assume? Explain.

5. How would you, as a new or future school principal, develop an effective model for training mentors? Support your answer by incorporating the 10 measures proven effective for training mentors as described in the chapter.

CASE STUDY APPLICATION

ODYSSEUS IMING.COM–THE MENTORING PHENOMENON!

The Valley Ridge Public Schools superintendent had been working collaboratively with district administrators on a plan to increase awareness in the region's teacher education and preparation programs of Valley Ridge's need for additional teachers. Valley Ridge Public Schools, along with 12 other school districts in the greater Urbanville metroplex, constantly competed for first-year teachers graduating from three area state universities and two local "for-profit" alternative teacher certification programs.

The Valley Ridge Public Schools had consistently lost the teacher recruitment battle and therefore decided that a new induction and mentoring program for first-year teachers was the key to reversing their poor recruiting efforts. This strategy became the "calling card" of the Valley Ridge human resource officers when recruiting at the teacher preparation programs. This new promotion tactic was unveiled with much fanfare and great attention at Union State University, home to the largest teacher preparation program.

The new Valley Ridge induction and mentoring program, *Odysseus IMing*, was presented at Union State in both video and Web-based formats. The *Odysseus IMing* catch-name immediately captured the attention of the graduating seniors who readily expressed employment interest in the Valley Ridge Public Schools. These students quickly realized that *Mentor* was the Greek mythology character whom Odysseus trusted to run his household and see to his son's education when Odysseus went off to fight the Trojans. Now, some 3,000 years later, Odysseus's name and Mentor's initial were being used, with the initial *I* (for Induction), to promote Valley Ridge Public School's new induction and mentoring program. The potential recruits were impressed with the marketing strategy. Equally important, the merits of the induction and mentoring program prominently served as an effective recruitment tool.

(Continued)

(Continued)

Lisa Natches, one of the graduating seniors at Union State University and an education major, eagerly received and viewed the electronic advertisements detailing the Valley Ridge Public Schools induction and mentoring plan. What really caught her attention were the topic links showcased within the *Odysseus IMing* plan. These topic links included the following:

- Why Valley Ridge Public Schools was a good employer for graduating education majors
- Why Valley Ridge Public Schools had an outstanding induction and mentoring program
- Why the Valley Ridge Public Schools pay schedule and benefits package were very competitive with the other area school districts

Of the three topic links, Lisa focused on why Valley Ridge Public Schools had an outstanding induction and mentoring program. This topic was important to Lisa because one of her roommates, Amanda, had entered the teaching profession the previous semester and had a terrible first-year experience teaching eighth grade at an area middle school. Amanda was so frustrated and "burned-out" with the experience she had submitted her resignation and was planning on "waiting tables" at the local Kershey Lane Café where she had worked while attending college.

Lisa thought of Amanda's bad experience and said to herself, "I want what Amanda didn't have at her school: an induction program and a really good mentor!"

Application Questions

1. Stephen P. Gordon (2004) writes in his book, *Professional Development for School Improvement: Empowering Learning Communities*, that "some experts maintain that the assignment of formal mentors to beginning teachers should be unnecessary because the entire learning community ought to provide a caring and supportive environment for the beginner" (p. 112). Based on your own experiences as a first-year teacher, and considering what the research reveals regarding mentoring, explain why such experts are right or wrong in this instance, especially as you consider the case study and the thoughts of Lisa Natches. Support your answer.

2. The developmental needs of Lisa, as a beginning teacher, will be a consideration of her mentor at Valley Ridge Public Schools. The professional and developmental needs of Lisa must be accurately assessed by her mentor. Reflect upon the chapter contents and consider how an effective induction and mentoring program will better ensure Lisa's chances of becoming an outstanding educator.

3. The current era of accountability dictates that schools have high standards of performance for all teachers, including those in their first year of teaching. Ubben, Hughes, and Norris (2007) suggest that setting performance standards (high expectations) in collaboration with the principal, mentor, and protégé has been a most effective mentoring practice. How can a principal establish high expectations without overstressing and overburdening a beginning teacher? Relate your answer to the essential responsibilities of mentors and explain how your answer relates to the research literature regarding the mentoring of school personnel.

4. It is revealed in the case study that Lisa's roommate Amanda "had a terrible first-year experience teaching eighth grade at an area middle school." How would you, the principal mentor, have helped Amanda relative to a positive teaching experience?

5. Effective mentors advise, counsel, guide, promote, and protect protégés. Mentors must also take an active role in monitoring the progress and performance of a protégé. Would you argue that the monitoring of progress and performance is the responsibility of the "teacher" mentor or the "principal" mentor? Explain your answer.

6. The National Commission on Teaching and America's Future (2008) reveal in their policy brief, *The High Cost of Teacher Turnover,* that the high cost of teacher attrition (calculate the cost for your own school district by using the *NCTAF Teacher Turnover Cost Calculator* at www.nctaf.org) could be avoided with the implementation of effective induction and mentoring programs. Research the effective induction and mentoring models noted within this chapter and then identify key components in each of the model programs that serve to keep beginning teachers in the profession.

8

*Personnel and
Adverse Situations*

NO RULES—NO WORRIES

A nationwide chain of steakhouses, specializing in an Australian flair and ambiance, dispenses dinner drinks on table coasters that boast the company slogan of "no rules—no worries." This flashy catchphrase is seemingly intent on reminding the diner that life can be, at least for those few short minutes in the restaurant, a momentary break from the complexities of real world headaches, anxieties, and problems. Principal-leaders know in reality that such a catchphrase, while cleverly deceptive, is never the case, especially when working with school personnel. If there were no rules, no policies, no regulations, no leadership, there would in fact be plenty of worries—as if the principal doesn't have enough worries to turn an auburn mane gray! Therefore, this chapter devotes itself to addressing the rules as well as attempting to solve the worries of principal leadership when it comes to handling adverse personnel issues and situations at school.

LEADING PERSONNEL IS HARD WORK

Research continues to provide evidence that a leader cannot motivate personnel or improve morale on the basis of fear or intimidation (Hughes, Ginnett, & Curphy, 2002; Yukl, 2001). While the introductory quote to this chapter may seem quite amusing, if not well-worn, it causes the school leader to pause and reflect upon the fact that it takes a great deal of courage, introspection, and consistency in purpose and effort to lead personnel effectively, especially when handling adverse situations. Lazear (1992) said it best: "Tyranny is easy" (p. 150). However, what we really know and understand is exemplified in a dated, yet relevant quote—even by today's standards: "Leading is hard work" (White, 1942). Effective leadership, to be certain, is a 10,000-aspirin job—most notably when working with personnel in adverse situations. Leading an organization may not be an easy task, but it is a necessary one if the organization wishes to move, as Jim Collins (2001) suggested, from "good to great"!

Effective leaders recognize the need to maintain a positive perspective when working with marginal staff in adverse situations. Webb and Norton (2003) note that "the personal worth and dignity of troubled employees must be protected" (p. 339). However, the question remains: What does it take to be an effective leader when handling adverse personnel issues? As noted in Chapter 3, it takes a leadership model that is based on respect, trust, honesty, responsibility, consideration of the rights of others, and the highest of expectations of self and others.

Effective leaders who expect to administer to and supervise personnel in troublesome times must be prepared for and anticipate conflict and controversy. However, the principal who emphasizes achievement, recognition, responsibility, professional growth and development, and the work itself creates a work environment that personnel find intrinsically rewarding and appealing. School personnel, like all human beings, have what McClelland (1961) decades ago, yet so relevant today, called a need for achievement, empowerment, and affiliation. These basic terms are reflected in expressions such as "the drive to strive," "the need to succeed," "the desire to aspire," and "the benefits of friendly and close interpersonal and professional relationships" in the workplace. The principal who does less is not a leader; he or she is, simply, a manager—a boss who ensures that the menial tasks are completed. Recall, B-O-S-S spelled backwards is nothing more than a "double S-O-B"!

PROACTIVE AND CORRECTIVE ACTIONS

School systems across the nation have clear procedures for disciplining personnel; however, some principals still ignore or simply do not understand such procedures when working with faculty and staff. Unfortunately, a principal's minor oversight can lead to a major legal entanglement, often

Figure 8.1   Important Steps in the Proactive Discipline of Personnel Process

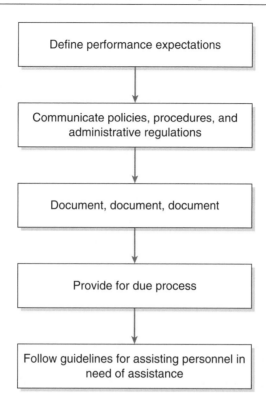

including a monetary damage award to a former employee. Before disciplinary action is taken relative to any campus personnel, take our advice and line your ducks up in a nice, neat row. You'll be glad you did!

When working with school personnel who are in trouble for whatever infraction, small or large, consider the following criteria before ever moving forward with disciplinary action against an employee. Contemplate what we label *proactive discipline*, which is a process that entails more than just discussing performance problems with an employee. Proactive discipline is a process implemented through a series of five interactive steps (see Figure 8.1) that are essential to correcting unsatisfactory personnel behaviors through appropriate support, genuine respect, and personnel-centered leadership.

PERFORMANCE EXPECTATIONS

Accountability standards, mandated assessments, budget limitations, increased student diversity, and changing social mores make the principal's task of defining and clarifying performance expectations for personnel even more daunting. A sequential model outlining the establishment of personnel performance expectations is identified in Table 8.1.

Table 8.1   Sequential Model Establishing Personnel Performance Expectations

Step	Leadership/Administrative Activity
1	Define, clarify, communicate, and articulate expectations for personnel performance through employee orientations, personnel handbooks, district policies, campus regulations, and faculty meetings and newsletters.
2	Regularly assess the school's overall needs in the context of both personnel and instructional expectations. This process can be accomplished through an analysis of the campus improvement or action plan in collaboration with a prioritized needs assessment, and through perception data collected via personnel, student, and parent survey and principal evaluative instruments.
3	Develop an action plan based upon a data collection process, needs assessments, and personnel, student, and parent perceptions relative to performance expectations.
4	Implement a plan of action that effectively establishes the highest performance expectations for campus personnel and the leadership team.
5	Monitor, adjust, and constantly reevaluate the action plan relative to administrative expectations of personnel, employee performance, and student achievement.

The desire for effective resolution of personnel issues, concerns, and problems continually resonates in our schools today. The question that begs an answer in an era of instructional and organizational reform, restructuring, decentralization, and personnel management is quite simply this: What's a principal to do? The answer, while complex in nature can be readily, if not effectively addressed by the principal who has knowledge and understanding of the Sequential Model Establishing Personnel Performance Expectations noted in Table 8.1. Remember, education is all about students and their academic achievement and educational success. The principal who engages personnel in establishing high performance expectations sets a standard of excellence.

SCHOOL POLICIES, PROCEDURES, AND ADMINISTRATIVE REGULATIONS

Principals shape the learning environment in addition to the day-to-day pressures of leading. The complexities of local dictates, federal and state mandates, and the general duties of the principalship often lead to frustration and even burnout, despite the best efforts of the leader.

On any given day, a principal is faced with a barrage of issues and problems, not only from personnel, but from members of the school community. From a personnel perspective, a principal might deal with any or all of the following considerations during the course of a single school week:

- Copyright laws
- Appraisals of performance
- Communicable diseases
- Hiring considerations
- Absences
- Inappropriate Internet activities
- Sexual harassment
- Disciplinary actions, sanctions, and appeals
- Academic freedom
- Employee assistance programs
- Confidentiality and right-to–privacy issues
- Intoxication
- Alcohol and drug testing
- Grievances
- Resignations
- Suspensions and dismissals
- Lawsuits
- Arrests and convictions

Incredibly, this list is just a sampling relative to the adverse personnel issues and situations that a principal must handle. Imagine managing one of these issues, let alone several during the course of a school day, week, or month! If you have been taken aback, consider how principals are supposed to solve each of these critical issues. As a rule, the development, implementation, and following of school board policies and administrative regulations are crucial to the school principal and the personnel involved. Webb and Norton (2003) wrote, "A school district's personnel policies and regulations are a direct reflection of how it values its human resources," that is, personnel—to include the campus principal (p. 134).

Following and complying with school board policies and administrative regulations promote intelligent decision making and enhance administrative effectiveness, organizational efficiency, and further strengthen principal-personnel relations. It is essential that principals be knowledgeable of board policy, because policy statements are based on the requirements of law. Failing to understand this basic premise carries the potential for legal entanglements and monetary penalties. Before we delve further into the examination of school board policies and administrative regulations, from a personnel perspective, let's consider how these terms are defined and applied.

Board Policies

Statements of decisions, principles, or courses of action related to the guidance and governance of a school district.

Administrative Regulations

Statements as to how board policy is to be applied and implemented by the administrative team of a school district.

School laws are enacted in education code and are binding rules mandated by either the U.S. Congress, a state legislature, or through state or federal court action. Such laws and codes are compiled and reviewed at the state level by legal teams who serve organizations such as the Texas Association of School Boards. Laws and codes are then disseminated in the form of policy briefings to local school boards for approval and ultimate distribution to every campus across a school district. Now consider the ramifications for not following school board policy as depicted in a fictitious account based upon an actual legal proceeding.

HELLO: ANYBODY AT HOME?

Ima Missen, a probationary teacher, claimed that her notice of nonrenewal from her school district was received late and therefore she was entitled to reemployment for the following year. The facts of this case reveal that Ima Missen was provided a written notice by her principal who wrote: "You have not done well enough for me to recommend that you come back next year." However, there were two problems with this form of notification: (1) The written notice was not in the form of appropriate documentation as required by board policy and state law and (2) when the principal attempted to deliver the notice, nobody was at home to receive the nonrenewal letter, and thus Ima Missen did not receive notice within the policy-dictated time frame.

Source: Adapted from *State ex rel. Curry v. Grand Valley Local School Board of Education* (1978) and *Johnson v. Selma Board of Education* (1978).

Imagine the possibility of additional legal entanglements as a result of a court ruling as relatable to this scenario. Consider what may have happened to the principal.

Board policy is recognized as legal and binding statements that evolve from important educational issues. Principals must recognize that without board policies and administrative regulations, a school district would cease to function, as policies and regulations provide direction for effective school leadership. Webb and Norton (2003) relate that "the challenges surrounding the human resources processes of selection, assignment, evaluation, welfare, and protection demand the direction and guidance that personnel policies and regulations can provide" (p. 171). Good board policy equates to good administrative decision making, which equates to good business in education.

DOCUMENTATION OF PERSONNEL

Remember the cardinal rule when working with school personnel: Document, document, document! A principal can never have too much documentation, especially if moving toward the nonrenewal or termination of an employee because of performance shortcomings or reasons for *good* or *just cause* dismissal, which will be examined in more detail in the next section of this chapter.

Concrete, indisputable documentation indicative of unsatisfactory personnel performance is imperative for three reasons. First, the burden of proof lies with the school district (i.e., the campus administrator). Second, campus personnel are more likely to improve a specified behavior if presented, in writing, with facts regarding poor performance. Third, if the employee decides to file a grievance (a very likely occurrence) indicating that the disciplinary action was unjust, the district human resource officer, the superintendent of schools, the school board of trustees, and probably the employee's lawyer will look very closely at the documentation collected by the campus principal. When documentation at the campus level is questionable, or has been carelessly recorded, any ruling will most likely favor the employee.

Identified below are seven tactics associated with effective and appropriate documentation, as recommended by Kemerer and Crain (1998).

1. *Promptness is essential!* Responding in writing to an incident, within a matter of hours, sends a clear message to the employee in question: "This is a serious matter!"

2. *Specificity is essential.* Carefully and exactly document what has occurred. Be very objective and nonjudgmental. Respond with tact and professionalism. Statements of fact often go unchallenged, most certainly have an appearance of accuracy, and thus ease the burden of proof on the principal, the school board, and the school district lawyer.

3. *Always note the individual's statutory right to file a grievance.* The individual cannot say, "You never explained to me my rights!" This is related to due process owed to all personnel.

4. *Identify and list any specific board policies, administrative regulations, educational code provisions, evaluation instrument indicators, and so forth that are implicated.* The more factual the documentation and the more it is related to school district policies and regulations, the stronger the case from an administrative perspective.

5. *Be direct in issuing a directive.* "You are hereby directed . . ."; "I direct you to . . . ."

6. *Conclude the directive memorandum on a positive note.* "I welcome your comments and I look forward to an early and equitable resolution to this situation. Remember, we are here for the benefit of our students."

7. *Always sign and date any piece of documentation and provide for the required "working days" response.* Concluding paragraphs to a piece of documentation might state:

I have received a copy of this memorandum. I understand that my signature does not necessarily indicate that I agree with its contents. I further understand that I have a right to respond within [district designated] working days if I disagree.

Please sign and date both copies. Keep one copy for your records and return the other copy to this office.

DUE PROCESS

No area within the scope of public school education generates more interest, more concern, and more legal disputes than personnel. This is not surprising, since school districts employ so many people and have to comply with so many federal and state mandates.

—Jim Walsh, Attorney
(Walsh, Kemerer, & Maniotis, 2005, p. 180)

Ask any public school employee, what is the number-one cause for school district litigation, and invariably, their answer will be "special education." While special education ranks high as a "student issue" reason for litigation, the vast majority of court cases involving school administrators evolve from personnel issues, and most notably, due process as associated with nonrenewal and dismissal (see Table 8.2).

Cunningham and Cordeiro (2006) reveal that the most important issues that school principals will face are "due process, freedom of expression, student discipline, records, and tort liability" (p. 317). It is interesting to note that the first (due process) and the last (tort liability) of these issues are personnel-centered and reflect a civil wrong done by one individual to another—for example, a breach of contract whereby a property right (due process) has been denied.

Table 8.2   Legal Issues, Personnel and District Administrators

Legal Issue Considered	Percentage of Lawsuits	Percentage of Lawsuits Ruled in Favor of District
Personnel issues (total)	**42.6**	**81.4**
Dismissal/nonrenewal	14.2	93.3
Contract negotiations	11.6	75.0
Disciplinary	10.5	88.8
Hiring	1.0	100.0

Source: Adapted from Underwood and Noffke (1990, pp. 18–20) as cited in Cunningham and Cordeiro (2006).

The Fourteenth Amendment to the U.S. Constitution stipulates a person cannot be deprived arbitrarily of "life, liberty, or property, without *due process* of law." In other words, before the state or a state entity (a school district, for example) can damage these rights, due process must be afforded. Due process means allowing an individual his or her "day in court." Simply speaking, an individual must be permitted to present his or her side of the story, or the situation, or the issue (whatever the case may be) that has created or resulted in a problem for said individual.

Personnel finding themselves in conflict with school administration must be assured that a "fair process" is in place, and that such a process is implemented appropriately and applied fairly. In the school business, *fair process*, from an employment-of-personnel perspective, is known as due process. Due process, simply defined, is a course of action by which the school principal in collaboration with other district officials must ensure justice for all personnel as related to employment actions or other employee-related considerations. Walsh et al. (2005) state, "It is a commonly accepted notion among legal scholars and lawyers that a right without adequate processes and procedures to protect and enforce said right is no right at all" (p. 128). School leaders are required to understand that such a statement is more than just an author's sentiment or a lawyer's recommendation. This statement must be a declaration of fact and, just as important, an applied practice. Since the courts have regularly stated that the purpose of educational employment laws, codes, and related district policy is to maintain a competent teaching staff that is free from political or arbitrary interference so that capable and competent personnel can perform their instructional duties, the incorporation and application of due process could very well be the difference between a satisfying and lengthy career in public education or the potential for the prompt termination of a school principal resulting from unwanted legal entanglements.

The Due Process Minimum

The handling of personnel issues, from an employment perspective, has been heavily influenced by court decisions (*Ferguson v. Thomas*, 1970; *Brosette v. Wilmer-Hutchins ISD*, 1984; *Cleveland Board of Education v. Loudermill*, 1985; *Williamson v. Dallas ISD*, 1998; *Gonzales v. Donna ISD*, 1998), through the collective bargaining process, and through adversarial, combative situations involving lawyers, professional advocates, negotiators, and mediators (Walsh et al., 2005). As previously examined in Chapter 5, far too many school principals are ill prepared and ineffectively trained to handle conflict and conflict resolution. As a result, it is imperative that campus leaders be adept at understanding certain *dos* associated with due process minimums in school personnel matters. In other words, the principal is mandated by law, code, and policy to recognize that school personnel must be prepared as follows:

1. Advised, in sufficient detail, of the cause or causes for potential discipline or termination

2. Advised of the names and the nature of the testimony of witnesses to be called against him or her

3. Provided a meaningful opportunity to be heard in self-defense

4. Provided an opportunity for a hearing before the board of trustees, as such group possesses academic expertise and is moreover considered impartial in their deliberations

Additionally, formal levels of due process must be accorded school personnel relative to any employment decision. Such levels include the following:

1. Timely notice of why an employment decision (e.g., termination) is being sought

2. A fair hearing whereby school personnel can present a defense and further question district officials, witnesses, or the evidence used against him or her

GUIDELINES FOR WORKING WITH PERSONNEL IN NEED OF ASSISTANCE

One of the most challenging tasks of any principal is to work humanely, reasonably, and positively with personnel who are not performing to expectation. Being fair and ensuring that an employee's self-esteem remains intact are easier said than done. The following guidelines can make a difficult situation less stressful for all parties.

- *Provide personnel with the benefit of the doubt.* When a campus employee makes a mistake, provide the employee a fair chance to succeed. This is especially true with new personnel. A principal might state, "I really want you to be successful at our school, so I want to make it clear that I understand what, why, and if you did such and such. Also, here's what I expect of you in your new role/position. Finally, here are some mutual goals that I believe we can agree on to better ensure you will have an excellent school year."

- *Make it crystal clear that expectations are not being met.* Proactive leadership permits a principal to deal with personnel issues while they are small, long before such issues increase in magnitude and become difficult to manage. By addressing concerns and reasons for the concerns in the context of campus expectations, the principal provides the employee with an opportunity to improve. Required expectations must always be the focus of the school leader. Expectations can be couched in statements such as "I am certain that you are capable of improvement in this particular area. However, at this time you are not meeting the expectations of this school or district. Continued failure to do so could have an adverse affect on your career. Let's talk about how you can begin necessary improvements immediately." Follow up such a conversation with immediate documentation for the purpose of clarity, reinforcement, and evidence of remediation. Interestingly, in a significant study of 200,000 school employees, Buckingham (2000) found that teachers consider four leadership behaviors as foundational to a positive school climate and culture, including (1) a caring, interested, and concerned principal, (2) teachers knowing what is *expected* of them, (3) teachers engaged in roles that fit their abilities, and (4) teachers and other campus personnel receiving positive feedback and recognition for good work, along with prompt and responsible feedback for less than adequate work.

• *Act quickly and responsibly.* Don't wait until it is too late to offer necessary assistance to personnel in need. Principals can't sit in their offices and hope their personnel in need are improving their performances on their own. Principals are responsible for providing necessary guidance and direction. Professional growth plans must mean more to an employee than receiving a sheet of paper from the principal. These plans must serve as the basis for genuine improvement. Meet with the employee in need of assistance immediately and discuss your concerns while placing the employee at ease. Address the necessary point(s) in a reasonable and responsible fashion, always maintaining desired expectations. Describe the problem in detail, using facts and emphasizing the problem, not the employee. Obtain agreement on the problem, involve the employee in resolving the problem, and then conclude by reviewing the problem and the solution. Finally, end on a positive note: "Donna, you were hired at our school for your strengths. Target this particular problematic area for improvement and let's move on for the benefit of the students we serve! Any questions?"

• *Provide a reasonable response time for performance improvement.* Give the employee in question a reasonable amount of time to rectify performance shortcomings. The amount of time considered reasonable should be influenced by the nature of the concern. For example, if the problem relates to Ms. Rowe getting her third-grade class to Ms. Miller's music room on time, a principal would expect this issue to be resolved immediately. However, if the problem is more complex, demonstrating improvement may take a longer period of time and require more in-depth support and assistance. An example would be a teacher who possesses the instructional skills and methodologies for students to excel but fails to incorporate strategies to effectively or appropriately manage or discipline students.

- *Stipulate the availability of an appeal process.* Due process requires that employees have an opportunity to respond to any allegation or performance problem. Typically, the appeal process begins with the immediate supervisor (campus principal) and then proceeds to higher management (human resource officer, superintendent, or school board). This appeal process should be stipulated in district policy, personnel handbooks, and in any documentation provided to the employee whose performance has been questioned. The appeals process is a very important aspect of supervising personnel, as even the best of principals are often too close or too emotionally involved to the problem at hand. Only someone not so personally involved can readily perceive a positive, reasonable solution to the situation.

The implementation of these guidelines is essential to the development of positive leader-follower relationships and will enhance organizational culture and climate. This is especially true when the principal handles controversial personnel issues. Note the words of Webb and Norton (2003): "In fact, human resources management is the *principal behavior* most highly correlated with a positive school climate" (p. 116, italics added).

CONTROVERSIAL PERSONNEL ISSUES

Behavioral scientists consistently agree that controversial issues provide leaders with the opportunity to explore different points of view, discover how diverse perspectives complement and oppose each other, and gain insight into some of the debates currently taking place within organizations (Van Knippenberg & Van Knippenberg, 2005; Tjosvold, 1987). While the research may support such an assertion, the authors, as former principals, would much rather have made a career of administrative leadership through positive personnel interactions as opposed to gaining insight about campus employees via the handling of controversial personnel issues. Nevertheless, controversy is an absolute in any organization as long as people continue to make up organizations. We will now examine controversial personnel issues such as discrimination, sexual harassment, sexual orientations, and alcohol and drugs. This examination is not exhaustive; rather, it identifies the more troublesome concerns a principal handles when working with personnel.

Discrimination

Bigotry and racism remain alive in our society. Newspapers are filled with hate-crimes, acts of covert discrimination, and other discriminatory practices, including violations of the Title IX Education Amendments (1972), which prohibit discrimination against persons on the basis of gender. The latter is a major concern of school districts across the nation (Valente & Valente, 2005). Discrimination on the basis of race, religion, national origin, gender, age, and disability is prohibited by federal and state laws. Discrimination quickly becomes a controversial issue when personnel are denied employment and other related benefits on the basis of recruitment, hiring, promotion, and compensation practices that conflict with legal statutes. Principals must be extremely cautious of any practice that could result in an employee successfully winning a discrimination suit. Court action could result in "affirmative action against a district as may be appropriate, which may include, but is not limited to reinstatement or hiring of employees, with or without pay," along with other "equitable relief," including attorney fees, court costs, and litigant damages (42 U.S.C. § 2000e-5g, as noted in Potter-Norton, 2006, p. 114).

Sexual Harassment

While sexual harassment is typically associated with females, males have also been subjected to sexual harassment in the workplace. Sexual harassment from a personnel perspective can be male to female, female to male, female to female, male to male, male to student, and female to student. The bottom line: Sexual harassment is no small source of stress for the victim and for the principal who must, by law, intervene.

From a female perspective, a woman can easily find herself in a no-win situation whether complaining openly or silently enduring the abuse. Principals must recognize that since the 1980s sexual harassment litigation has made it easier for victims to recover damages from school districts under Title VII of the Civil Rights Act of 1964, which protects personnel against employment discrimination based on gender (Sergiovanni, Kelleher, McCarthy, & Wirt, 2004). If successful in their litigation against a school district, aggrieved employees can be compensated monetarily for injuries suffered.

Naturally, more legal difficulties can be brought against a district when the harassment is employee-to-student. The 1992 court decision, *Franklin v. Gwinnett County Public Schools*, served as the judicial impetus to offer students monetary damages from school districts for sexual harassment or abuse by a school district employee. It is important for the school leader to understand that the U.S. Department of Education's *Office for Civil Rights Sexual Harassment Guidance* (1997) stipulates that a sexual relationship between a campus employee and an elementary school student can never be defended as consensual, and there is little doubt that a relationship between a campus employee and a secondary student is not consensual (Fisher, Schimmel, & Stellman, 2003).

Sexual Orientation

The term "sexual orientation" is used in this passage to refer to both male (homosexual) and female (lesbian) sexual behaviors and relationships. A question often posed by school administrators is, Can a teacher be terminated for his or her sexual orientation? The answer is possibly yes, depending on individual state statutes. The basis for this response is judicially bound when the sexual orientation violates an individual's efficiency or ability to function as a teacher and as a role model for students. For example, in Nebraska, a high school teacher was terminated for making homosexual advances to a salesman in the teachers' workroom. Although there was no direct evidence that the incident impaired the teacher's ability to perform the instructional tasks of the position, the courts ruled in favor of his dismissal as such sexual behavior in a school is "a clear departure from moral behavior and professional standards" and served to prove that the individual exhibited an "unfitness to teach" (*Stephens v. Board of Education, School District No. 5*, 1988).

In an Oregon case, a teacher was dismissed for his sexual orientation on the basis of violating contemporary moral standards by which "his ability to function as a teacher was severely impaired" (*Ross v. Springfield School District No. 19*, 1984).

Most recently, in the state of Texas, the sexual orientation of a high school Teacher of the Year and girl's basketball coach, who had led the team to four state final championship series, resulted in the school district seeking termination of the employee's contract. The teacher/coach lived with a same sex teacher's aide/school bus driver. In Texas, same-sex couples are offered no legal protection in the workplace from discrimination based on sexual orientation. While 16 states have amended their employment laws to offer such safeguards, and 7 others have mandated these protections only for their state employees, the remaining 27 states have not done so (Colloff, 2005).

Alcohol and Drugs

Many school districts have adopted employee health provisions in an attempt to protect the welfare of the students and other personnel at the campus level. Such provisions or policy requirements include wording related to eyesight, hearing, and mental fitness, as well as disease transmission stipulations, and alcohol and drug specifications to include testing, interdiction, intervention, and employee assistance programs.

Schools are a true reflection of the norms of society, including the ills of alcohol and drug use, abuse, and addictions. As former principals, the authors believe that the campus leader must model behavior that directly influences campus personnel and students. In today's society, students need to observe how moral and ethical adults conduct themselves. The importance of positive adult role models cannot be overestimated.

Carrell, Kuzmits, and Elbert (1992) relate alcohol and drug use will not only lead to marital problems, family abuse, and estrangement, but can create the following work-related difficulties:

- Accidents and injuries to students and colleagues
- A disregard of performance details, the use of poor judgment, and bad decision making

- Irresponsible performance in terms of quantity and quality
- Upwards of five times greater likelihood of workers' compensation claims
- Absenteeism of more than 10 workdays per year
- Greater likelihood of an employee filing a grievance

Additionally, policies regarding alcohol and drug use in the workplace cannot be justified only for social and moral reasons; one has to weigh the monetary issue (what it costs a district) as well. Nationwide, $25 billion is lost annually due to absenteeism, accidents, sick leave, and decreased productivity related to the use of alcohol and drugs by our work force (Council on Alcohol and Drugs-Houston, 2007). Researchers recognize that certain working conditions can lead to alcoholism and drug use, and these conditions are magnified in workplaces that are unstructured in their employee expectations or where leaders are nonsupportive of their personnel and create stressful and anxiety-ridden atmospheres (Filipowicz, 1979).

Finally, rehabilitation or employee assistance programs for school personnel who are suffering from addictions are generally available and are designed to help with the challenge, stress, and conflict inevitable in the modern school setting. School administrators often wonder if these programs work. The Kemper Insurance Companies (2005) report that the majority of employees suffering from alcohol and substance abuse can fully recover as a result of rehabilitation efforts, with success rates of up to 80%.

THE SUPERVISION OF MARGINAL EMPLOYEES

Smith (1998) defines marginal teachers as those individuals who fail to perform satisfactorily in one or more of the following areas and thus inhibit student learning. The teacher fails to

- teach the mandated curriculum;
- reveal an interest in or dedication to students and teaching;
- exhibit interpersonal skills with students and colleagues;
- demonstrate effective and appropriate teaching skills;
- maintain an organized classroom, lessons, and plans;
- establish expectations for student management and behavior; or
- exhibit knowledge of the subject matter. (p. 184)

Most marginal teachers fail to recognize that their instructional performance is less than adequate. This issue poses an even more serious dilemma for the school principal when trying to help these teachers in need of professional assistance. To better serve marginal personnel, a school principal must

- be positive in assisting and developing the potential of personnel by showing empathy and understanding, yet never negating organizational expectations;

- provide support that is caring and personal;
- look for signs of dysfunction, such as irritability, nonmotivation, lack of interest or commitment, minimal energy, loss of concentration or effort, and unusual or bizarre behavior(s);
- assist with referrals to internal programs or external agencies;
- be sensitive to adjustments in position assignments and workloads; and
- use appropriate mentors.

Effective school principals realize that at various times during their tenure a great deal of their responsibility in interacting with campus personnel will relate to their ability to handle and counsel employees who are struggling with troublesome factors. These factors include, but are not limited to, the following areas of serious consideration:

- Marital issues
- Personnel illnesses
- Family problems
- Financial issues
- Alcohol and drugs
- Adultery and affairs
- Sexual harassment
- Death
- Peer relationships
- Assaults/fights
- Dating problems
- Gossip and innuendos
- Abortion
- Inappropriate language
- Outside employment
- Spouse interference
- Religious convictions
- Bigotry and racism
- Child care
- Mental health
- Nonsupportive spouse
- Abusive spouse

Supervision of marginal employees is not easy. Supervision can be viewed as a process of managing functions intended to promote the achievement of institutional goals and to enhance the personal and professional capabilities of the marginal employee. Supervision of marginal employees is an ongoing aspect of the supervisory process that offers a mechanism for principals to provide for optimal working and learning conditions. Supervision of marginal employees and dealing with troublesome factors brought to school by campus personnel necessitate effective administrative leadership along with a cooperative relationship between the principal and the followership. Without such, the foundation necessary to build upon instructional improvement will ultimately collapse.

The principal's role, relative to supervisory practice, is constantly evolving. The principal has a key responsibility in the improved performance of all personnel, most notably those who are marginal by definition. Words such as leadership, collaboration, cooperation, and inspiration must be manifested in the principal's action and not confined to the spoken word. The principalship is a tough job, but those who do it and do it well wouldn't work in any other occupation.

Supervision is a special practice, worthy of the best. Northouse (2004) suggests that leadership, from a supervisory perspective, must be defined as "a combination of special traits or characteristics that individuals possess that enable them to induce others to accomplish tasks" (p. 269). Effective principals must possess and demonstrate the qualities they are trying to instill in marginal employees and in their team as a whole. One of the most important aspects of the principal role is leading by example. It is a principal's responsibility to serve as a role model for not only those who need the modeling most, but for all school personnel. Remember, everyone is watching!

GRIEVANCES

Principals new to any school can mark their calendars and readily expect to be personally tested early in the school year! Such a test can very well come in the form of personal confrontations with campus personnel. Often a confrontation occurs unexpectedly and unannounced, until a filed grievance comes across a principal's desk. Only then does the principal realize there is a problem with personnel.

A grievance has been defined by Young (2008) as a "relief valve" (p. 388). In other words, an employee is seeking relief through a procedural process that will resolve a violation, or a purported violation that has created personal dissatisfaction with the school administrator. For this reason, it is imperative that the new or the tenured leader incorporate each of the six personnel principles (respect, trust, honesty, responsibility, rights, and expectations) identified in the Principled Personnel Model for Effective Leader-Follower Relationships, introduced in Chapter 3.

Webb and Norton (2003) describe the grievance procedure as a process that permits campus personnel the opportunity to express a complaint to their administrator without fear of reprisal. The grievance procedure provides for due process, which in turns allows for the complaint and grievant to be heard, and often heard by "successively higher levels of management, until an answer is provided that the grievant can or must accept" (McCollum & Norris, 1984, p. 106). Shown in Figure 8.2 is a procedural model for grievance resolution.

Personnel grievances should be received, reviewed, and resolved in a serious and legitimate manner. The procedures noted in Figure 8.2 provide campus personnel with fair consideration and equitable resolution of their grievances. These procedures safeguard the rights of the building principal and other district officials involved in the process.

CAUSES FOR TERMINATION

Sufficient evidence must be presented by a school principal and other district officials to establish *good* or *just cause* for employee termination. The courts have stipulated what constitutes good or just cause relative to the

Figure 8.2   Procedural Model for Grievance Resolution

Step 5 – Should the grievance involve the appointment, employment, evaluation, reassignment, duties, discipline, or dismissal of the grievant, the hearing may be held in a closed session unless the grievant requests that it be heard in public. It is the superintendent of schools who determines whether the grievance satisfies the criteria for an open or closed meeting.

Step 4 – Should the school board choose to respond to the grievance, the board shall then make and communicate its decision to hear the grievant either orally or in writing. However, a lack of a response or the denial of a hearing by the board upholds the administrative decision rendered at Step 2. Any proceeding before the board is typically recorded.

Step 3 – Should the outcome of the Step 2 conference not be to the employee's satisfaction, the employee may request in writing that the matter be placed on the agenda of an upcoming school board meeting.

Step 2 – Should the outcome of the Step 1 conference not be to the employee's satisfaction, the employee may request and be granted a conference with the superintendent of schools or a designee to discuss the grievance.

Step 1 – The grievant shall request and be granted a conference with the principal by submitting a grievance in writing.

termination of school personnel. Such good or just cause actions include but are not necessarily limited to the following causes listed in Table 8.3.

In most states, an additional good or just cause for termination is the violation of a code of ethics and standard practices for public educators.

As a concluding activity to the Causes for Termination section of this chapter, read the true scenario noted in You Be the Judge on page 169, reflect upon the due process minimums and the good or just cause actions, and then answer the questions that follow.

Table 8.3   Good or Just Causes for Termination

Good or Just Cause	Specified Actions
Incompetence (Alexander & Alexander, 2001)	• Lack of knowledge of subject matter • Inadequate teaching • Failure to manage students • Use of unreasonable discipline • Physical or mental disability • Willful neglect of duty
Immorality (Fisher et al., 2003)	• Sexual conduct with a student • Sexual conduct with nonstudents • Homosexuality • Sexually explicit remarks to students • Distribution of sexually explicit materials to students • Use of obscene, profane, or abusive language • Possession, distribution, or use of controlled substances • Dishonesty
Violent and unprofessional conduct (Walsh et al., 2005)	• Assaulting a student, parent, or professional colleague • Inappropriate use of corporal punishment • Aggravated assault on spouse or children • DWUI convictions and other forms of public intoxication
Insubordination (Garner, 1999; Valente & Valente, 2005)	• Refusal to follow established policies and regulations • Refusal to obey principal or school official directives • Unwillingness to cooperate with campus principal or other school officials • Encouraging student disobedience • Unauthorized absence from duty • Refusal to accept a school or teaching assignment

(Continued)

Table 8.3 (Continued)

Good or Just Cause	Specified Actions
Misappropriation of public funds (Sorenson & Goldsmith, 2006)	• Utilizing school budgetary funds for personal gain or benefit • Embezzlement, fraud, or mismanagement of school budgetary funds, including but not limited to the campus activity account
Criminal violations (Valente & Valente, 2005)	• Possessing a criminal record at the time of employment • Abuse of or other unlawful acts with a student or a minor • Withholding criminal information at the time of employment or failure to disclose a conviction during employment • Convicted of a felony • Convicted of a misdemeanor involving moral turpitude
Obtaining district services for personal benefit (Walsh et al., 2005)	• Using an official administrative capacity to acquire school personnel services for personal benefit or for political alliance
Discrimination (Lunenburg & Ornstein, 2004)	• Employment • Race and gender • Sexual harassment • Disability • Religious • Age • Maternity

YOU BE THE JUDGE

Following a campus evacuation by a fire alarm, an elementary school teacher sent a student back into the building to retrieve her grade book, guessing correctly that the alarm was only a drill. The teacher is terminated after the child's parents cite their expectation that their child should be safe with teachers, and a school district should not be required to provide a second chance if a teacher injures or potentially injures a child. The teacher demands reinstatement and remediation following several meetings with the school principal and a district human resources official after the incident. Later, the teacher presents an appeal to the local school board but is nonetheless terminated.

Questions for Consideration

1. Does this action (sending a child back into the school building during a fire drill) present a possible legal entanglement for the teacher, the principal, the school district? If so, how and why?
2. Which of the formal levels of due process were afforded the teacher in this scenario?
3. Which of the due process "minimums" were presented by administration to the teacher in question?
4. Which one of the eight good or just cause actions identified in the chapter served as the basis for the termination of the teacher?

Note: See the final court rulings relative to this particular scenario at the conclusion of the chapter.

Source: Adapted from *Ruiz-Garcia v. Houston ISD* (2000), and *Adair v. Cumby ISD* (2001).

Schools, like all other institutions in our society today, operate within a legal framework of codes, legislative mandates, and court decisions. One of the legally centered tasks that all school principals face is that of disciplining campus personnel. It is a task that is certainly unpleasant and distasteful—the dark side of school administration, so to speak. However, it is one task that must be undertaken to ensure quality instruction. When the act of disciplining school personnel becomes necessary, it is imperative that the various legal requirements of due process be met. The entire disciplinary process is in jeopardy unless various legal requirements are met. Therefore, the practicing school leader should be keenly aware of all due process procedures and recognize the legal implications of ignoring due process assurances to campus personnel.

UNION-MANAGEMENT RELATIONSHIPS

A major responsibility of teacher unions is to influence school district decisions relative to conditions of employment through the collective bargaining process. This process relates to the negotiation and administration of an agreement or negotiated contract between the union and the school district. Collective bargaining agreements are specific in listing the rights and duties of school personnel, along with principals, with respect to wages, hours of employment, working conditions and other identified terms within a contract. This agreement serves as a major influence on the day-to-day operations of a school (Sharp & Walter, 2003, 2004).

Bargaining issues include grievance arbitration, teacher evaluation, class size, school calendar, wages and benefits, good or just cause for dismissal, grievance definitions, and teacher and management rights. Through the collective bargaining process, the union attempts to negotiate items that represent the concerns of its members, and management bargains to advance the interests of the school district. The collective bargaining process can be tedious, lengthy, and outright antagonistic with the resulting document being as lengthy as several hundred pages. Negotiation tactics include initial proposals from both sides, followed by counterproposals, then tradeoffs, caucusing by both parties independent of the other to decide what actions to take on particular aspects of the bargaining process, concluding with costing proposals and eventual acceptance or rejection of the collective bargaining agreement by both sides (Lunenburg & Ornstein, 2004). The upside to the negotiation process is the development of trust and effective collaboration. The downside: distrust, resentment, and sometimes open hostility.

CONTRACTS FOR PUBLIC SCHOOL EMPLOYEES

Most school personnel, especially certified educators, are employed on a contract basis. Contracts are approved through either the collective bargaining process or by the local school board. For example, in Texas, a *right-to-work* state, public school employees are not permitted to engage in collective bargaining. States such as Texas may outlaw collective negotiation, but cannot prohibit unions from existing nor public school employees from joining them. Right-to-work states provide for contract standards with specific stipulations for length of contract period, teacher resignation, nonrenewal, termination, notice of intent, and hearing request and appeal. *Unionized* states have contract provisions relative to employment status, benefit agreements, buyout terminology, performance evaluation stipulations, impasse procedures, strike provisions, grievance procedures, arbitration, exclusive representation, and other employee benefits. Most contracts negotiated through the collective bargaining process consist of three functional categories: (1) organizational security, (2) compensation and working conditions, and (3) individual security.

Organizational Security

Young and Castetter (2004) note that one of the first steps in the collective bargaining process is the development and negotiation of security clauses in contract agreements. Such clauses may stipulate duration of the contract agreement, teaching or work schedules, promotion, transfer, discipline, dismissal, staffing assignments, appraisal, leaves of absence, and protection from union intimidation.

Compensation and Working Conditions

Central to any contract agreement are compensation and working conditions. Compensation includes remuneration (salary, wages, and collateral benefits) in exchange for services rendered. Specified working conditions might include class size, lunch or break periods, planning time, nonteaching functions, student discipline measures, academic freedom, and protection from physical assault (Keane, 1996).

Individual Security

Clay (1997) reveals that individual security clauses in a contract are designed to protect school personnel against arbitrary treatment from a school district, union or association, other personnel, and community groups. This security is important to both the individual educator as well as the school district, as the rights of an individual and the collective rights of an organization (school system) can be infringed upon. For example, consider the following vignette.

HE'S GOT TO GO!

Sam Austin was a good man and a really fine employee. He arrived at work earlier than most each day, offered additional help to his students, and was regularly involved in student activities at Natchin High School in Madisonville. He was admired and respected by his colleagues, by the school's administrative team, and by most parents and other members of the learning community. Sam did have the highest of expectations for his students. He was demanding, but caring and kind.

Justin Woodrow was one of those difficult students who happened to play lead guitar in a local rock band. Justin really had little interest in school. Justin had "locked horns" with Mr. Austin several times during the course of the first semester of school because Sam expected Justin to work, learn, and succeed. Justin would not

(Continued)

(Continued)

realize until later, after he inflicted quite a bit of pain on his teacher, that Mr. Austin, while firm, was fair and had the best interest of his students at heart.

Justin, one afternoon following class, began to circulate a bogus petition to remove Sam Austin from his teaching position on the grounds that Sam had used inappropriate language in class. Amazingly enough, Justin was able to collect over 200 signatures, many from students who had never been in Sam's class. Justin, with his mother in tow, presented the petition to the principal of Natchin High School. As you might expect, the principal was quite surprised and later, upon learning the news, Sam was quite devastated.

Later that week, a community rally—bolstered by Justin's parents—occurred at the Local 114 VFW Hall in Madisonville. The community group, made up mostly of 25 to 30 disgruntled parents of students who had been suspended or expelled from Natchin High School, ranted and raved, demanding "he's got to go!" This assemblage over the next few weeks became known as the "Concerned Citizens" group. The group made demands and threatened the principal, the superintendent, and several school board members until the "Concerned Citizens" realized that their initial case and other causes were simply frivolous. Finally, the group disbanded once they realized that Mr. Sam Austin, teacher at Natchin High School, was protected against such ridiculous charges by certain individual security clauses in his employment contract.

Sam, being the man of character that he was, moved forward, never bitter and actually worked to improve his relationship with young Justin. Justin ultimately apologized, matured into an excellent student under the tutelage of Mr. Austin, and today, some years later, Justin Woodrow is a leading attorney in Madisonville where he continues to stay in contact with his mentor and good friend, Sam Austin. Interestingly, Justin and Sam play guitar and trombone in a three-piece jazz combo every Friday night at the Local 114.

Now an important note: Principals need to carefully read and understand the provisions and clauses within district contracts. Many principals have found themselves in difficult personnel situations simply because they either did not read or misinterpreted the language in union contracts.

FINAL THOUGHTS

Webb and Norton (2003) suggest that perhaps no other aspect of public school administration is subject to the plethora of policies, regulations, and legal mandates that govern the administration of school personnel.

We couldn't agree more! Plenty of rules, lots of worries! In reality, the rules, policies, and regulations serve to ease the administrative burden and associated worries relative to the handling of personnel and personnel issues. Effective school principals follow the law and incorporate policies and regulations into the daily campus routine as a means of leading, supporting, and motivating school personnel to reach their highest levels of enthusiasm, responsibility, achievement, and excellence. Nevertheless, there will be times when even the best of school leaders must take proactive and corrective actions in handling personnel who find themselves in trouble for an infraction, great or small, that has occurred at the campus level. When such occurs, principals must affect the situation by (1) defining performance expectations; (2) communicating policies, procedures, and administrative regulations; (3) documenting said offenses; (4) providing for due process; and (5) following all guidelines for assisting personnel in need of assistance.

Unfortunately, controversial personnel issues abound because school leaders are dealing with human beings and human beings make mistakes. Recall from Chapter 5: Conflict is inevitable. Mediation is vital. Resolution is essential. Some of the more difficult conflicts and controversial issues a principal will have to confront, from a personnel perspective, relate to sexual harassment, alcohol and drug abuse, discrimination, and sexual orientation. These issues can interfere with an employee's ability to perform satisfactorily and thus negatively affect student learning.

Marginal employees often demonstrate ineffective and inappropriate behaviors as related to teaching and interacting with students and colleagues. When principals intervene, marginal employees, many of whom fail to recognize that their performance is less than adequate, often react defensively by filing a grievance in an attempt to shift attention from their performance to procedural issues associated with the school principal.

The grievance process is one that involves a series of steps by which employee-supervisor differences can be remedied. Sometimes, the remedy does not favor the employee, as the principal has good or just cause for the disciplinary action, including termination. Good or just cause has been defined in the law as relating to incompetence, immorality, violent and unprofessional behaviors, insubordination, misappropriation of public funds, criminal violations, obtaining district services for personal benefit, and discrimination.

Effective teacher-principal, union-management relations, including collective bargaining processes, can work to manage, if not solve, personnel problems. Nevertheless, when problems with personnel arise, the school principal must be proactive and ready to handle the situation through effective leadership styles and skills. This is not an easy task. Remember, leading is hard work, and hard work equates to leadership determination, personnel expectations, and employee considerations.

In closing, may we be among the very first to welcome you into the leadership-service role of being a school administrator. Become a better leader of personnel. Seek the challenges associated with human resources administration. Consider every principal-personnel situation to be a learning opportunity that opens the door to increased professional growth and leadership skill development. Finally, consider the leadership message found within the lyrics of the old hymn, "Life's Railway to Heaven."

Life is like a mountain railroad, with an engineer that's brave;
We must make the run successful, from the cradle to the grave;
Always mindful of obstruction, do your duty, never fail;
Keep your hand upon the throttle, and your eye upon the rail.
As we roll along the mainline, there'll be storms and there'll be strife;
There'll be sidetracks unexpected on the left and on the right;
But with a straight always before us and our heart upon the prize;
There'll be no disembarkation until we've done what is right.

—M. E. Abbey/C. D. Tillman (1890)

DISCUSSION QUESTIONS

1. Do principals have a moral obligation to provide all personnel with a meaningful job and campus responsibilities? What do *you* think and why?

2. What, in your opinion, is the most important step, as identified in Figure 8.1, Important Steps in the Proactive Discipline of Personnel Process? Explain your answer.

3. If documentation is the cardinal rule of working with school personnel, which of Kemerer and Crain's seven tactics of effective documentation, as identified on pages 155–156, would have effectively served the principal in the Hello: Anybody at Home? scenario?

4. What is due process, and why are due process procedures essential to leadership effectiveness when working with school personnel?

5. What controversial personnel issue have you personally witnessed at the campus you serve? Why do you believe the issue was controversial, and how did the principal leader handle this personnel matter? Was the eventual outcome positive or negative, and why?

6. Consider Table 8.3, Good or Just Causes for Termination, and then determine which good or just cause was willfully neglected in the You Be the Judge scenario. Explain your answer.

CASE STUDY APPLICATION

TRUTH CAN BE STRANGER THAN FICTION IN PERSONNEL ISSUES

He Said What?

Dr. Marie Corley, superintendent of schools, was sitting in her office one Monday morning during the second semester of school, finishing a much-needed cup of coffee to kick off the first day of the workweek, when Raphael Sanchez, the associate superintendent for personnel services, walked in with Principal Paul Reven and suggested that the three needed to talk. Dr. Corley, a very personable leader who always exuded much confidence and further had the highest of expectations for all her administrative team members, met Mr. Sanchez's frown with a "Good morning, Raphael. You and Paul pull up a chair!"

Dr. Corley listened carefully as the associate superintendent and the high school principal each related a story that one could only wish was a far-fetched fabrication or some sort of sadistic joke. Unfortunately, the story was true! Mr. Sanchez noted that one of the district's head football coaches, Nick Reid, had publicly stated to several male coaches on the previous Saturday afternoon during a winter meeting that "I'm going to slit their throats, slide them down the bank, and let them float down the river and bleed a slow death!"

Dr. Corley looked at Mr. Sanchez with disgust and blurted out, "He said what?"

Mr. Sanchez retorted, "That's right, he said it, and I have just received six grievances this morning filed by our female coaches."

Dr. Corley replied, "Let me guess, he made the statement in reference to our female coaches."

Mr. Sanchez responded affirmatively with a nodding of his head.

Dr. Corley looked dismayed and simply shook her head and then said, "What are the grievances about?"

Mr. Sanchez quickly produced each one from a file folder he held on his lap. Superintendent Corley scanned each of the six grievance forms and readily concluded that the basis for each grievance filed against Nick Reid was gender discrimination, sexual harassment resulting from a hostile work environment, true threats, as well as offensive or harassing speech.

"Surely, he didn't mean it, did he?" the superintendent asked.

"Whether he meant it or not, he said it," said Mr. Sanchez, "and three of our male coaches, who were present at the Saturday meeting, have confirmed to Paul and me already this morning that the statement was actually made by Reid."

Dr. Corley then asked, "The female coaches heard about this, I assume?"

(Continued)

(Continued)

Principal Reven replied, "Yes, Coach Bill Merritt told his wife, Thelma, who in turn called Jenda Marsh, the girls' head softball coach, who shared the word with the other female coaches—so here we are!"

"Oh, by the way," said Mr. Sanchez, "Paul has some additional documentation regarding Reid that he needs to share with you."

"Raphael, what have you done about this, other than telling me?" asked Dr. Corley.

Mr. Sanchez replied, "Well, the usual. After receiving the grievances this morning, I have made appointments with each of the female coaches, as well as Reid, and I will be taking their statements later this afternoon. I have three telephone messages from union representatives and one fax from a local attorney. It's going to be a long week—so much for having spring break off next week! I've also called Jerome Howard, the school district attorney, and made him aware of the situation."

Dr. Corley then asked, "What did Jerome say?"

"Pretty much the same response you offered: 'He said what?'" responded Mr. Sanchez. He went on to note that "Jerome has scheduled some time for us to meet with him later this morning. Paul has already canceled a parent conference so he can meet with us as well. Can you adjust your schedule to meet with him?"

Dr. Corley acknowledged his question with an affirmative nodding of her head. Thus began a difficult day that led to several more long and tedious days, eventually working into a stressful three additional weeks! Later that morning, the school district attorney—in his meeting with the administrative team—noted, "Truth can be stranger than fiction!"

Application Questions

1. *True threats* have been defined by the courts as "utterances which a *reasonable person* could view as a serious expression of intent to harm another" (Valente & Valente, 2005, p. 294, italics added). Would the statement made by Coach Reid be considered a "true threat" or "offensive or harassing speech" or "protected speech"? Support your answer.

2. What constitutes a *hostile work environment*? Have Coach Reid's statements provided the female coaches with the right to grieve the coach as well as the school district on the basis of gender discrimination? Explain your answer.

3. What must the high school principal do in this situation? How should Principal Reven document the head coach's actions? Compose a brief directive (no more than one page) illustrating the principal's written response to this particular incident.

4. One of the female coaches is planning to sue Nick Reid as well as the school district on the basis that the statement made by Reid was defamatory. According to Fisher et al. (2003), a statement is defamatory if the "law assumes that an individual's reputation has been injured" (p. 83). Do you believe Reid's remark about the female coaches was defamatory? Support your answer.

5. Which of the Principled Personnel Model principles (see Chapter 3), from the perspective of Principal Reven, relate to or are applicable to the situation in the case study presented? Explain your answer(s).

6. What type of "additional documentation" do you suspect Principal Paul Reven "needs to share" with the superintendent regarding Head Coach Nick Reid? What might be inferred by such a statement?

7. How is this case study representative of *controversial personnel issues*? Be specific in your answer. Also, have any specific actions by Head Coach Nick Reid provided the school district with good or just cause for termination? Explain your answer.

FINAL RULING: YOU BE THE JUDGE (FROM P. 169)

Neither remediation nor reinstatement by the school district is required for a teacher who, after a class is evacuated from a school building by a fire alarm, sends a student back into the building to retrieve a grade book, plan book, roll book, or any other item or material.

> While one can often guess that an alarm is only a drill, unless one pulls the alarm, one cannot be certain. Petitioner's (the teacher's) assumption about the alarm could have placed the student at risk. Remediation is not required when students are potentially placed at risk. (*Ruiz-Garcia v. Houston ISD*, 2000)

> Parents should have an expectation that their children will be safe with teachers. A school district is not required to give a teacher who injures or potentially injures a child a second chance. (*Adair v. Cumby ISD*, 2001)

Therefore, the teacher presented in the scenario should be denied reinstatement and remediation, and thus must be terminated by the school district.

OTHER RESOURCES

Dunklee, D. R., & Shoop, R. J. (2006). *The principal's quick-reference guide to school law: Reducing liability, litigation, and other potential legal tangles.* Thousand Oaks, CA: Corwin Press.

Kosmoski, G. J., & Pollack, D. R. (2005). *Managing difficult, frustrating, and hostile conversations: Strategies for savvy administrators.* Thousand Oaks, CA: Corwin Press.

Peine, J. (2008). *The educator's professional growth plan: A process for developing staff and improving instruction.* Thousand Oaks, CA: Corwin Press.

References and
Further Reading

Adair v. Cumby ISD, Dkt. No. 029-R2–1200 (Tex. Comm'r Educ. 2001).

Alexander, K., & Alexander, M. D. (2009). *American public school law*. Belmont, CA: Wadsworth Cengage Learning.

Allen, D. (2001). *Getting things done: The art of stress-free productivity*. New York: Penguin Books.

Alliance for Excellent Education. (2005). *Teacher attrition: A costly loss to the nation and to the states*. Washington, DC: Author. Available online at http://www.all4ed.org/files/archive/publications/TeacherAttrition.pdf

Anderson, W. (2006). Site-based management. In S. C. Smith & P. K. Piele (Eds.), *School leadership* (pp. 223–244). Thousand Oaks, CA: Corwin Press.

Arvey, R. D., & Faley, R. H. (1992). *Fairness in selecting employees*. Reading, MA: Addison-Wesley.

Baehr, A. (2005). *Would you lie on your resume?* Retrieved March 6, 2007, from http://www.articlealley.com/article_10671_36.html

Barth, R. S. (2003). *Lessons learned*. Thousand Oaks, CA: Corwin Press.

Bass, B. M. (1990). *Bass and Stogdill's handbook of leadership* (3rd ed.). New York: Free Press.

Beaudoin, M., & Taylor, M. (2005). *Creating a positive school culture: How principals and teachers can solve problems together*. Thousand Oaks, CA: Corwin Press.

Becker, G., Withycombe, R., Doget, F., Miller, E., Morgan, C., DeLoretto, L., et al. (1971). *Elementary school principals and their schools: Beacons of brilliance and potholes of pestilence*. Eugene: University of Oregon, Center for the Advanced Study of Educational Administration.

Beckner, W. (2004). *Ethics for educational leaders*. Boston: Pearson Education.

Bell, J. D., Castagnera, J., & Young, J. P. (1984). Employment references: Do you know the law? *Personnel Journal, 63*(2), 32–36.

Bennis, W., & Nanus, B. (1985). *Leaders: The strategies for taking charge*. New York: Harper & Row.

Blase, J., & Kirby, P. C. (1991). *Bringing out the best in teachers: What effective principals do*. Thousand Oaks, CA: Corwin Press.

Blum, R. E., Butler, J. A., & Olson, N. L. (1987). Leadership for excellence: Research-based training for principals. *Educational Leadership, 45*(1), 25–29.

Bolman, L. G., & Deal, T. E. (1997). *Reframing organizations: Artistry, choice, and leadership*. San Francisco: Jossey-Bass.

Bolton, T. (1997). *Human resource management: An introduction*. Cambridge, MA: Blackwell.

Bowers, D. G., & Seashore, S. E. (1966). Predicting organizational effectiveness with a four-factor theory of leadership. *Administrative Science Quarterly, 11*, 238–263.

Breaux, A. L. (2002). *101 "answers" for new teachers & their mentors: Effective teaching tips for daily classroom use.* Larchmont, NY: Eye on Education.

Bretz, R. D., & Judge, T. A. (1998). Realistic job previews: A test of the adverse self-selection hypothesis. *Journal of Applied Psychology, 83,* 330–337.

Brock, B. L., & Grady, M. L. (2007). *From first-year to first-rate: Principals guiding beginning teachers.* Thousand Oaks, CA: Corwin Press.

Brosette v. Wilmer-Hutchins ISD, Dkt. No. 190-R2-782 (Tex. Comm'r Educ. 1984).

Brown, G., & Irby, B. (1997). *The principal portfolio.* Thousand Oaks, CA: Corwin Press.

Buckingham, G. (2000). Some difference. *People Management, 6*(4), 45.

Buell, N. A. (1992). Building a shared vision: The principal's leadership challenge. *NASSP Bulletin, 76*(542), 88–92.

Burns, J. M. (1978). *Leadership.* New York: Harper & Row.

Camden, C., & Wallace, B. (1983). Job application forms: A hazardous employment practice. *Personnel Administrator, 28*(3), 31–32, 64.

Carrell, M. R., Kuzmits, F. E., & Elbert, N. F. (1992). *Personnel/Human resource management.* New York: Macmillan.

Caulfield, J., Kidd, S., & Kocher, T. (2000). Brain-based instruction in action. *Educational Leadership, 58*(3), 62–65.

Center for Teaching Quality. (2006). Why mentoring and induction matters and what must be done for new teachers. *Teaching Quality Across the Nation: Best Practices and Policies, 5*(2), 1–5.

Cerra, C., & Jacoby, R. (2004). *Principal talk! The art of effective communication in successful school leadership.* San Francisco: Jossey-Bass.

Charles A. Dana Center. (2006). *Application for teacher quality grants under the No Child Left Behind Act of 2002 Public Law 107–110.* Retrieved December 28, 2006, from http://www.utdanacenter.org/downloads/teacherquality/rfp_2007-2008.pdf

Clay, M. V. (1997). A collaborative approach to collective bargaining. *American School Board Journal, 3*(54), 19-21.

Cleveland Board of Education v. Loudermill, 470 U.S. 532 (1985).

Collins, J. C. (2001). *Good to great: Why some companies make the leap and others don't.* New York: HarperCollins.

Colloff, P. (2005, July). She's here. She's queer. She's fired. *Texas Monthly,* 52–61.

The Columbia world of quotations. New York: Columbia University Press, 1996. Retrieved December 15, 2006, from http://www.bartleby.com/66

Conger, J. A. (1989). *The charismatic leader.* San Francisco: Jossey-Bass.

Cooper, T. L. (1998). *The responsible administrator: An approach to ethics for the administrative role.* San Francisco: Jossey-Bass.

Corporate Wellness Programs and Employee Wellness. (2007). *Top 10 reasons why your company needs an employee wellness program.* Retrieved October 20, 2007, from http://www.wellnessquotes.com/top10-reasons-why-your-company-needs-an-employee-wellness-program.html

Council of Chief State School Officers. (1996). *Interstate school leaders licensure consortium: Standards for school leaders.* Washington, DC: Author. Available at http://www.educ.ksu.edu/EDADL928/ISLLCStandards.pdf

Council of Chief State School Officers. (2008). *Interstate school leaders licensure consortium: Standards for school leaders.* Washington, DC: Author. Available at www.ccsso.org/content/pdfs/elps_isllc2008.pdf

Council on Alcohol and Drugs-Houston. (2007). *You know someone who needs us: The high road.* Houston, TX: Author.

Covey, S. R. (1992). *Principle-based leadership.* London: Simon & Schuster.

Cunningham, W. G., & Cordeiro, P. A. (2006). *Educational leadership: A problem-based approach.* Boston: Pearson Education.

Daft, R. L., & Lengel, R. H. (1984). Information richness: A new approach to managerial behavior and organizational design. *Research in Organizational Behavior, 6,* 191–233.

Daft, R. L., & Lengel, R. H. (1986). Organizational information requirements, media richness, and structural design. *Management Science, 32,* 554–571.

Daggett, W. R. (2005). *Reforming American high schools: Why, what and how.* Retrieved June 21, 2008, from http://www.leadered.com/pdf/Reforming%20HS%20White%20Paper.pdf

Davis, B. L., Hellervik, L. W., & Sheard, J. L. (2001). *Successful manager's handbook.* Minneapolis, MN: Personnel Decisions.

Deal, T. E., & Peterson, K. D. (1994). *The leadership paradox: Balancing logic and artistry in schools.* San Francisco: Jossey-Bass.

Deal, T. E., & Peterson, K. D. (1999). *Shaping school culture.* San Francisco: Jossey-Bass.

DeCenzo, D. A., & Robbins, S. P. (2005). *Fundamentals of human resource management.* Hoboken, NJ: Wiley.

Dipboye, R. I. (1992). *Selection interviews: Process perspectives.* Cincinnati, OH: South-Western College Publishing.

Dirks, T. (2007). Cool Hand Luke (1967) [Review of the motion picture *Cool Hand Luke*]. Retrieved March 3, 2007, from http://www.filmsite.org/cool3.html

Drury, W. R. (1988). Entry-year administrator induction: A state and local school district model. *Spectrum: Journal of School Research and Information, 6*(1), 8–10.

DuFour, R. (1997). Functioning as learning communities enables schools to focus on student achievement. *Journal of Staff Development, 18*(2), 56–57.

DuFour, R. (2004). What is a professional learning community? *Educational Leadership 61*(8), 6–11.

DuFour, R., DuFour, R., Eaker, R., & Karhanek, G. (2004). *Whatever it takes: How professional learning communities respond when kids don't learn.* Bloomington, IN: National Education Service.

Dunklee, D. R., & Shoop, R. J. (2006). *The principal's quick-reference guide to school law: Reducing liability, litigation, and other potential legal tangles.* Thousand Oaks, CA: Corwin Press.

Dunn, L. A. (1999). Transforming identity in conflict. In C. Schrock-Shenk & L. Ressler (Eds.), *Making peace with conflict: Practical skills for conflict transformation* (pp. 38–46). Waterloo, Ontario, Canada: Herald Press.

Eagan, G. (2002). *The skilled helper: A problem-management and opportunity–development approach to helping* (7th ed.). Belmont, CA: Brooks Cole.

Elbot, C. F., & Fulton, D. (2008). *Building an intentional school culture: Excellence in academics and character.* Thousand Oaks, CA: Corwin Press.

Elkin, A. (1999a). *Stress-free living in the big city.* New York: Plume.

Elkin, A. (1999b). *Stress management for dummies.* New York: Wiley.

Elkin, A. (2004). *Relax in the city week by week: 52 practical skills to help you be stress and find peace.* London: Duncan Baird.

Fear, R. A., & Chiron, R. J. (2002). *The evaluation interview: How to probe deeply, get candid answers, and predict the performance of job candidates.* New York: McGraw-Hill.

Ferguson v. Thomas, 430 F.2d 852 (5th Cir. 1970).

Filipowicz, C. A. (1979). The troubled employee: Whose responsibility? *Personnel Administration, 24,* 18–19.

Fisher, L., Schimmel, D., & Stellman, L. R. (2003). *Teachers and the law.* Boston: Pearson Education Group.

Fisher, R., Ury, W., & Patton, B. (1991). *Getting to yes: Negotiating agreement without giving in* (2nd ed.). New York: Penguin Books.

Ford, J. D. (1981). Departmental context and formal structures constraints on leadership behavior. *Academy of Management Journal, 24,* 274–288.

Foster, W. P. (1984). Toward a critical theory of educational administration. In T. J. Sergiovanni & J. E. Corbally (Eds.), *Leadership and organizational culture: New perspectives on administrative theory and practice.* Urbana: University of Illinois Press.

Franklin v. Gwinnett County Public Schools, 503 U.S. 60 (1992).

Friedman, T. L. (2005). *The world is flat: A brief history of the twenty-first century.* New York: Farrar, Straus and Giroux.

Fullan, M. (1998). Leadership for the 21st century: Breaking the bonds of dependency. *Educational Leadership, 47*(8), 13–19.

Garner, B. A. (Ed.). (1999). *Black's law dictionary.* St. Paul, MN: West.

Geisel, T. S., & Geisel, A. S. (1957). *The cat in the hat.* Boston: Houghton Mifflin.

Gibson, L. (2003). Leadership with laughter. *Urologic Nursing, 23*(5), 364. Retrieved February 24, 2007, from the Academic Search Premier database.

Glanz, J. (2002). *Finding your leadership style: A guide for educators.* Alexandria, VA: Association for Supervision and Curriculum Development.

Glenn, R. E. (2002a). Keys to better communication. *Educational Digest 68*(3), 4. Retrieved May 25, 2007, from Academic Search Premier database.

Glenn, R. E. (2002b). Using brain research in your classroom. *Educational Digest, 67*(7), 27–30.

Gonzales v. Donna ISD, Dkt. No. 120-RI-698 (Tex. Comm'r Educ. 1998)

Gordon, S. P. (2004). *Professional development for school improvement: Empowering learning communities.* Boston: Pearson Education.

Goulet, M. (2005). How to hire: The legal perspective. *Texas Study of Secondary Education 15*(1), 2–4.

Guskey, T. R. (2000). *Evaluating professional development.* Thousand Oaks, CA: Corwin Press.

Halawah, I. (2005). The relationship between effective communication of high school principal and school climate. *Education 126*(2), 334–345.

Hallinger, P., & Leithwood, K. (1998). Unforeseen forces: The impact of social culture on school leadership. *Peabody Journal of Education, 73,* 126–151.

Harris, B. M., McIntyre, K. E., Littleton, V. C., Jr., & Long, D. F. (1985). *Personnel administration in education: Leadership for instructional improvement.* Boston: Allyn and Bacon.

Harris, S. (2005). *Best practices of award-winning elementary school principals.* Thousand Oaks, CA: Corwin Press.

Harris, S. (2006). *Best practices of award-winning secondary school principals.* Thousand Oaks, CA: Corwin Press.

Hays Consolidated Independent School District. (2008). *Induction/mentoring program.* Kyle, TX: Author.

Heifetz, R. A. (1994). *Leadership without easy answers.* Cambridge, MA: Harvard University Press.

Heifetz, R. A., & Linsky, M. (2002). *Leadership on the line: Staying alive through the dangers of leading.* Boston: Harvard Business School Press.

Heller, F., & Yukl, G. (1969). Participation, managerial decision-making, and situational variables. *Organizational Behavior and Human Performance, 4,* 227–241.

Hemphill, J. K., & Coons, A. E. (1957). Development of the leader behavior description questionnaire. In R. M. Stogdill & A. E. Coons (Eds.), *Leader behavior: Its description and measurement.* Columbus: Ohio State University, Bureau of Business Research.

Hilgert, R. L., Truesdell, J. L., & Lochhaas, P. H. (2002). *Christian ethics in the workplace.* St. Louis, MO: Concordia Publishing House.

Hogan, J. (1992). The view from below. In R. T. Hogan (Chair), *The future of leadership selection.* Symposium conducted at the 13th Biennial Psychology in the DoD Conference, United States Air Force Academy, CO.

Holcomb, E. L. (2004). *Getting excited about data: Combining people, passion, and proof to maximize student achievement* (2nd ed.). Thousand Oaks, CA: Corwin Press.

House, R. J., Woycke, J., & Fodor, E. M. (1988). Charismatic and noncharismatic leaders: Differences in behavior and effectiveness. In J. A. Conger & R. N. Kanungo (Eds.), *Charismatic leadership: The elusive factor in organizational effectiveness* (pp. 98–121). San Francisco: Jossey-Bass.

Houston, P., & Sokolow, S. (2006). *The spiritual dimension of leadership: 8 key principles to leading more effectively.* Thousand Oaks, CA: Corwin Press.

Hoy, A. W., & Hoy, W. K. (2006). *Instructional leadership: A research-based guide to learning in schools.* Boston: Allyn & Bacon.

Hoyle, J. R., English, F. W., & Steffy, B. E. (1998). *Skills for successful 21st century school leaders: Standards for peak performers.* Arlington, VA: American Association of School Administrators.

HR-Guide.com. (1999). *HR guide to the Internet: Personnel selection: Interview questions: Difficult questions.* Retrieved March 6, 2007, from http://www.hr-guide.com//data/G353.htm

Huber, G. P., & Daft, R. L. (1987). The information environments of organizations. In F. M. Jablin, L. L. Putnam, K. Roberts, & L. W. Porter (Eds.), *Handbook of organizational communication: An interdisciplinary perspective* (pp. 130–164). Newbury Park, CA: Sage.

Hughes, R. L., Ginnett, R. C., & Curphy, G. J. (2002). *Leadership: Enhancing the lessons of experience.* Columbus, OH: McGraw-Hill.

Institute for Teacher Renewal and Growth. (2003). *Staff development, induction, mentoring.* Retrieved on June 23, 2008, from http://www.flowingwellsschools.org/filestore/StaffDev-InductionMentoring.pdf

Johnson, R. S. (2002). *Using data to close the achievement gap: How to measure equity in our schools.* Thousand Oaks, CA: Corwin Press.

Johnson v. Selma Board of Education, 356 So. 2d 649 (Ala. 1978).

Jonas, P. (2004). *Secrets of connecting leadership and learning with humor.* Lanham, MD: Rowman & Littlefield.

Kapadia, K., & Coca, V. (with Easton, J). (2007). *Keeping new teachers: A first look at the influences of induction in Chicago Public Schools.* Consortium on Chicago School Research, 3 (ERIC Document Reproduction Service No. ED498332).

Kaser, J., Mundry, S., Stiles, K. E., & Loucks-Horsley, S. (2002). *Leading every day: 124 actions for effective leadership.* Thousand Oaks, CA: Corwin Press.

Keane, W. (1996). *Win-win or else: Collective bargaining in the age of public discontent.* Thousand Oaks, CA: Corwin Press.

Kelley, L. M. (2004). Why induction matters. *Journal of Teacher Education, 55*(4), 438–448.

Kemerer, F., & Crain, J. (1998). *The documentation handbook.* Austin, TX: University of Texas Press.

The Kemper Insurance Companies. (2005). *Guidebook on alcoholism and drug abuse.* Long Grove, IL: Author.

Kosmoski, G. J., & Pollack, D. R. (2005). *Managing difficult, frustrating, and hostile conversations: Strategies for savvy administrators.* Thousand Oaks, CA: Corwin Press.

Kramer, J., & Schaap, D. (2006). *Instant replay: The Green Bay diary of Jerry Kramer.* New York: Doubleday.

Krone, K. J., Jablin, F. M., & Putnam, L. L. (1987). Communication theory and organizational communication: Multiple perspectives. In F. M. Jablin, L. L Putnam, K. Roberts, & L. W. Porter (Eds.), *Handbook of organizational communication: An interdisciplinary perspective* (pp. 18–40). Newbury Park, CA: Sage.

Lambert, L. (1995). *The constructivist leader.* New York: Teachers College Press.

Lambert, L. (1998). *Building leadership capacity in schools.* Alexandria, VA: Association for Supervision and Curriculum Development.

Lashway, L. (2006). Visionary leadership. In S. C. Smith & P. K. Piele (Eds.), *School leadership* (pp. 153–177). Thousand Oaks, CA: Corwin Press.

Lazear, J. (1992). *Meditations for men who do too much.* New York: Fireside/Parkside.

Likert, R. (1961). *New patterns of management.* New York: McGraw-Hill.

Lindsey, R. B., Roberts, L. M., & CampbellJones, F. (2005). *The culturally proficient school: An implementation guide for school leaders.* Thousand Oaks, CA: Corwin Press.

Lindstrom, P. H., & Speck, M. (2004). *The principal as professional development leader.* Thousand Oaks, CA: Corwin Press.

Lombardi, V., Jr. (2001). *What it takes to be #1: Vince Lombardi on leadership.* New York: McGraw-Hill.

Lunenburg, F. C., & Ornstein, A. C. (2004). *Educational administration: Concepts and practices.* Belmont, CA: Wadsworth/Thomson Learning.

MacArthur, J. (2005). *The heart of the Bible: Explore the power of key Bible passages.* Nashville, TN: Thomas Nelson.

Martin, C. (1993). Hiring the right person: Techniques for principals. *NASSP Bulletin, 77,* 79–83.

Maurer, S. D. (2002). A practitioner-based analysis of interviewer job expertise and scale format as contextual factors in situational interviews. *Personnel Psychology, 55*(2), 267–306.

Maxwell, J. C. (2003). *Leadership: Promises for every day*. Nashville, TN: Thomas Nelson.

Maxwell, K. (2007). *Reminiscing about the leadership role*. Unpublished interview, Department of Education, Abilene Christian University, Abilene, TX.

McClelland, D. C. (1961). *The achieving society*. New York: Van Nostrand Reinhold.

McCollum, J. K., & Norris, D. R. (1984). Nonunion grievance machinery in southern industry. *Personnel Administrator, 29*(11), 106.

McGue, M., & Bouchard, T. J., Jr. (1989). Genetic and environmental determinants of information processing and special mental abilities: A twin analysis. In R. J. Sternberg (Ed.), *Advances in the psychology of human intelligence* (pp. 7–45). Hillsdale, NJ: Erlbaum.

McKee, R. (1997). *Story: Substance, structure, style, and the principles of screenwriting*. New York: HarperCollins.

Merriam-Webster, Inc. (2000). *Webster's new collegiate dictionary* (11th ed.). Springfield, MA: Author.

Moir, E., & Gless, J. (2003). *Meeting the challenges of recruitment and retention*. Washington, DC: National Education Association.

Morden, M. E. (2001). *Delphi: The Oracle of Apollo*. Retrieved October 6, 2007, from http://www.odysseyadventures.ca/articles/delphi/articledelphi.htm

Morgan, M. M., & Kritsonis, W. A. (2008). A national focus: The recruitment, retention, and development of quality teachers in hard-to-staff schools. *National Journal for Publishing and Mentoring Doctoral Student Research, 5*(1), 1–7.

Mosher, F. (1968). *Democracy and the public service*. New York: Oxford University Press.

Murphy, J., & Shipman, N. J. (1998, April). *The interstate school leaders licensure consortium: A standards-based approach to strengthening educational leadership*. Paper presented to the annual conference of the American Educational Research Association, San Diego, CA.

National Commission on Teaching and America's Future. (2003). *No dream denied: A pledge to America's children*. Retrieved May 21, 2008, from http://www.nctaf.org

National Commission on Teaching and America's Future. (2008). *The high cost of teacher turnover*. Retrieved May 21, 2008, from http://www.nctaf.org

National Policy Board for Educational Administration. (2002). *Instructions to implement standards for advanced programs in educational leadership for principals, superintendents, curriculum directors, and supervisors*. Arlington, VA: Author.

National Staff Development Council. (2001). *Standards for staff development* (Rev. ed.). Oxford, OH: Author.

National Staff Development Council. (2006). *National staff development council code of ethics*. Retrieved December 21, 2006, from http://www.nsdc.org/connect/about/ethics.cfm

Neely, E. (2005). Communication with parents: It works both ways. *Leadership 34*(5), 24–27.

Northouse, P. G. (2004). *Leadership: Theory and practice*. Thousand Oaks, CA: Sage.

Northwest Regional Educational Laboratory. (1984). *Effective schooling practices: A research synthesis*. Portland, OR: Author.

Norton, M. S. (2005). *Executive leadership for effective administration*. Boston: Pearson Education.

Ottensmeyer, E. J., & McCarthy, G. D. (1996). *Ethics in the workplace*. New York: McGraw-Hill.

Patterson, K., Grenny, J., McMillan, R., & Switzler, A. (2002). *Crucial conversations: Tools for talking when stakes are high*. New York: McGraw-Hill

Pawlas, G. E. (1997). Vision and school culture. *NASSP Bulletin, 81*, 587.

Payne, J. (n.d.). *Information for employers: Best practice guidelines for recruitment and selection: Interviewing*. Retrieved June 26, 2008, from http://www.hreoc.gov.au/info_for_employers/best_practice/recruitment.html

Peine, J. (2008). *The educator's professional growth plan: A process for developing staff and improving instruction*. Thousand Oaks, CA: Corwin Press.

Philbrick, N. (2006). *Mayflower*. New York: Penguin Books.

Picciano, A. G. (2006). *Data-driven decision making for effective school leadership*. Upper Saddle River, NJ: Pearson Education.

Pink, D. H. (2006). *A whole new mind: Why right-brainers will rule the future*. New York: Penguin Books.

Potter-Norton, S. (2006). *Employment litigation: Model jury instructions*. Chicago: American Bar Association.

Public Education Foundation. (2006). *Lessons learned: A report on the Benwood initiative*. Washington, DC: Author.

Quotes of G. K. Chesterton. (n.d.). Retrieved December 7, 2007, from http://www.chesterton .org/acs/quotes.htm

Rebore, R. W. (2007). *Human resources administration in education: A management approach*. Boston: Pearson Education.

Robbins, S. P. (2004). *Organizational behavior: Concepts, controversies, and applications* (8th ed.). Englewood Cliffs, NJ: Prentice Hall.

Roberts, W. (1990). *Leadership secrets of Attila the Hun*. New York: Warner Books.

Ross v. Springfield School District No. 19, 691 P.2d 509 (Or. Ct. App. 1984).

Ruiz-Garcia v. Houston ISD, Dkt. No. 044-R2–1199 (Tex. Comm'r Educ. 2000).

Rutherford, P. (2005). *21st century mentor's handbook: Creating a culture for learning*. Alexandria, VA: Just ASK Publications.

Sanderson, B. E. (2005). *Talk it out! The educator's guide to successful difficult conversations*. Larchmont, NY: Eye on Education.

Sashkin, M., & Huddle, G. (1988). Recruit top principals: Tips for spotting and coaching key players. *School Administrator 45*(2), 8–15.

Schlechty, P. (1997). *Inventing better schools: A plan of action for educational reform*. San Francisco, CA: Jossey-Bass.

Schmitt, N., Noe, R., Meritt, R., & Fitzgerald, M. (1984). Validity of assessment center ratings for the prediction of performance ratings and school climate of school administrators. *Journal of Applied Psychology, 69*(2), 207–213.

Schneider, E. J., & Hollenczer, L. L. (2006). *The principal's guide to managing communication*. Thousand Oaks, CA: Corwin Press.

Scoolis, J. (1998). What is vision? *Thrust for Educational Leadership, 28*, 20–21, 36.

Senge, P., Cambron-McCabe, N., Lucas, T., Smith, B., Dutton, J., & Kleiner, A. (2000). *Schools that learn: A fifth discipline fieldbook for educators, parents, and everyone who cares about education*. New York: Doubleday.

Sergiovanni, T. J. (1992). *Moral leadership: Getting to the heart of school improvement*. San Francisco: Jossey-Bass.

Sergiovanni, T. J. (1994). The roots of school leadership. *Principal 74*(2), 6–9.

Sergiovanni, T. J. (1996). *Leadership for the schoolhouse*. San Francisco: Jossey-Bass.

Sergiovanni, T. J., Kelleher, P., McCarthy, M. M., & Wirt, F. M. (2004). *Educational governance and administration*. Boston: Pearson Education.

Shannon, G. S., & Bylsma, P. (2007). *Nine characteristics of high-performing schools: A research-based resource for schools and districts to assist with improving student learning* (2nd ed.). Olympia, WA: Office of Superintendent of Public Instruction. Retrieved July 29, 2008 from http://www.eric.ed.gov/ERICDocs/data/ericdocs2sql/content_storage_01/ 0000019b/80/3c/7e/48.pdf

Shapiro, J. P., & Stefkovich, J. A. (2005). *Ethical leadership and decision making in education*. Mahwah, NJ: Lawrence Erlbaum Associates.

Sharkey, B. J., & Gaskill, S. E. (2006). *Fitness and health*. Champaign, IL: Human Kinetics.

Sharp, W. L., & Walter, J. K. (2003). *The principal as school manager*. Lanham, MA: The Scarecrow Press.

Sharp, W. L., & Walter, J. K. (2004). *The school superintendent: The profession and the person*. Lanham, MD: The Scarecrow Press.

Shipman, N. J., Topps, B. W., & Murphy, J. (1998, April). *Linking the ISLLC standards to professional development and relicensure*. Paper presented to the annual conference of the American Educational Research Association, San Diego, CA.

Sitzler v. Babers, Dkt. No. 092-PPC-1191 (Tex. Comm'r Educ. 1992).

Slaikeu, K. A. (1996). *When push comes to shove: A practical guide to mediating disputes*. San Francisco: Jossey-Bass.

Smith, R. E. (1998). *Human resources administration: A school-based perspective.* Larchmont, NY: Eye on Education.

Smith, S. C., & Piele, P. K. (Eds.). (2006). *School leadership* (4th ed.). Thousand Oaks, CA: Corwin Press.

Sorenson, R. D. (2002). The novice principal: How to avoid the pitfalls leading to career derailment. *Texas Study of Secondary Education, 12*(1), 28–33.

Sorenson, R. D. (2004a). *Answering reference checks: Some do's and don'ts for the campus principal.* Unpublished course materials, University of Texas at El Paso.

Sorenson, R. D. (2004b). *They talk: Voices from the field of school administration.* Unpublished interviews of school principals and lead teachers, The University of Texas at El Paso. The Department of Educational Leadership and Foundations Department.

Sorenson, R. D. (Summer 2005a). Productive teamwork: Tips for school administrators. *TEPSA Journal,* 9–10, 23–26.

Sorenson, R. D. (2005b). The seven keys to effective communication. *NAESP Principal Online, 85*(2). Retrieved June 25, 2008, from http://www.naesp.org/Content Load.do?contentId=1768

Sorenson, R. D. (2007). Leading by interviewing. *AASA Journal of Scholarship and Practice* 4(2), 33–43.

Sorenson, R. D., & Goldsmith, L. M. (2006). *The principal's guide to school budgeting.* Thousand Oaks, CA: Corwin Press.

Sorenson, R. D., & Goldsmith, L. M. (in press). Essentials to the effective principal mentoring of beginning teachers. *TEPSA Journal.*

Stanton, E. S. (1988). Fast-and-easy reference checking by telephone. *Personnel Journal* 67(11), 123–130.

Starratt, R. J. (1977, June). *Apostolic leadership.* San Jose, CA: Jesuit Commission on Research and Development Workshop.

State ex rel. Curry v. Grand Valley Local Schools Board of Education, 375 N.E.2d 48 (Ohio 1978).

Stein, J. (Ed.). (1967). *The Random House dictionary of the English language* (Unabridged ed.). New York: Random House.

Stephens v. Board of Education, School District No. 5, 429 N.W.2d 722 (Neb. 1988).

Stogdill, R. M. (1948). Personal factors associated with leadership: A review of the literature. *Journal of Psychology 25,* 35–71.

Stone, D., Patton, B. N., & Heen, S. (1999). *Difficult conversations: How to discuss what matters most.* London: Penguin Books.

Tallerico, M. (2005). *Supporting and sustaining teachers' professional development.* Thousand Oaks, CA: Corwin Press.

Tanner, L. N. (1999). The practical affairs of improving teaching. In L. W. Hughes (Ed.), *The principal as leader* (pp. 190, 194). New York: Macmillan.

Tate, J. S., & Dunklee, D. R. (2005). *Strategic listening for school leaders.* Thousand Oaks, CA: Corwin Press.

Tindal, G., Duesbery, L., & Ketterlin-Geller, L. R. (2006). Managing data for decision-making: Creating knowledge from information. In S. C. Smith & P. K. Piele (Eds.), *School leadership: Handbook for excellence in student learning* (pp. 380–400). Thousand Oaks, CA: Corwin Press.

Tjosvold, D. (1987). Controversy for learning organizational behavior. *Organizational Behavior Teaching Review, 11*(3), 51–59.

Tolkien, J. R. R. (1937). *The hobbit.* Boston: Houghton Mifflin.

Ubben, G. C., Hughes, L. W., & Norris, C. J. (2007). *The principal: Creative leadership for excellence in schools.* Boston: Pearson Education, Inc.

U.S. Department of Education. (1997). *Office for civil rights sexual harassment guidance (4000-0-P).* Washington, DC: Author.

U.S. Department of Education. (2005). *Teacher attrition and mobility: Results from the 2004–2005 teacher follow-up survey.* Washington, DC: Author.

Valente, W. D., & Valente, C. M. (2005). *Law in the schools*. Upper Saddle River, NJ: Pearson Education.

Van Knippenberg, B., & Van Knippenberg, D. (2005). Leader self-sacrifice and leadership effectiveness: The moderating role of leader prototypicality. *Journal of Applied Psychology, 90*, 25–37.

Villani, S. (2006). *Mentoring and induction programs that support new principals*. Thousand Oaks, CA: Corwin Press.

Walsh, J., Kemerer, F., & Maniotis, L. (2005). *The educator's guide to Texas school law*. Austin: University of Texas Press.

Warren, R. (2002). *The purpose driven life*. Grand Rapids, MI: Zondervan.

Wayne, A. J., Youngs, P., & Fleischman, S. (2005). Improving teacher induction. *Educational Leadership, 62*(8), 76–77.

Webb, L. D., & Norton, M. S. (2003). *Human resources administration: Personnel issues and needs in education* (4th ed.). Upper Saddle River, NJ: Pearson Education.

Webb, L. D., & Norton, M. S. (2009). *Human resources administration: Personnel issues and needs in education* (5th ed.). Upper Saddle River, NJ: Pearson Education.

White, J. (Director). (1942). *Three smart saps* [Motion picture]. Los Angeles: C3 Entertainment.

Williamson v. Dallas ISD, Dkt. No. 095-R2-498 (Tex. Comm'r Educ. 1998).

Wilmot, W. W., & Hocker, J. L. (2007). *Interpersonal conflict* (7th ed.). New York: McGraw-Hill.

Within, A. (1980). Commonly overlooked dimensions of employee selection. *Personnel Journal 59*(7), 573–575.

Young, I. P. (2008). *The human resource function in educational administration*. Upper Saddle River, NJ: Pearson Education.

Young, I. P., & Castetter, W. B. (2004). *The human resource function in educational administration*. Upper Saddle River, NJ: Pearson Education.

Young, I. P., & Chounte, P. F. (2004). The effects of chronological age and information media on teacher screening decisions for school principals. *Personnel Evaluation in Education 17*(2), 157–172.

Yukl, G. A. (2001). *Leadership in organizations*. Englewood Cliffs, NJ: Prentice Hall.

Index

CORWIN PRESS

The Corwin Press logo—a raven striding across an open book—represents the union of courage and learning. Corwin Press is committed to improving education for all learners by publishing books and other professional development resources for those serving the field of PreK–12 education. By providing practical, hands-on materials, Corwin Press continues to carry out the promise of its motto: **"Helping Educators Do Their Work Better."**